Bargain Hunting in the Bay Area

Bargain Hunting in the Bay Area

5th Revised Edition

by Sally Socolich

Wingbow Press • *Berkeley*

For late additons to this revised, updated revision, see page 247. It's always best to call ahead to verify hours and addresses.

ISBN 0-914728-48-2

Wingbow Press books are published and distributed by Bookpeople, 2929 Fifth Street, Berkeley, California 94710.

Designed by Bonnie Jean Smetts
Cover photographs by
Elliott Varner Smith
Back cover photograph
courtesy of Esprit de Corp.

Thanks to Stroud's Linens, Shoe Town, Pioneer Home Supply, Bluxome Factory Outlet and Esprit for permission to use their stores' photographs on the cover.

Revised Edition
First Printing, April 1976
Second Printing, September 1976
Third Printing, April 1977
Fourth Printing, September 1977

Second Revised Edition
Fifth Printing, July 1978
Sixth Printing, December 1978
Seventh Printing, June 1979

Third Revised Edition
Eighth Printing, June 1980
Ninth Printing, February 1981

Fourth Revised Edition
Tenth Printing, June 1982
Eleventh Printing, March 1983
Twelfth Printing, February 1984

Fifth Revised Edition
Thirteenth Printing, September 1984

Contents

PART THREE
**Related Services, New
Trends And Information,
Late Additions, Updates
and Index**

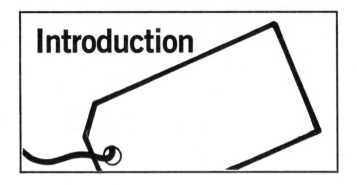

Introduction

The first four editions of *Bargain Hunting in the Bay Area* were so well-received it was clear readers wanted to know yet more about where to find good shopping values. It's hard to believe that each year bargain resources for consumers have continued to develop. In 1984/85 the growth promises to explode. *Off-price* is the new game in town. Inspired by the successful growth of off-price chains in the east and mid-west, Bay Area developers are wooing these successful companies with hopes of adding new off-price locations (with the success and profits that go along with them) to local developments. The off-pricers, as the stores are called in the retail industry, are the fastest growing segment of retailing — a revolution that won't go away. Industry analysts expect them to continue to grow at an average pace of 20-25% a year. *See Off Price Shopping Centers page 223.*

Savvy bargain hunters realize that you can save money on most of the things you buy — if you know *where* to buy. Sale buying is not confined to just a few weeks a year, but is possible every day, and almost monthly from traditional department stores. Armed with *Bargain Hunting in the Bay Area* you can stretch your dollar on everyday necessities: food, clothing, housewares, furniture, as well as on luxury items like diamonds, gold, sterling silver and hobby and sporting goods, too. Bargain hunting is an interest that appeals to shoppers at all income levels. As the cost of living continues to rise and more demands are put on our family budgets we must look for ways to make our dollar do more. That is the purpose of this book.

While some stores have closed, new stores have opened, and old stores continue to thrive as more enlightened consumers seek them out. You will find that branches of larger stores have opened in your neighborhood shopping centers saving you costly trips around the Bay Area. Re-evaluating and updating old listings, and researching new listings resulted in many changes for this edition. In going back over old territory, I find some retailers no longer *measure up* to the price/value requirements for this book. Others have blossomed with bigger and better values and selection, while many have vanished without a trace.

This revision leads you in the same direction as previous editions: to over 400 stores offering the *best quality goods for the lowest prices*. Of these entries I have kept my basic bargain criteria of "at least 20% off the retail price," though *most* entries offer far greater reductions. Many readers of the first five editions have shared their bargain discoveries with me and I have researched and included a number of them. This book is intended as a guide, of course, and not as an endorsement of the stores listed. Those included are strictly personal selections for which I have accepted no kindnesses or gratuities to insure their inclusion. To maximize the number of entries for this book I have avoided lengthy descriptions of each store or business, just wordy enough to reveal its "personality" and spark your interest.

A word of warning, before you shop

Even a seasoned bargain hunter has trouble keeping up with the outlets and discount stores that move and seem to play hopscotch around the Bay Area. Outlets have been known to quietly move across the street, or even close permanently on a few days notice. Rent increases, changes of building ownership, or management shifts can force a bargain outlet to seek new, lower priced locations. **Since store hours are subject to change, I recommend that you call those shops you intend to visit before driving miles across town**. Addresses and phone numbers were correct at the time of publication, but these may change. Subsequent printings will include corrections, and readers are encouraged to notify the author, in care of the publisher of any such changes.

Please glance over the *Hints for the Bargain Hunter* that follow. You're probably already aware of the basic rules, but the caveat emptor rule cannot be overemphasized. I trust that your innate good shopping habits will caution you to comparison shop before buying and always to ask

that number one, all-important question: "How can they sell it so cheap?." I've answered this question in most cases and have tried to lead you to stores that will give you an honest answer. But don't let your guard down — not for a minute.

Remember, too, that just because an item is cheap, it's not necessarily a bargain; and to turn the coin over, some merchandise is going to be expensive, even when priced at 20% or more under retail. Finally, nothing is a bargain if you don't need it. One of the biggest problems in shopping outlets and discount stores is the compulsion to buy everything simply because it all seems so cheap. I've had to learn self-restraint to avoid unjustified and unnecessary expenditures while being sorely tempted!

I have quoted specific prices in some listings to give you a clue to the kinds of bargains available at the various stores. The prices mentioned are based on research conducted in the spring of 1984, but because of changes in the economy, those prices may be higher by the time you visit the stores. Still, chances are the ratio of the discount to the retail price will hold.

So if you're determined to "beat the system," I'm with you. Once you get into the swing of buying at these prices, you'll soon discover that paying straight retail is for the unenlightened!

Hints for the bargain hunter

It's difficult to make specific recommendations about where *you* should shop. Shopping is a highly personal activity and reflects many facets of your personality. Some prefer the tranquil atmosphere of the "better" stores, the sometimes higher quality product and the attentiveness of the personnel that go with it; others are namebrand aficianados and many are just plain budget-conscious. You'll discover that I've listed stores of every possible description; my own personal taste in bargain hunting is quite varied. I shop a chic apparel boutique one day and a bare bones factory outlet the next. I adore rummaging in salvage and surplus outlets *and* relaxing in an elegant decorator's showroom. Limited facilities, goods, and services don't cause me to blink an eye; my goal is a *bargain* — and hang the tranquility. And if you've bought this book, you probably have one main objective in your shopping ventures: to get the most for your dollar.

Questions to ask

Whenever an item is for sale to the public at 20-50% under retail, common sense tells you there must be a reason. I have tried in each entry to give you an explanation, and the answer generally falls into one or more categories described by the following terminology used in retailing.

● **Discontinued or manufacturer's close-out:** A product that is no longer being manufactured. In most instances this does not effect the merchandise, but where parts may need to be replaced, it could cause a problem.

● **Floor sample:** A model displayed in the store.

● **Freight damage:** Even if only one or two items in a shipment are broken, burned, chipped, marred, etc., for insurance purposes the entire lot is designated "damaged." This merchandise may be noticeably damaged; often, however it is actually in A-1 condition but part of a shipment that met with physical mishap.

● **Irregular:** Merchandise with minor imperfections, often barely discernable.

● **In-season buying:** Most retailers buy pre-season, whereas a discounter will often purchase in-season, relieving the manufacturer of merchandise that is old to him but still new to the public.

● **Jobber:** A person who buys goods in quantity from manufacturers or importers and sells them to dealers.

● **Job lot:** Goods, often of various sorts, brought together for sale as one quantity.

● **Liquidated stock:** When a company or business is in financial trouble, the stock they have on hand is sometimes sold to merchandisers — often the lot — at prices much lower than retail in order to liquidate the assets of the company.

● **Loss leader:** An item purposely priced low to get you into the store.

● **Odd-lots:** A relatively small quantity of unsold merchandise that remains after an order has been filled.

● **Open stock:** Individual pieces of merchandise sold in sets, which are kept in stock as replacements.

● **Overruns:** An excess of products, similar to surplus and overstocks, but generally due to a manufacturer's error.

● **Past Season:** Goods manufactured for a previous season.

● **Retail:** The selling of merchandise directly to the consumer.

● **Returns:** Orders returned to the manufacturer by retail stores because they do not arrive on time. Fashion discounters are able to buy this merchandise below cost from the manufacturer, thereby helping him to alleviate his losses.

● **Samples:** An item shown by the manufacturer's representative to the prospective merchandiser/buyer for the purpose of selling the product.

● **Seconds:** Merchandise with more than minor flaws which may effect the aesthetic appeal or performance of the product.

● **Surplus overstocks:** An excess quantity, over and above what is needed by the retailer.

● **Wholesale price:** Wholesale price refers to the cost of goods to the retailer, except in discount shopping when consumers can buy at or near this price.

In addition to the above, the business acumen of one retailer buyer in purchasing merchandise may be superior to his competitors'; a better original buy generally is reflected in the price. Low overhead can also effect the price; stores in low rent districts with few frills and no advertising can often undersell those in the high rent areas. The necessity to keep goods moving sometimes forces a retailer into cutting prices — space is a problem in merchandising just as it is in your home. They're in it for the long haul, not the the quick profit. Bless them!

Once you have determined the reason the price is low, your next question should be: "Is there anything wrong with the item that will effect its performance or use to me?" Look for flaws before you buy. And if you find one, be realistic about whether you can repair it or have it repaired and still save money. If you've answered all these questions honestly and find the bargain value there, plunge, you've bagged a buy. Now you can relish that delicious feeling of beating the system, you've earned it.

Maps

In this edition I have included maps for areas of San Francisco where there are many outlets and resources for bargains in close proximity to each other. (See page 1).

Timing

Many of the shops have specific days that new merchandise comes in. Knowing what those days are will enable you to get the pick of the new crop. When you find a store or outlet that sells merchandise that you're particularly interested in, be sure to ask if they have a mailing list and get on it. This will give you advance notice of sales and new arrivals. For many of these stores, mailing lists are their only form of advertising.

How to use this book

Bargain Hunting in the Bay Area is arranged by categories, very much like the Yellow Pages of your telephone directory. Beneath the subject heading the name of each bargain shop and service is listed in alphabetical order. Also included is such information as address, telephone number (unless specified phone numbers are in the 415 area), store hours, the means of purchasing (cash only, cash or check, and which credit cards, if any, are accepted). The credit card code is MC — MasterCharge, AE — American Express, and VISA. Also listed are the other cities in Northern California where a branch store or similar service is offered.

Because many stores sell a wide variety of merchandise I have not attempted the mammoth job of a complete cross-reference system. I have, however, made a limited number of cross references where I felt they would be most helpful to the bargain hunter. Please be sure to look at the "also see's" when they appear under the main headings. Please consult the index at the end of the book:

SUBJECT INDEX: (See page 242)
Arranged by product or service supplied.
ALPHABETICAL LISTINGS: (See Page 227)
GEOGRAPHICAL LISTINGS: (see page 232)
Arranged by the name of the city in which it is located.

Updates

Those interested in keeping abreast of new stores, outlets, private sales by manufacturers and changes in existing listings, that will occur after publication of this edition, may want to subscribe to **The Bargain Hunter's HOTLINE.** This newsletter is published 10 times a year. To subscribe please forward a check or money order for $15 (annual rate or $1.50/issue) made out to *Bargain Hunting*, Post Office Box 144, Moraga, Ca. 94556.

I would be delighted to hear from other bargain hunters regarding new listings for future editions or other suggestions you may have. Please forward any comments to my publisher, *Wingbow Press*, **2929 Fifth Street, Berkeley, Ca. 94710.**

Sally Socolich

It's clearly impossible to include maps for all the businesses listed in Bargain Hunting in the Bay Area. Because of the close proximity of many San Francisco businesses, three maps are provided to help you locate outlets in the primary resource areas within San Francisco.

South of Market

1. Fritzi Factory Outlets
2. Gunne Sax Outlet
3. End of the Line
4. Raincoat Outlet
5. Fashion Factory Outlet
6. Sprint Wholesale Apparel
7. Kutler Bros.
8. Patti Quinn's
9. Clothes Rack
10. Pioneer Home Supply
11. AAA Luggage Repair Depot
12. Harband's Luggage
13. Cottage Tables
14. Terry McHugh Outlet,
    Lady Like Factory Outlet
15. Photographic Supply
16. Bluxome Factory Outlet,
    C. P. Shades Outlet
17. Maternity Factory Outlet
18. Fantastico
19. Flower Mart
20. Clothing Clearance Center
21. Rucker Fuller South
22. Jeffrey Kriger Framing
23. Jadel Inc.
24. Four Star Apparel,
    International Household Export,
    General Bead
25. House of Karlson
26. Western Fur Traders Outlet,
    Solo Factory Outlet
27. Soloco
28. Cosmetic and Fragrance Outlet
29. Factory Store
30. Flax's Warehouse
31. House of Louie
32. Derby Factory Outlet
33. San Francisco Apparel Mart Sales
34. San Francisco Ski & Sportswear
35. Fashion Gift Outlet
36. Spare Changes
37. Bear Factory
38. Luggage Clearance Center
39. Coast Florist Supply
40. Japanese Weekend
41. Men's Wearhouse
42. San Francisco Galleries

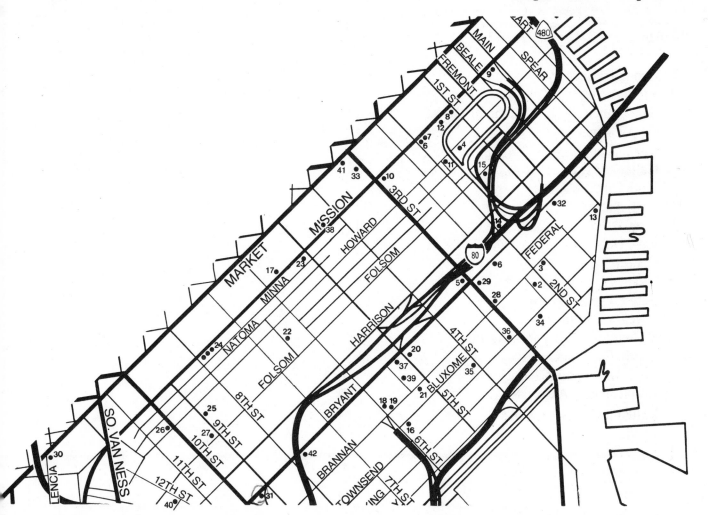

Mission and Potrero

1. Canned Foods
2. S. Beressi
3. San Francisco Manufacturers Outlet
4. Arvey Paper
5. Linen Depot
6. Gallery West
7. Patti Quinn's Outlet
8. Lilli Ann
9. S & R Fashion Center
10. Sew Help You Shop
11. Cherin's
12. Clothes Encounter II
13. Better Dress Outlet,
    Jewels of Light
14. Wallcovering & Fabric Outlet
15. Esprit Factory Outlet
16. Western Contract Furnishers
17. Don Ermann Associates
18. Contempo Factory Outlet

Union Square

1. Deovlet Furniture
2. Nigel's Furniture
3. Cresalia Jewelers,
   Daniels
4. Azevedo Jewelers
5. S. Christian of Copenhagen
6. Niederholzer
7. Jeanne Marc Fabric Outlet
8. A Small Things Co.,
   Zwillinger Jewelry
9. My Favorite Clothing Store
10. Executive Clothes
11. Silky Bee
12. Clothes Rack
13. Clothes Encounter
14. Sharper Image Sale Store
15. Clothes Vault
16. Patti Quinns
17. Vogue Alley
18. United Tool

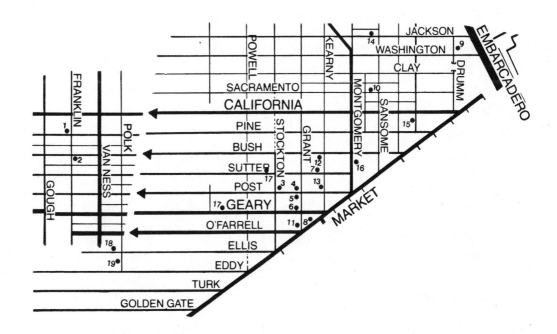

Part One

Almost All New, Sometimes Irregular, But Otherwise First Class Merchandise

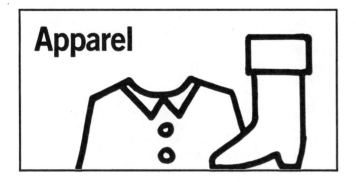

Apparel

Apparel Mart Sales

SAN FRANCISCO APPAREL MART SATURDAY SALES

22 Fourth Street (between Market & Mission), San Francisco 94103. Hours: Saturday's Only l0am-4pm. Four times a year. Purchases: Cash preferred, checks with proper I. D. Parking: 5th & Mission Garage. *Admission Charge = $l./person.*

Following the example of the *California Mart* in Los Angeles, the *San Francisco Apparel Mart* has decided to go "PUBLIC". Not every day, not all the time, in fact sales are scheduled four times a year usually in March, May or June, September and December. For the uninitiated, there are over 300 reps representing 1,400 lines of apparel and accessories who have showrooms in the Mart.

From there, fashions are sold to retailers throughout the West. At the end of each season, the sales reps are left with their "samples." For instance, at the March sale most samples will be from the spring and early summer lines; you're actually buying in-season or ahead-of-season merchandise. On Saturday sale days the reps will set up booths in Market Hall 1 & 2 (lower level of the building) to give the public a chance to buy samples at wholesale prices. Many reps have hundreds of garments, so there is a tantalizing selection.

Will you fit a sample size? Chances are you will if you're an 8 or l0 in misses; 7/8 or 8/9 in Juniors; 40 top, medium, or 32-34 waist in men's; or children's sizes, infant to toddler, 3-6X, 7-14. This is not exact, rather a general indication since there are exceptions in many lines. Many reps have complete size ranges. By far the biggest selection is in women's apparel which includes sportswear, outerwear, dresses, separates, sweaters and accessories, etc. The lines of men's and children's apparel include a little bit of everything, from suspenders to bathrobes, from kid's overalls to precious party dresses. Teen boys can have a field day buying shirts and jackets. Many women who have little hope of fitting sample sizes zero in on the handbags, scarves, belts, jewelry, etc. I've promised not to mention specific labels, but many are the most prominent found in retailing today, plus many you've never heard of before.

A word about dressing rooms: they don't have any. Because of security considerations most try-ons take place in the most rudimentary, barely private spaces. If you must try on, come wearing leotards to provide some measure of modesty.

Plan ahead, most reps will only accept cash, others will

accept checks with proper I. D. (There are probably as many different policies as there are reps doing business at the sale). Because of the crowds they do not allow strollers. One way to beat all the hassle of traffic and parking is to take BART, exit at the Powell/Market station and walk around the corner. All in all, it's an impressive event eagerly anticipated by the thousands who attend. Do come early!

Finally, if you're worried about missing the dates for these sales, which are usually advertised in major metropolitan papers a few days in advance, take note. To get on their mailing list, send a postcard to the *San Francisco Apparel Mart* at 821 Market, Room 222, San Francisco, Ca. 94103. Attention: Saturday Sale.

Active Sportswear

(Also see **Sporting Goods**)

T. L. BRODERICK CO.

2605 Lafayette St., Santa Clara 95050. Phone: (408) 748-0880. Hours: M-Fri 10am-8pm, Sat 10am-6pm, Sun Noon-5pm. (Closed from May 1st to September 1st.) Purchases: MC, VISA. Parking: Lot.

If price is your main consideration in outfitting the family for the slopes, rather than the latest jet set apparel, there's some hope at trimming those costs by shopping at the *T. L. Broderick Co.* Associated with the well known *P. F. McMullin Co.* in Santa Ana, they also discount namebrands of apparel, goggles, gloves, socks, caps, sweaters, turtlenecks and thermals. Additionally, they also sell their own lines of well-made, moderately priced down jackets, bibs, and pants for men, women, and children. Prices are reduced 30-60% on the first quality selection that is sold on a selfserve, no frills basis. They carry toddler and smaller children's sizes; kid's sizes 8-16; women's 6-16 or S,M, & L; men's 30-38, or S,M,L, & XL; plus tall sizes for men and women. They're located between the Central Expressway and El Camino, but they're set back from the street and easy to miss.

FILA FACTORY OUTLET

821 Industrial Road, San Carlos 94070. Phone 595-1750. Hours: T-F 11am-5:30pm, Sat 10am-5pm. Purchases: MC, VISA. Parking: Lot.

I don't know if wearing expensive tennis clothes will improve your game, but if you're willing to try anything, consider the clothing at the *Fila Factory Store*. At this distribution center, a small factory store exists for the purpose of selling past season merchandise, samples, and some seconds that have been repaired.

I'm hard pressed to justify the high retail prices on Fila sportswear. In fact, I think they're outrageous, but there is no disputing the fact that they use quality fabric, they're well-made and do wear well. At the factory store, prices are reduced approximately 50% which makes them more affordable but still not inexpensive. Tennis skirts, men's suits, warmup suits, ski vests, sweaters, bathing suits, shorts and everything else they make are in this selection of clothing, which is limited in styles and sizes, but changes frequently. Men's sizes range from 26-44 and women's sizes are 4-14. All sales final.

L & L OUTLET (ADIDAS)

967 Contra Costa Blvd., Pleasant Hill 94523. Phone: 689-4150. Hours: M-F 11:30am-8pm, Sat 9am-6pm, Sun 11am-6pm. Purchases: MC, VISA. Parking: Lot.

☞ **Other Store:** 926 El Camino Real, San Carlos, 592-8465.

If you have to have Adidas sportswear or athletic shoes you're going to get a price break at last! Instep which has several Adidas stores in the Bay Area has converted their former Pleasant Hill store into an outlet that is kept well supplied by Adidas with closeouts, irregulars, and salesman's samples. All merchandise is reduced at least 30% off of original retail and a major part of the overall selection is reduced 50%. Everyone in the family can find bargains from infants (a few T-shirts), boys, girls, teens, and moms and dads. All the familiar shirts, jackets, shorts, tennis apparel, jogging suits, warmup suits, bathing suits and everything else Adidas makes is usually in the store. Shipments from the factory arrive on a weekly basis so that the selection is constantly changing. Athletic shoes at 30-50% off are discontinued or have cosmetic flaws. These flaws are usually confined to a misprinted logo and are not associated with sizing or fabric imperfections. Children's sizes start at size 3 1/2 and go right through men's sizes 14. Basketball, tennis, jogging, football, soccer and all around athletic shoes are available. Sales on irregulars are final. Returns on closeouts are allowed for exchange within

seven days. This store is at the intersection of Willow Pass/Taylor Blvd. and Contra Costa Blvd. right across from the Sun Valley Shopping Center.

PURE SWEAT

2530 Bancroft Ave. (off Telegraph) Berkeley 94704. Phone: 548-7388. Hours: Purchases: MC, VISA. Parking: Street.

If you're into Jazzersize or aerobics, or if you'd like people to think you are because you love the comfort of loose fitting sweats, here's one place where you'll never have to sweat the prices. *Pure Sweat* is stocked with *basic* sweats in a dazzling rainbow selection of colors. Basic, in that there are no cutsey screen prints, labels, logos etc., just plain ol' solid colors. The super buy is the sweat set with plain crew neck top and draw string bottom for $15.00. (You can buy separate sizes if your bottom and top just don't match the way they should.) Other styles and prices: Hooded sweat with zipper $12.90; Pullover hood $10.90; Muscle top (finished edges) $5.90; Shimmel (unfinished edges) $5.90; Shorts $4.90; Crew neck top $7.90; Drawstring bottom $7.90. Between the walls, that are covered with shelves of sweats, there are tables piled high (but neatly) with overruns, closeouts, and off dye lots from other manufacturers and from their own inventory. Everything in this grab bag selection is priced at $5.90 — adding up to super bargains. All their own sweats are made in the U. S. of 50% cotton, 50% acrylan. Their sweats have no side seams — typical in the construction of better sweats made in the U. S. (Foreign made sweats usually have side seams because they lack the machinery to fabricate in this manner.) A smaller selection of 100% cotton sweats are carried, also nylon running shorts with lining for $10.90, plus socks, headbands, wrist bands etc. Unisex sizes in S,M,L & XL. Wonderful store!!

SAN FRANCISCO SKI & SPORTS

148 Townsend St. (between 2nd & 3rd Streets), San Francisco 94107. Phone: 543-5164. Hours: M-Sat 9:30am-6pm. Extended hours ski season. Purchases: MC, VISA. Parking: Street.

This company sells their own designer-direct active sportswear and accessories manufactured in their own factory directly to the consumer at substantial savings over comparable quality clothing in conventional retail stores. In addition, they offer samples lines and special purchase closeouts of activewear with other labels appealing to the budget conscious shopper at 20-60% off. Their basic selection is usually made up of ski apparel for men and women: parkas, stretch pants, bib overalls, Goretex clothes and one piece suits, plus warmup suits, tennis togs, activewear and bathing suits in summer. They always have an assortment of totes, daypacks, sunglasses, tights, leotards and other accessories for the sports oriented consumer. Sizes for Junior, Misses, and Men.

Children's Apparel (New)

(See **Baby Furniture — New and Used**)

BABYWEAR OUTLET

873 Blossom Hill Road. (at Pearl across from Oakridge), San Jose 95123. Phone: (408) 629-6021. Hours: M-F 10am-9pm, Sat 10am-6pm, Sun Noon-5pm. Purchases: MC, VISA. Parking: Lot.

☞ **Other Store:** 10 Abbott Avenue, Milpitas, (408) 263-5739.

Parents need all the help they can get in terms of resources and bargain prices when they shop for their children. Now those in the South Bay can add the *Babywear Outlets* to their list. These two stores are well stocked with clothing for dress and play, infant and layette accessories, and baby furniture and equipment.

I was very impressed with the many well known labels like Polly Flanders, Healthtex, Carters, Rob Roy, Cinderella, Jordache, Pierre Cardin, Billy the Kid, Thomas, Doe Spun, Nanette, etc. With such great lines you might wonder if these are old, leftover, outdated or damaged. They're not. The owners are operating on the premise that if prices are lower, people will buy more, and they'll make their profit on volume. Accordingly, all Carters are discounted at least 20%, except when they're having a promotion and prices are reduced another 10% off. The other apparel lines are discounted 30% off retail every day.

Their infant furniture like Jenny Lind cribs, high chairs,

strollers, etc., are very competitively priced. Each week a "special" is offered on one or two furniture items, plus special lines of apparel or seasonal merchandise where the price may be as close to wholesale as you can get. These specials are featured in the *San Jose Mercury*, and local media. To really be on the safe side, call and get on their mailing list. A word about sizes: boys sizes up to size 7, girls go through 6X. The infant and toddler selection is wonderful! Also, no cash refunds, but exchanges are cheerfully made within 15 days of purchase or a store credit will be given.

BRIGHT IDEAS FACTORY OUTLET

112 Commercial Ct., Santa Rosa 95404. Phone: (707) 523-0461. Hours: M-F 10am-4pm. Purchases: Cash or Check. Parking: Street.

Keep the kiddies dry and warm by shopping the bargain racks at *Bright Ideas*. Manufacturers of darling raincoats for the 2-6X crowd, they also import washable sweaters with delightful designs typically sold through major department stores or boutiques. Prices at the outlet are always wholesale or less on their seconds, seasonal overruns, and discontinued styles. The dresses, skirts and blouses combine contemporary styles with an old fashioned feeling. The outlet is a charming cubby hole in front of the factory.

CARTER'S FACTORY OUTLET STORE

2329 Buchanan Drive, Antioch 94509. Phone: 757-8623. Hours: M-Sat 10am-5pm, Sun 1pm-5pm. Purchases: Cash or Check only. Parking: Lot.

The Carter's Outlet Store is large, beautifully merchandised and well stocked. You will find a complete selection of everything Carter's makes: infant and layette goods, diapers, bibs, rubber pants, blankets, crib accessories, as well as playclothes, special occasion clothing and even Christening outfits. You'll be pleased to discover all the other manufacturers who use *Carter's Outlet Stores* to dispose of their overruns and end-of-season merchandise. Osh Kosh, Jack Tar, London Fog, Lee, Wrangler, Youngland, Polly Flanders, Pretty Please and Wonderalls are just a few worth mentioning.

The discounts at *Carter's* are not as great as the "outlet" title would suggest. By far the largest part of their selection is discounted a modest 20-30% off retail, while the rest is discounted 30-60%. Rather than discourage a visit, I'm only trying to give a realistic expectation about what you'll find after making what, for many, is a very long trek to Antioch.

Most of the clothing is from the previous year's stock, but only a retail fashion buyer would know the difference. The *Carter's* irregulars are clearly marked and priced accordingly. Your best buys will always be found on their special clearance merchandise. Sizes encompass infants (including preemie sizes through size 14 in girls and up to 18-20 in boys). For harried parents, the children's playroom, with toys and TV, is a welcome addition. Reach the outlet by taking the Somersville offramp South from Hwy. 4 and turning left on Buchanan.

CARY'S FACTORY OUTLET

102 Linden Street (off 3rd St. in Jack London Sq. area), Oakland 94607. Phone: 839-3329. Hours: M-F 10am-3pm. Purchases: MC, VISA. Parking: Street.

Cary's Factory Outlet is in a warehouse setting. This line which has a European or American country look (sizes infant — size 10) is high priced at retail since it is sold primarily to fine department and specialty stores nationwide. In the outlet, prices are a refreshing 40-50% off. The inventory consists of samples, irregulars, and end-of-season merchandise. Complementing the style of their own line and extending the size range is the Bearware line from Aspen, Colorado. Made from 100% cotton the infant apparel is delightful for gifts, plus there's bonnets, baskets and bibs at less than wholesale prices.

CHOCOLATE MOOSE

821 Petaluma Blvd., North, Petaluma 94952. Phone: (707) 763-9278. Hours: Mon-Sat 10am-4pm. Purchases: MC, VISA. Parking: Street.

Sonoma County has few resources where residents can purchase clothing at close to wholesale, but this manufacturer's outlet will save some a drive into the "City". *Chocolate Moose* is a specialty line for infants through size 10. Winter fashions are usually made in soft colorful velours while the summer clothing is primarily cotton knits or cotton wovens in sporty, casual styles appropriate for playwear. In addition to the *Chocolate Moose* line, the owner utilizes her connections with other manufacturers of specialty lines to extend the selection of merchandise to include precious party dresses, T-shirts and quilted infant goods. These are all sold at 30-50% discounts. The discounts reflect the fact that these are end-of-season, samples, and overruns. Clothing from other manufacturers extends the size range to include a few 14's.

FACTORY OUTLET

1509 San Pablo Ave. (North of Cedar), Berkeley 94702. Phone: 527-7633. Hours: M-Sat 10am-5pm. Purchases: MC, VISA. Parking: Street.

Sweet Potatoes fashions are truly *sweet*. They're perfect for the pre-school set in sizes 6mos. through 6X. The seconds, overruns, samples and past season styles are discounted 30-60% which doesn't make them cheap by any means since they are "boutique" priced at retail. Quilters can often pick up charming little fabrics for their projects that are left over from factory production.

FROCKS AND KNICKERS

603 Soquel Ave., Santa Cruz 95060. Phone: (408) 425-8463. Hours: M-Sat 10am-5:30pm. Purchases: MC, VISA. Parking: Lot.

Nestled in the front room and parlor of a charming renovated Victorian, *Frocks and Knickers* is where mothers in the Santa Cruz area go who want the "dress for success" look for their daughters. YSL, Chocolate Moose, Wild Flowers, Polly Flinders, Petite Gamine and other status lines in childrens dress and playwear are carried in infant sizes through pre-teen. Most of these adorables are samples so you won't find a complete size range in many lines. Precious dresses are plentiful for Easter and Xmas. Discounts range from 30-50%.

IZZIE'S KIDS

160 Raley's Towne Centre, Rohnert Park 94928. Phone: (707) 584-8771. Hours: M-Sat l0am-6pm, Thurs till 9pm, Sun Noon-5pm. Cash or Check Only. Parking: Lot.

You'd think being right next to a *Ross Store* would be a disadvantage for someone selling children's clothes at discount. Not so if your prices are as good or even better than those at *Ross*. Using their "good connections" the two owners are buying namebrands like Cinderella, Carters, Buster Brown, Esprit and others, then selling these current goods at discounts of 30-60% off retail. Some are samples, some are just good inside buys. There is a great selection of infant to toddler boys' and girls' dress and playwear, a good selection of girls' clothing up to size 14. Their active sportswear lines are very popular, with the latest looks in sweats geared for the very young, along with sweaters, party dresses, and mud puddle clothing. This is a good place to buy gifts if you don't mind paying 50 cents for a gift box. Mothers can shop without fear because exchanges are allowed; cash refunds are given except on sale clearance merchandise. The store is on the small side, but the selection is delightful.

JAMBOREE

5630 Geary (betw. 20th & 21st Ave.), San Francisco 94121. Phone: 751-9000. Hours: M-Sat 9:30am-6pm, Sun Noon-5pm. Purchases: MC, VISA. Parking: Street, City Lot.

☞ **Other Stores:** 204 E. 2nd Ave, San Mateo, 342-5555; 1649 Hollenbeck Ave., Sunnyvale, (408) 739-3337; 1690 Locust, Walnut Creek, 935-5252.

Jamboree was the first elegant children's discount store in the Bay Area several years ago. Even with the advent of many competitors, they still hold their own as a purveyor of quality children's clothing at solid discount prices. Their stores have been redecorated, their lines expanded, their service increased — all aimed at retaining their fair share of the market. Their infant and toddler departments are especially well stocked with activewear and basics. *Jamboree* has always been a reliable resource for special occasion clothing and they still are, with many impressive designer lines. They've rounded out the "basics" with gift items, underwear, socks, lingerie, as well as jewelry, hair goods, and other accessories. Sizes for boys range from infant through size 7; girls sizes are infant through size 14. In terms of savings, count on 20-50% off retail. Exchanges are allowed, but no cash refunds. No children of your own? Give one of their gift certificates.

KIDS CLOTHING CO.

216 Northgate One (Freitas Pkwy. exit off 101), San Rafael 94903. Phone: 479-4932. Hours: M-Sat 10am-5:30pm, Sun Noon-5pm. Purchases: MC, VISA. Parking: Lot.

This looks like any other children's store, but there's one important difference. All the very good quality, name brand merchandise is marked down at least 15-20%. The owners buy some samples, some overruns, and take a smaller markup on other merchandise to offer discount prices. At their sales they take an additional 20-25% off so you want to get on their mailing list. *Kids Clothing Co.* specializes in better 100% cotton domestic and European brands at moderate prices. Sizes: infant through preteen for girls, infant through toddler 4 for boys.

KIDS MART

2020 El Camino Real (Mervyns Plaza), Santa Clara 95051. Phone: (408) 984-5215. Hours: M-F 10am-9pm, Sat 10am-6pm, Sun Noon-5pm. Purchases: MC, VISA, Layaway. Parking: Lot.

☞ **Other Stores:** Daly City, Dublin, Fairfield, Mountain View, Petaluma, Pinole, Pleasant Hill, Redwood City, Salinas, San Jose - 3 stores, San Leandro, Santa Clara, Vallejo.

A sign on the wall at *Kids Mart* says, "Our goal is to buy quality overproduction from famous brand manufacturers, to pass our buying skills on to the public in the form of low prices, and to sell at smaller profits so our prices are always sale prices." They do all of this and more.

Their stores are immaculate, beautifully merchandised and well staffed. Their brands include many of your favorite traditional namebrands (usually never sold to off-price stores), plus those status trendsetters even the youngest child seems determined to wear. Size range is infant through 14. The overall selection is geared towards providing the basics for school or play. You'll find a good selection of dresses for infant and toddler girls but few in larger sizes. Prices are 30-70% off retail. The *Kids Mart* operation has moved into the Bay Area after opening over 60 stores in Southern California. They now have over 100 stores in California and Arizona which accounts for their volume buying power and great prices!

MOUSEFEATHERS FACTORY OUTLET

1235-A Fourth Street (off Gilman), Berkeley 94710. Phone: 527-7381. Hours: M-F 10am-3pm. Purchases: Cash or Check. Parking: Limited street.

Do call before visiting: occasionally the owner must leave to make deliveries and attend to other business and it would be a shame to miss an opportunity to buy the charming girls' dresses, play clothes, plus raincoats, jumpsuits, and pants. My favorite styles are the adorable prints in 100% cotton that are often utilized in creating a perfect tea party dress like the one you buy for portrait sittings. The outlet is small and selection limited to five or six racks of seconds, past season, and sample merchandise in sizes 2-10 at 40-50% off retail. Leftover fabrics too, at tempting prices!

PATTY CAKES FACTORY OUTLET

830 Cleveland (West side of 101 between 9th & College.), Santa Rosa 94501. Phone: (707) 526-2778. Hours: M-Sat 10am-5pm. Purchases: Cash or Check. Parking: Street.

Bright, clever, colorful and fun describe the original *Patty Cakes* line for infants and toddlers. For new babies, special birthday gifts, and just everyday adorable clothing, the line is every bit as cute as the name would suggest. The high prices at retail reflect the use of many hand dyed quality cottons, fleece, and knits plus extraordinary detailing that results in these little treasures. They'd melt the heart of any grandma! Prices on current lines are discounted 20%, while the past seasons, and seconds are wholesale or less. Sizes 6mos to 4T. All sales final.

PRICE CLUB

(See **General Merchandise — Discount Stores**)

SUCH A BUSINESS

5533 College Ave., Oakland 94618. Phone: 655-6641. Hours: M-Sat 10am-5:30pm, Thurs eve till 8pm, Sun Noon-5pm. Purchases: MC, VISA. Parking: Street.

There are many reasons why I like this store. I can always find great little toys, the kind of toys you use just as a little pick-me-up for the unhappy child. I also appreciate the samples and irregulars of brands like Buster Brown and Healthtex that I find on their racks at 20-30% discounts. First quality clothing at regular prices is also mixed in with the bargains, which can be confusing. Prospective parents will be delighted with the selection and competitive prices on new infant furniture and equipment. You can also shop leisurely after depositing the kids in the play area. This shop is about two blocks from the Rockridge BART Station.

Children's Apparel (Used)

Not wishing to be overly redundant, or end up sounding hackneyed while attempting to list the merits of resale and consignment shops for children, I think it's better to deal with this category with a general approach and leave you to take advantage of whichever is closest to you. There's no doubt in my mind that if you really want to bundle up the kids without spending a bundle, you should consider the many consignment shops specializing in children's clothes around the Bay Area. Many offer a mix of new and used clothing, some even carry maternity clothing. Prices are usually 75% off the original price. The discriminating shopper with good timing can often find clothing that is as good as brand new just because there are types of clothes that get little wear or use like frilly dresses or fancy coats. Each shop may have different times or days when clothing will be accepted for consignment (if you're more interested in selling than buying) so call ahead before packing up your leftover, outgrown, but still wearable clothing.

ALAMEDA KIDS STUFF & BALLOON CO.

1422 Park St., Alameda 94501. Hours: M-Sat 10am-5:30pm. Purchases: MC, VISA. Parking: Street.

Consignment clothing for kids sizes 0-14. Small selection of maternity plus lots of helium balloons!

CINNAMON BEAR

1309 Solano Ave., Albany 94706. Phone: 524-3649. Hours: M-Sat 11am-5pm. Purchases: Cash or Check. Parking: Street.

New clothing discounted at least 10%, samples and special purchases 20-50% off retail. Good selection of *used* clothing (sizes 0-14), toys, books, and maternity clothes.

CHILDREN'S CORNER

1147 So. Saratoga/Sunnyvale Rd. (Huntington Village Shopping Ctr.), San Jose 95129. Phone: (408) 257-5332. Hours: M-Th 10am-5pm, Fri 1pm-5pm, Sat 10am-5pm. Purchases: MC, VISA. Parking: Lot.

New samples from quality lines discounted 30-50%. Consignment clothing in infant through pre-teen plus maternity fashions.

KIDS CLOSET

721 Camino Plaza, San Bruno 94066. Phone: 589-6400. Hours: T-Sat 10:30-4:30pm. Purchases: Cash or Check. Parking: Street.

From "closet to closet" consignment children fashions, maternity clothes and gift items. Sizes 0-14.

THE KIDS ROOM

115 Manor Drive, Pacifica 94044. Phone: 355-5009. Hours: T-Sat 10am-5pm. Purchases: MC, VISA. Parking: Street.

Good selection of consignment clothing and lots of extras: used baby furniture, handmade items, toys, books, rentals on cribs and bassinets plus cheerful owners.

OUTGROWN

1417 4th Street, San Rafael 94901. Phone: 457-2219. Hours: M-Sat 10am-4pm. Purchases: Cash or Check. Parking: Street, Lot. Well stocked with consignment clothing in sizes 0-14. Maternity clothing too! Occasionally, baby equipment and furniture.

POPCORN

1201-C Solano Ave., Albany 94706. Phone: 524-6488. Hours: T-Sat 10am-5pm. Purchases: Cash or Check. Parking: Street.

Discounts on new clothes in sizes 0-7; consignment bargains in sizes 0-14, and maternity clothes. Special gifts, toys, and fantastic helium balloons.

2r2s.

SECOND TIME AROUND
979 W. Winton (Hunter Shopping Center), Hayward. Phone: 783-4832. Hours: M-F 10am-5pm, Sat 10am-4pm. Purchases: Cash or Check. Parking: Lot.

Bring in clothes, baby furniture or equipment (by appointment) and leave with cash in hand or a store credit for future buying. Sizes accepted: 0-14, plus maternity clothes on consignment.

Family Apparel

(Also see **Men's** and **Women's Apparel, Sporting Goods**)

CLOTHES DIRECT
3589 Industrial Drive (near K-Mart), Santa Rosa 94501. Phone: (707)523-2730. Hours: M-Sat 10am-6pm, Th to 9pm, Sun Noon-5pm. Purchases: MC, VISA. Parking: Lot.

☞ **Other Stores:** 322 Front St., Santa Cruz; 2801 Mc Henry Blvd., Modesto; 241 No. Mc Dowel Blvd., Petaluma.

The *Clothes Direct* stores are like neighborhood emporiums for casual family clothing. These warehouse stores offer few frills, but their brightly painted ceiling ducts, immaculate merchandising, and bold use of colors through-out their stores, all say "welcome" to their shoppers. Their speciality is popular labels in sportswear with a special emphasis on junior and young men's fashions. Most merchandise is first quality closeouts and overruns from Bay Area and national manufacturers, or seconds and irregulars that are super bargains. First quality merchandise is usually discounted from 30-45%. Clearance racks are always in evidence with drastic markdowns on merchandise that has been around too long. To outfit the whole family, especially teens, for casual clothing, i.e. tops, bottoms, jackets, you can't do better for discount prices in these towns than a shopping expedition to *Clothes Direct*. Sizes: Children 4-6X; boys and girls 7-14/8-18; juniors 3/4-13/14; and men S,M,L, XL.

GOOD BUY STORE
Broadway at 20th Street (at Bart 19th St. exit), Oakland 94612. Phone: 891-5000. Hours: M-F 10am-8pm, Sat 10am-6pm, Sun Noon-5pm. Purchases: Checks, store charge. Parking: Pay Lots.

☞ **Other Store:** 1789 Hillsdale Ave, San Jose 95124. (408)265-1111, ext. 305.

After the sales and markdowns at the 21 Northern California *Emporium-Capwell* stores, the "dogs of war" that are left are sent to the *Good Buy* shops. In Oakland there's a smattering of everything: some mens, some kids, and gobs of misses and junior apparel. Their price tags are titillating! The tickets reflect a 50% discount from the original price for starters. Then 3 other prices are listed reflecting what you'll pay in 30, 60 or 90 days if your *Good Buy* hasn't been snapped up. As you might expect some pieces are a "little worse for wear", while others equal a dynamite buy. If you find a gem of a bargain, don't try to wait till the lowest price in 60-90 days, because if it's that good it won't last that long. The San Jose store has only women's apparel, but hopefully that will change before the end of '84. Oakland also offers a fairly tempting selection of shoes from their upstairs shoe department. Parking at Oakland doesn't have to be a problem if you take BART to the 19th St. Station exit that leads you right into the basement *Good Buy Shop*. All sales are final.

KEALY STORE

8000 Capwell Dr. (Across Fwy. 17 from Oakland Coliseum), Oakland 94621. Phone: 635-9328. Hours: M-Sat 9:30am-5pm. Purchases: Cash or Check. Lay-a-Way. Parking: Side of building.

The *Kealy Store* has been around for a number of years. It was originally created as a service for their employees and as a vehicle for clearing out sample merchandise acquired in selling many manufacturers' lines to the military. Basically, everything they sell is reduced at least 30% off retail, often as much as 50% on lines that are not discounted in other stores. They carry radios, stereos, and TV's; luggage, briefcases, watches and clocks; linens; small electric appliances, and clothing. I feel that their clothing selection is geared more to the mature customer, men and women who are shopping for basics rather than trendy styles sought by the younger set. However, their current junior and misses styles in swimsuits and coverups, (from a popular swimsuit company) are irresistible for all ages, especially at almost 50% off. Sizes for women are fairly complete in 8-18, for men, S, M, L, & X-L. For special deals be sure to get on their mailing list. Directions: From the Nimitz Fwy., take Hegenberger Rd. West, Right on Edgewater, Left on Pendleton, Right on Capwell Dr. The store is on the side of the building. The next time you're heading in for an event at the Coliseum, leave a little extra time for a looksee at the *Kealy Store*.

MACY'S FURNITURE CLEARANCE PLACE
(See **Furniture and Accessories**)

MARSHALL'S

5160 Stevens Creek Blvd. (at Lawrence Expressway), San Jose 95129. Phone: (408) 244-8962. Hours: M-S 9:30am-9:30pm, Sun Noon-5pm. Purchases: MC, VISA. Parking: Free Lot.

☞ **Other Stores:** Newark, Pleasant Hill, Sacramento, San Jose, Stockton.

At *Marshall's*, it's department store selection (minus atmosphere) with many brand names selling for less than retail. Their clothing departments for men, boys, girls, infants and women are the largest part of *Marshall's* inventory. Their shoe department has excellent buys and lo and behold, they even have a lingerie and robe department. 20-60% savings are offered on merchandise categorized as irregulars, samples or overruns. Some labels are cut. *Marshall's* has a full money back refund policy within 14 days of purchase with a sales slip verification. That's nice! Not to be overlooked are the linens, housewares, gift departments where you can purchase sheets, spreads, and dust ruffles, etc., at prices that should make white sale admakers blush. Conveniently, *Macy's Furniture Clearance Place* is next door to this San Jose store — two great bargain places side by side.

MONTGOMERY WARD CLEARANCE CENTER
(See **General Merchandise — Liquidators**)

ROSS DEPARTMENT STORES
7888 Dublin Blvd., Dublin 94566. Phone: 829-5995. Hours: M-F 10am-9pm, Sat 9am-6pm, Sun 11am-5pm. Purchases: MC, VISA. Parking: Lot.

☞ **Other Stores:** Carmichael, Castro Valley, Concord, Fremont, Novato, Oakland, Pacifica, Redwood City, Rohnert Park, Roseville, San Jose (Westgate Mall & Almaden Plaza), San Rafael, Santa Rosa, South Sacramento, Sunnyvale.

To the layman, "off-price" may seem like just another word for "discount." To *Ross* stores it means selling brand name merchandise at prices 20-60% less than traditional department and specialty store prices. Average prices will be 30-35% less. Their strategy: buy opportunistically. The opportunism often means buying from big-name manufacturers at the end of the season, often at less than the manufacturers' cost. The manufacturers are frequently happy to get rid of the merchandise because they have overproduced, are unable to meet a delivery date, need space for next season's line or have an order cancellation. *Ross* also accepts a lower markup than traditional stores, and puts the merchandise into a low-cost enviornment. *Ross* has avoided the high-rent districts such as regional shopping malls and instead opted to recycle space in older stores and to put new stores into strip shopping centers.

You can satisfy many needs at *Ross* stores. Not only do they have clothes for *every* member of the family, for all occasions, they also sell linens (or domestics), shoes, hosiery and handbags. I love their price tags which note whether an item is irregular (very few), past season, current season and the comparable price in other stores. After just a few minutes in the store you'll probably round up a shopping cart to pile in the bargains. *Ross* is where I go to fill in the spaces in my closet. Perfect for a replacement pair of basic pants, a spruce-up-your-wardrobe blouse, and especially panty hose and lingerie. Young mothers appear ecstatic at the prices and children's clothing selection, while a neighbor reported finding the lowest prices on flannel sheets in their domestics department. All the amenities of full service stores are available, such as lay-a-way, exchange, cash refunds, private dressing rooms, etc.

WEAR WITH ALL
75-J Bellam Boulevard, Marin Square, San Rafael 94901. Phone: 454-GOSH. Hours: M-Sat 10am-6pm, Sun Noon-5pm. Purchases: MC, VISA. Parking: Lot.

As the owner says "All her genes and jeans come from Oshgosh, Wisconsin". The loyalty to her hometown is evident with the opening of her store devoted exclusively to the Oshkosh line including accessories such as back packs, bandanas, jackets, bib overalls, engineer caps, canvas aprons, pants, shirts, sweaters, jackets and jumpers. Prices are reduced a modest 15-20% off regular retail prices (but not department store sale prices). Sizes and styles are available for the whole family from baby to grandpa. Not in evidence at press time was her own line of maternity wear which will also be well priced for bargain hunters.

WHITNEY'S/MCO

470 East Brokaw, San Jose 95112. Phone: (408) 279-3855. Hours: M-Sat 9:30-5:30pm, Sun Noon-5pm. Purchases: MC, VISA. Parking: Lot.

☞ **Other Stores:** One Monterey Road, Monterey; 4165 Stevens Creek, Santa Clara; 5759 Pacheco Blvd., Concord; 747 First St., Gilroy.

Brad Whitney took over operation of two *MCO* stores in the Bay Area in 1984. It's a little hard during the transition to get a clear picture of just what their operation will look like in six months. At present, it's a mixed bag. Some good stuff, some stuff so old, I can't imagine where they found it, or why they bought it. Yet, they bear watching. They always have sportcoats, blazers, and western style coats for men and women from their own manufacturing plant in Monterey, and these are very nice. They have a sprinkling of prestigious labels on their racks, but it appears at this time that these are frequently well past season. Clothing for the whole family is sold plus accessories, nightwear, underwear, nylons, etc. You'll have no complaints about the prices which are discounted 40-70%

off original retail. Womens sizes 4-16; Men's tops-46; Children's-infant to teen.

Men's Apparel

(Also see **Active Sportswear & Family, Women's Apparel and Sporting Goods**)

ATHLETIC SHOE FACTORY STORE
(See — **Shoes**)

BELMONT CLOTHES

915 Ralston Ave., Suite B, Belmont 94002. Phone: 591-8760. Hours: T-F 10am-5:30pm, Sat 10am-5pm. Purchases: MC, VISA. Parking: Home Federal Savings Parking Lot.

Professional and career men who are interested in dependable, enduring fashion rather than the latest fads and trends will be impressed with the fine quality and modest prices at *Belmont Clothes*. Discreetly tucked away behind a bank, the store is immaculate and simply furnished with most available space taken up by racks of suits, sportcoats, and slacks. In fact, they only sell these three items. Each item has a letter code on the hand tag which you compare to their posted price list which reflects their reduced prices compared to a suggested retail price. With lower overhead, and minimal advertising expenses, they still make a respectable profit and their customers reap a tidy savings!

Suits range in price from $139-$269, sportcoats, $80-$219, and slacks, $19-$44. Most of the selection is obtained from well known American manufacturers. Their selection is very extensiv℈ in all three categories with hard to find sizes available in good quantities. At these prices it's understandable that they charge extra for alterations. Once you get on their mailing list you'll be kept informed of their latest shipments and special sales. Bring the ladies when you shop, they've added a nice selection of career apparel for women. Finally, their low-key, no pressure approach to selling is very refreshing and most appreciated.

CLOTHING CLEARANCE CENTER
695 Bryant Street, San Francisco 94105. Phone: 495-7875. Hours: M-F l0am-8pm, Sat 9am-6pm, Sun l0am-5pm. Purchases: MC, VISA. Parking: Street — difficult at S. F. store.

☞ **Other Stores:** 2995 Junipero Serra Blvd., Daly City; 2660 El Camino Real, Santa Clara; 255 El Portal Shopping Center, San Pablo; 942-A Blossom Hill Rd., San Jose; 505 Contra Costa Blvd., Pleasant Hill; 34 E. 4th Ave., San Mateo.

The man who has never ventured out into the bargain environment for his clothing needs may feel skeptical when first entering the warehouse — no frills — atomsphere of *CCC*. If he stays awhile and objectively considers the merchandise, he cannot fail to be impressed that the selection of suits, sportcoats, pants, shirts, sweaters and ties, etc. He will be pleased at the quantity and amount of

quality garments in even hard-to-fit shorts, portlies, longs and extra longs.

With savings that average a pleasing 40%, you may wonder how they do it. *CCC* is associated with 250 outlets throughout the U.S., all buying through one centralized buying office. April-Marcus buys the overstock inventories of manufacturers and retailers throughout the country and these tremendous savings are passed on to their customers. Their success has been noted by articles in *Newsweek* and *Money* magazines.

Their salesmen are not on commission so you won't have jackets forced off your body by aggressive salesmen, and they will give you as little or as much help as you need. I think it's wise to ask for assistance. You'll save time as they can steer you to those manufacturers that have a cut that is suited to your body type. At these prices any alterations are extra. They can be done on the premises for a minimum charge with fast, reliable service.

All the merchandise is first quality with a fashion orientation geared primarily to the MOR (middle-of-the-road) customer. However, I've observed men from all income levels, age groups and with varying tastes doing business here. You are unlikely to spend more than $99 for a sportcoat, or more than $199 for a suit. They have frequent special markdowns.

DERBY FACTORY OUTLET
333 Bryant St. (off 2nd St.), San Francisco 94107. Phone: 543-6393. Hours: W-F llam-4pm, Th Noon-5pm, Sat 9am-2pm. Purchases: MC, VISA. Parking: Street.

The *Derby Factory Outlet* is first on my list when shopping for a new blazer or sportcoat. The name, which may not ring bells, is usually sold under private label through major department stores and fine specialty shops. You'd be surprised and impressed if I dared to reveal where you're likely to find their merchandise. Their Harris Tweeds, 100% wool herringbone, assorted wool shetlands, wool flannels, and summer weight wool-blend hopsacking (linen look), are beautifully tailored, most fully lined, and with prices that make this a mecca for money-saving, savvy shoppers. "Classic" is the style of record. If you want a basic Navy blue blazer, for men or women, you'll want to dash right in. The selection is about equally divided between men's and women's jackets and blazers. In addition, they carry 100% wool slacks at $33 for men and some matching dirndl skirts for women. Occasionally, they will cut matching wool fabric at $12/yard for those women wishing to make their pants or skirts. You're not limited to stock in the outlet, when available they will pull additional sizes from their warehouse, so do inquire if you don't see what you want in your size. There's also several racks of their well known floating shoulder casual jackets for about $30-$35 in boy's sizes 8-20 and men's sizes. Their range is extensive. In men's: 36-56 in regular, 36-44 in short, and 40-56 in Long; Women's Petite 2-14, and regular 4-18.

EXECUTIVE CLOTHES
520 Washington St., San Francisco 94111. Phone: 433-7818. Hours: M-F 9:30am-5:30pm, Sat 10am-3pm. Purchases: MC, VISA. Parking: Street or Pay Lot.

You're greeted at this store across from the Transamerica Building by a loud jarring buzzer as you open the gate into the sales area. After you've calmed your pounding heart and nerves you can start to appreciate the selection of men's suits, sportcoats, slacks, shirts, raincoats, belts, and ties. Most of the merchandise sports their private label making comparison shopping difficult. However, if you're familiar with the merchandise sold in other retail stores you will recognize at *Executive Clothes*, the same quality and fine tailoring, but at a much lower price. Their selection of three piece wool suits in the $160 price range is extensive, and the stylish camel hair sportcoats at $179 were excellent values.

Most of their merchandise is purchased from American manufacturers whose styles are designed for the professional or executive mien. They maintain a complete size range (35-50) which includes many hard-to-find sizes. Alternations are extra, but they will have them done for you at a very reasonable cost.

FASHIONS UNLIMITED
(See **Apparel, Women's — Neighborhood Store**)

GOLDEN BEAR LEATHER FACTORY OUTLET
475 Valencia (2nd Floor), San Francisco 94103. Phone: 863-6171. Hours: M-F 9am-5pm. Purchases: MC, VISA. Parking: Street.

If approximately $80-$145 sounds like a good price range for better quality leather jackets (in bomber, western and blazer styles), or suede and shearling outerwear then stop by *Golden Bear's* factory showroom where samples, imperfects, closeouts and first quality overruns are 40% off retail. Sizes for men range from 36-46 and for women 6-16. If you're buying for a gift, discuss exchange arrangements with them before buying, they're very reasonable. The *Golden Bear* line is sold through better stores, specialty shops, and mail order catalog houses across the country, in Europe and the Orient. There's no guarantee you'll find exactly what you want on the first visit because they only have about five racks of jackets and vests to choose from in their sale room.

KUPPENHEIMER FACTORY STORES

455 Paseo Grande (San Lorenzo Village), San Lorenzo 94580. Phone: 278-0213. Hours: M-F 10am-9pm, Sat 9am-6pm, Sun 11am-6pm. Purchases: MC, VISA. Parking: Lot.

☞ **Other Stores:** 651 Contra Costa Blvd., Pleasant Hill; 797 E. El Camino Real, Sunnyvale; 81 El Camino Real, San Carlos; 5151 Broadway, Oakland; 1330 Howe Ave., Sacramento, 5300 Sunrise Blvd., Fairoaks.

Kuppenheimer is a division of Hercules Manufacturing, who for over 70 years, has been making men's clothing and selling it to retailers nationwide. Now they have eliminated the middleman and are selling directly to the public through their factory owned stores. Controlling retail overhead allows them to reduce prices by operating basic no-frills stores. They offer a wide selection of suits, slacks and sportcoats in a complete size range whether your build is trim, regular, tall or portly. They've got other basics too, like shirts, ties, belts and outerwear. Initially, I was not that impressed with this outfit, but in the last few years they've upgraded their quality with better fabrics and more 100% wool styles and offer a very good value for the price you pay. If you're just getting started in the business world, this is a good place to acquire the required look without spending your first few months salary. Alterations will cost extra like they do everywhere else, so hope for a perfect fit.

KUTLER BROS.

585 Mission Street, San Francisco 94105. Phone: 543-7770. Hours: M-F 9am-5pm, Sat 9am-3pm. Purchases: MC, VISA. Parking: Street or Pay Lots.

Kutler Bros. has a most impressive selection of fine quality men's clothing at discount prices (30-50%). Although I can't mention specific brands or labels, be assured that you will see many of their designer suits, sportcoats, slacks, and raincoats, along with dress shirts, sport shirts, sweaters, ties and belts, selling in only the "best" men's stores or departments. *Kutler Bros.* does most of its business with executives and professionals. Accordingly, a large part of their inventory may seem high priced even at discount pricing. That $425-$450 suit can be a bargain for one customer at $269-$289, and out of reach for the next who will choose among the more modestly priced lines. Their size range is extensive and includes the hard-to-fit in any dimension. Alterations are not included in the discount price, but are done at a minimal charge right on the premises. The shoe department contains the best names in imported and domestic footwear at 25-50% below retail. They carry a full range of styles — from penny loafers to fine Italian dress shoes, from crepe soled casuals to wing tips. My one frustration at *Kutler Bros.* is that all their prices are coded to protect the manufacturer. Therefore, if you're on a tight budget, let the salesman know and he'll keep you in your price range.

In order for *Kutler Bros.* to acquire these fine lines and to sell them at reduced prices, they have an agreement with their manufacturers to exclude the public and to restrict their business to a select clientele which is based on personal referrals, or to employees of large companies that have had entry arrangements made for them. While I find it hard to believe they'd turn a prospective customer away, I've always been asked for my card and cleared before gaining entrance to the showroom. Check with your company to see if customer privileges have been arranged. If they haven't, suggest that they do.

MEN'S CLOTHING CO.

1684 Locust Street, Walnut Creek 94596. Phone: 935-3321. Hours: M-S 10am-6pm, Th till 9pm. Sun 11am-5pm. Purchases: MC, VISA, AE. Parking: Street.

Savings from 25-50% off suggested retail price on a large selection of quality designer and famous brand men's apparel can be found in this converted garage in downtown Walnut Creek. The location affects their prices, however they do not buy closeouts, seconds, factory overruns or unlabeled merchandise. They buy regular designer and better quality, natural fiber, in-season clothes at the regular cost and just charge less for it than other stores. They offer Calvin Klein, Pierre Cardin, John Henry, Henry Grethel, Givenchy and others in a full range of men's clothing and apparel. Although this is intended to be a no frills opera-

tion, the service is excellent. There is a charge for alterations.

MEN'S SHIRT AND SWEATER OUTLET

8200 Capwell Drive, Oakland 94621. Phone: 635-8400. Hours: M-Th 11am-3pm, Fri 11am-4pm, Dec. Xmas hours, M-F 10am-4pm. Purchases: Cash Only. Parking: Free Lot.

A pleasing selection of men's ski sweaters, mod T-shirts, golf shirts, and sportshirts is available at this manufacturer's outlet for a well-known brand (think of a famous golf course in the Carmel area) found in better men's stores and department stores.

Finding this outlet takes all your investigative skills, since it is obscurely located at the side back corner of the building. A small hand-lettered sign saying "Open" is the only indication of the treasure trove of men's wear within. Merchandise is neatly arranged on tables or racks in sizes S-XL. There are dressing rooms. Exchanges are permitted, but no cash refunds or credit slips. P. S. They're just a few doors down from the *Kealy Store*.

MEN'S WEARHOUSE

5355 Almaden Expressway #39 (Almaden Plaza), San Jose 95118. Phone: (408) 723-1900. Hours: M-F 10am-9pm, Sat 10am-6pm, Sun Noon-5pm. Purchases: MC, VISA. Parking: Lot.

☞ **Other Stores:** 2550 W. El Camino Real, San Antonio Center, Mt. View; 508-K Contra Costa Blvd., Pleasant Hill; 5572 Newpark Mall, Newark ; 655 Market (Sheraton

Palace); San Francisco; Peninsla Boardwalk Center, Redwood City.

The Houston based *Men's Wearhouse* is a fast breeding chain with over 30 stores and more to come. Most of their merchandise bears their own private label. However, they select the fabrics and styles for their stores and have them made by such well known designers as Pierre Cardin, Botany 500, Cartier, Nino Cerruti, YSL, Givenchy and Adolfo. Because they deal with these manufacturers on a volume, cash basis, they buy "right" and can pass on considerable savings to value-conscious men. Additionally, they do purchase regular inventory from these and other manufacturers. Overall the discounts range from 20-40% off retail prices on their suits, sportcoats, ties, shirts, sweaters, raincoats and belts. Sizes in men's clothing ranges from 36S-52X-Long. Alterations are not included in the purchase price but often can be done while you wait depending on the complexity of the job. Alterations are guaranteed to your satisfaction. Full refunds will be given on unaltered merchandise if returned within 30 days accompanied with a receipt. I liked their prices and their quality.

MERCHANDISERS INC.

343 Golden Gate Ave., San Francisco 94102. Phone: 864-0515. Hours: M-F 9am-5:30pm, Sat 10am-4pm. Purchases: MC, VISA. Parking: Limited street, pay lots.

This is where the "Feds" shop on their lunch hour and also potential legal beagles from Hastings Law School. Customers are typically those that are sportsminded, just stopping in for some golf balls, athletic shoes, tennis gear;

or racquet ball, camping, backpacking and team sport equipment. Of course, they don't overlook the apparel. Good prices on socks, underwear, and a fairly complete active wear department posting prices that yield a 20-45% savings. This results from low rent, low markup, and good buying skills. Not a big outfit, but not to be overlooked when you're in the area.

OPTIONS

3985 17th St. (corner of Market & Castro), San Francisco 94114. Phone: 863-7818. Hours: M-S 11am-7pm, Sun Noon-6pm. Purchases: MC, VISA. Parking: Very Limited Street.

Take the #8 or 33 bus, underground Muni, or the Market Street Trolley from downtown, and you'll avoid the headaches of parking in this part of town. *Options* is a wonderful off-price boutique specializing in better quality fashions for men and women. They carry wonderful sportswear for men who want "classic casual", but no suits or sportcoats. Their sweaters and shirts are from the best makers. Women love their stylish apparel that allows them to look up-to-date without feeling foolish (if they're inclined to be conventional). Their shirts, blouses, leisure/fun fashions, accessories, and career apparel are all discounted 20-50% off retail. Everything is first quality, typically current overruns or sample lines from well known favorites. Natural fibers predominate in the selections for both men and women. Sizes for women: 3/4 to 15/16; men 14 1/2-17, 28-36 or S-XL. The store is a pleasure to shop in because everything is beautifully displayed and the service is very gracious. After bagging your bargains, try some of the delightful restaurants and cafes that abound in this colorful area!

SHEEPSKIN OUTLET

68 Coombs St. (off Imola), Napa 94559. Phone: (707) 252-0923. Hours: Th-M 10am-4:30pm. Purchases: MC, VISA. Parking: Lot.

☞ **Other Store:** Sawyer Sheepskin Company, Freeport, Maine.

Sawyer of Napa does very well as a by-product industry. That is, turning sheepskin from lambs grown on the Western slopes of the U.S. for food consumption into beautiful coats, vests, jackets, and car seat covers. Their fine quality apparel sells in Harrods of London, Bloomingdales, Lord and Taylor plus many other fine stores. The outlet store which is the repository of samples, discontinued styles, overruns, and occasionally seconds — all sold for approximately 40% off retail.

Be prepared for the prices: even at 40% off, a quality full length woman's coat can range from $480 up. Men's jackets start at $210, and vests are $39-$130. If you're a Perry Ellis customer, you'll be delighted over the prices on his exciting coats and jackets which he designs for *Sawyer*. To maximize profits, leftover sheepskin is made into hats, golf club covers, booties, purses, etc. and also sold for discount prices. Sold for about $70 a pair, their car seat covers are hot items.

Sheepskin can last for 25 years if properly cared for. The high cost of these garments can be attributed to the 65 processes involved in taking raw skin and turning in into a perfect finished product. Sizes in women's garments range from 4-16, men's sizes are 34-50. Recently they've expanded their selection to include leather coats and the finest leather handbags and luggage all at savings up to 30%. Exchanges are accepted within 30 days of purchases. Et cetera: If you ever get to Freeport, Maine don't miss the opportunity to check their store, and the other outlets like *L. L. Bean, Ralph Lauren, J. G. Hook and Designer Fashions.*

Women's Apparel

(Also see **Family Apparel**)

With 73 separate listings for women's clothing I divided the listings into three categories. Hopefully, this will enable you to locate the resources that best suit your shopping needs, while saving time, gas and money.

Factory Outlets: Stores that are typically owned and operated by a clothing manufacturer or distributor, usually located on or near the manufacturer's plant. Their popularity is often due to their ability to offer the lowest prices that you'll find anywhere on *their* merchandise. Some manufacturers offer little in the way of retail store amenities like sales staff or even try-ons. Most of these stores elect to keep a low profile, and depend on word-of-mouth advertising. Many prefer to go nameless or choose an innocuous name like "Factory Outlet" or "Factory Store" which makes it difficult sometimes to figure out who they really are and what labels they sell. Factory outlets do not always take credit cards and may have unconventional hours. Many manufacturers have chosen to develop a thriving and profitable side business by operating not just one, but several factory owned stores throughout the country. These stores are listed under the *chain store* category.

BETTER DRESS OUTLET

777 Florida Street (at 20th), San Francisco 94110. Phone: 821-4422. Hours: M-Sat 10am-5pm. Purchases: MC, VISA. Parking: Limited Street.

For the sophisticated woman of any age who desires a nice dress with subtle details, good fit, in beautiful colors, a dress that will be a wardrobe basic for years, this is *the* place. There are dresses for working women that are perfect for dazzling days leading right into elegant nights, dresses in high voltage colors, rich jeweled tones, wonderful 2-piece combinations, comfortable casual summer cottons, subtle wool crepes, soft linens, plus their renowned silks in crepe de chine, charmeuse, crepe, and raw silk. The look each season is updated to reflect the latest trends with perhaps a little more shoulder padding, more fullness in the sleeve, pleats, tucks, etc. but not enough to date the dress. I'm still wearing the first two dresses I bought at this outlet five years ago!

Care should be taken to check each garment for flaws. If you spot this line in a store you'll have to wait a few months till the style is past season to find it in the outlet. Infrequently, shipments are delayed from the Orient, and some fairly current merchandise may end up on the racks. Prices at the factory range from $30-$80, while at retail, prices go up to $200. Sizes range from 2-14 in Misses and Petite.

Angling for a glimpse in their dressing room mirrors challenges your civility, they really need about ten more. Also, the dressing room area is defined by a a wall of lockers five feet high, and if you're modest you may feel that everyone is watching. Certainly if the factory workers were so inclined they could get an eyefull. Yet, they seem far too busy and possibly immune to the activities of all the ladies trying on armfulls of dresses.

Finding this outlet is not easy. Drive down Florida, stop and park (if you can) just before 20th Street. The entrance is on the side of the building set back 30 feet from the sidewalk, the outlet is on the third floor. Do by all means, get on their mailing list for special discounts during sale days.

BLUXOME FACTORY OUTLET

173 Bluxome (3rd Floor), San Francisco 94107. Phone: 974-1250. Hours: 10am-2pm. Purchases: Cash or Check Only.

If *fashion forward* is descriptive of your fashion orientation and bargain prices are your goal, you'll love Carol Miller's line of better quality separates. Her line also includes the basics for the more conventional. Prices on her related separates range from $16-$45. On Saturday, you have a chance to buy the end-of-season overruns and closeouts if you fit sizes 4-14. Typical of better quality, higher priced garments, sizes run larger and lengths are more adequate for taller gals. Her choice of fabrics is especially appealing to those who like natural fibers, or lovely blends of linen and silk and wool. You'll want to start each season with a trip to this outlet. *Bluxome* is an alley-type street sandwiched between Bryant and Townsend, off 5th St. Once through the bright blue door, follow the maze of stairs up to the 3rd floor. All sales final.

CAPP STREET OUTLET
160 Capp Street, San Francisco 94110. Phone: 861-3098. Hours: W-S 11am-4pm. Purchases: MC, VISA (no checks). Parking: Very limited street.

The *Capp Street Outlet* customer is typically a young woman (college student or working) who wants more than the formula look. Their styles reflect a state of mind or fashion expression that is unique, fun, and perfect for hip-trendsetters. While not fitting into those categories, even I find their fashions delightful and from time to time have purchased one of their dresses, or outfits just to have something a little different in my wardrobe. Many styles are loose, flowing, with unusual sleeve, shoulder, or hemline treatments, and other clever design details. *Cingano* imports all their clothing from their own factories in India and China, but they are designed at corporate headquarters in San Francisco. Their use of natural fibers, unusual textures, and many handwoven fabrics imparts a unique quality to their designs. Chances are, when you're wearing one of their designs, people will want to know where it was bought. At the outlet, samples, irregulars, and overruns are sold for wholesale or much less. Sizes in S-M-L fit 3-13 or 4-14. Prices range from $2-$35. Check their $2 bargain tables (the source for one of my favorite skirts with matching top at a total of $4.26). Be sure to try everything on. I've tried on small pants that were not as

tight as the large size I tried. Get on their mailing list for fashion previews and special sales. The outlet is located between Mission & South Van Ness, off 16th St. or take BART to the 16th St. Station.

CHIHUAHUA FACTORY OUTLET
2362 San Pablo Ave., Berkeley 94702. Phone: 644-2839. Hours: Fridays by appointment 10am-4pm. Purchases: Cash Only. Parking: Street.

The *Chichuahua* line is for women and teens who like to play with clothes, who like to be just a little different or just one step removed from conformity. Their contemporary fashions are currently oversized, many are silkscreened, and all are made from natural fibers. Most don't need to be ironed — how liberating! You can layer their popular tunic T-shirts over leggings, skirts or jeans, or wear them bloused over belts with shorts or over swim suits for perfect weekend wear. Their dresses, coordinated separates and wonderful tops are neat for the office if you're a trendsetter. At their outlet, located in a cozy back room behind their small factory, you can pick and choose from their eclectic selection of seconds, overruns, and samples. Prices are wholesale or less, generally between $5-$30. Sizes S-M-L or 4-14. You must call ahead for an appointment, (that's just to make sure they have time for customers), otherwise everyone is very relaxed and helpful.

CLOTHES BY DEBORAH

701 Bermuda Drive, San Mateo 94403. Phone: 574-1344. Hours: T-F 11am-4pm, Sat 11am-5pm. Purchases: MC, VISA.

☞ **Other Stores:** Persuade, 2435 Polk, San Francisco, 441-4454; USO/Ultrasuede Outlet, 4125 Piedmont Ave., Oakland, 655-4984.

Inside connections go a long way towards making *Clothes by Deborah* "almost" a factory outlet. The reason: Dad manufactures in San Diego all the Ultrasuede clothing for men and women that they sell at 35-50% discounts. The line is usually sold to small specialty shops around the country at very hefty prices. The quality is excellent and with Skinner Ultrasuede, you're buying the best. They offer very special services and options. One, you can buy separates in mixed sizes. For instance, if you're an eight top and a ten bottom, you can finally buy a suit that fits. Additionally, they can custom order any garment for you that they carry in a wide color range. This may take 4-6 weeks depending on the cutting schedule at the factory. Sizes for women run from 4-20; men's 35-50 in short, regular, long and XLong.

Any garment in ultrasuede is going to be expensive. The fabric alone at retail sells for $57/yard. Here are a few examples of their discount prices: Ladies blazers for $235, skirts at $135, Men's blazers at $265, and Western blazers at $275. The shop is tucked away in the Fiesta Garden Shopping Center, one block south of Hwy. 92, and off of So. Delaware St.

END OF THE LINE

275 Brannan St., San Francisco 94107. Phone: 989-0234. Hours: M-Sat 10am-4:30pm. Purchases: MC, VISA. Parking: Street.

Timing is the key to success here. One visit I'm pleased, the next, put off. Shoppers seem evenly divided about their experiences and success at shopping here, so I have to conclude that if you like their fashion orientation "decidedly Junior" you'll be one of the happy ones. Their two labels are Coquille and Coquille Sport, a line they say is sold in better department stores across the country. The end of season overruns, irregulars are discounted 40-60%. Basically, you can buy skirts, blouses and junior dresses in sizes S,M, & L, or 5-13. Parking is this area is grim during the week: check the pay lot down the street, or better yet, wait till the weekend when the area is free of workers.

SUSANA ENGLAND DESIGNS

10855A San Pablo Ave., El Cerrito 94550. Phone: 235-4660. Hours: By appointment only. Purchases: Checks. Parking: Street.

Susana England designs very special garments for fashionable boutiques. You might call them "limited editions". Jackets, vests and coats are quilted with fabric appliques, all in natural fibers. Because of their unique "art in wearing" qualities, the garments are not inexpensive even at her factory store. Factory prices range from $25-$200 ($5-$40 on children's) and represent discounts from 20-50% off retail. Her "little" store has a very limited selection of garments. At any one time there are not more than 100 pieces on the racks. Sizes range from 6/8-12/14 in misses, some children's sizes.

ESPRIT FACTORY OUTLET

16th & Illinois, San Francisco 94107. Phone: 821-2000. Hours: M-F 10am-6pm, Sat 10am-5pm, Sun Noon-5pm. Hours subject to change during special sales and holiday season. Purchases: MC, VISA. Parking: Limited Street.

Little girls in kindergarten up to big girls in college, plus women up to ??? love the *Esprit Outlet*. No wonder, it's San Francisco's most dazzling, dynamically merchandised outlet store that exhilerates you as soon as walk in and will surely leave you exhausted when you leave. The high tech display units, vibrant colors and background music give an air of razzle-dazzle to the whole environment. This is where students head when they are having one of their "many" school minimum days or holidays. Xmas, spring vacation, back-to-school, and ski week bargain hunting hordes approach pandemonium. During these hectic days, they run out of shopping baskets (yes, shopping baskets!), and the lines for dressing rooms give one time to make considerable headway if reading *War and Peace*.

For the uninitiated (if such a person exists), *Esprit* has several apparel and accessory lines which include: shoes, belts, blouses, handbags, sweaters, pants, jackets, blazers, dresses, related separates, activewear, well, just about everything. If you order their catalog from one of their magazine advertisements, or buy one at the store, you can get a peek at what "may" be coming into the outlet, but always a few months behind the retail stores. The clothing at the outlet is classified as seasonal overruns, returns, production samples and seconds.

Discounts at the outlet range from 15-60% off retail. Naturally, the more recent the merchandise is, the smaller the discount. If you think *Esprit's* prices are higher than other outlets, bear in mind that *Esprit* is higher priced than many Junior lines at retail, therefore outlet prices are proportionally higher. Irregulars, bargain bins, and production samples yield the biggest price cuts. However, their unadvertised sales, where cards are sent inviting the recipient to come on a specific date for discounts on selected merchandise, or on anything in the store, are coveted by all their regular customers. This is *Esprit's* way of dealing with sales. A sale advertised to the "world" would bring such crowds (and did in the past) that the facilities and personnel would be completely overwhelmed.

The Esprit and Esprit Sport junior lines are for sizes 1-11, (although some styles that are loosefitting will fit larger sizes); PreTeen's 6-14; and Esprit Kids in children's sizes 7-14. The big hitch: no exchanges, no returns, all sales final — somewhat risky for moms shopping for their daughters — which probably accounts for the crowds on weekends.

FACTORY OUTLET

446 W. Francisco Blvd. (side of building), San Rafael 94901. Phone: 459-4944. Hours: M-F 9am-5pm, Sat 11am-5pm. Purchases: MC, VISA. Parking: On side of building.

Whizzing down the freeway in San Rafael you'll notice the *Factory Outlet* sign on the Chair Store which will lead you to a bright blue door on the side of the building which is the entrance to the outlet for Gurmeet of San Francisco, the company importing a popular line called New Options. Prominent this last season in all major department stores, this updated misses sportswear is distinctive for the unusual fabrics made in India that are used in their designs. I would call this a very trendy line, certainly a departure from such fashion staples as Villager, Lanz, Evan Picone et al. Recent popular styles were made from Ikat prints, hand woven cottons, cotton batiste and sheeting. Skirts, dresses, pants, and tops (many in dramatic, oversize proportions), fill most of their racks, while others hold the remnants of seasons past. Current fashions sell for current "full retail prices", however, end-of-season overruns and past season styles are reduced 40-50% off retail. Sizes fit 3/4 to 11/12 for women depending on the style. This is one of those outlets that has some good, some great, and some ho hum buys and merchandise. All sales final!

FARR WEST
2444 Old Middlefield Road (between San Antonio and Rengstorff), Mountain View 94043. Phone: 968-7440. Hours: M-F 10am-4:30pm, Sat 10am-2pm. Purchases: Checks. Parking: Lot.

If you want to "buy American" go to *Farr West*, a manufacturer of lingerie with slips, camisoles, panties, robes, hostess pajamas, elegant and Tom Boy types of sleepwear and coverups. Their little factory store obscurely located at the back of this commercial building has the leftovers, irregulars, and salesmen's samples from their factory. Peninsula shoppers are enticed by the prices which are 50% off retail if they're perfect, with everything else about 75% off. Prices start at $2.25 and rarely exceed $40. Shipments from the factory arrive weekly so there's always something new from visit to visit. For those seeking 100% cotton in lingerie, they have many styles. Women's sizes come in Petite through Large or 5/6 to 16/18.

FASHION FACTORY
493 3rd Street (at Bryant), San Francisco 94107. Phone: 543-2244. Hours: M-Sat 10am-5pm. Purchases: MC, VISA. Parking: Street.

There are occasions when you want something a little unconventional: a party, a holiday, a cruise, for poolside or patio, or when you're a hostess. The "ethnic" feeling conveyed by the garments at the *Fashion Factory*, which are designed in America but made in India, will provide the solution. Usually you will see their unique apparel sold in their own stores located in major shopping malls in the Bay Area. At their factory store (where all the shipping is done for accounts nationwide), you can buy the overruns for about 50% off retail. The dresses, skirts, blouses, jumpsuits, vests, etc., are made in 100% cotton or silk, often in vibrant colors, with wonderful prints, many gauze fabrics, with embroidery, metallic threads and sensuous, soft free flowing designs — perfect for a Club Med vacation! At first glance, the merchandise in the outlet may not be appreciated. The outlet is crowded with racks and only those willing to muscle their way through the inventory will find the "jewels". Detracting from the "good stuff" is the sportswear they've brought in from local manufacturers (pants, sweaters, mostly polyester) that are not nearly as exciting as their own Arabian Nights/ethnic peasant apparel. Misses and Junior sizes.

FOUR STAR APPAREL

1153 Mission St., San Francisco 94103. Phone: 552-8400. Hours: M-Sat 10am-4pm. Purchases: Cash Only. Parking: Street.

Small fashion dress shops throughout Northern California hand pick their merchandise in the quantities and sizes that are appropriate for their stores from this jobber. *Four Star* welcomes extra business from bargain hunters, who will pay a little more but still save 40% off retail (more or less) depending on whom you use for comparison prices. They focus on providing moderately priced casual sportswear, and career separates including wool blend blazers and suits. Blouses range from $10-$20; skirts $12-$18, and blazers $30-$40. Sizes extend from 3-13 or 4-16. Styles seem to appeal to younger working women. *Four Star* makes few accommodations for retail business, it's strictly cash only: all sales final.

FRENCH CONNECTION

1110-B Burnett Ave., Concord 94520. Phone: 827-4309. Hours: Friday afternoons only. Noon-5pm. Purchases: Cash or Check. Parking: Street Only.

This importer of fine quality fashion accessories, i.e., belts, scarves, handbags, shawls, etc., sells discontinued merchandise, samples, seconds and current overstock on Friday afternoons, and then only when they're not on the road. You should call before making a trip. The line, imported from France, is sold in elegant boutiques and prestige stores throughout the country. Their selection always includes a line of classic belts in calfskin, cowhide and reptile leathers which range in price from $7-$18 at wholesale. The Couture line is more expensive with the wholesale prices ranging from $24-$50. Their customer is typically a career woman or fashion sophisticate who wants and appreciates quality in fashion accessories. Quarterly sales are held during the year where prices and selection are best. *The French Connection* is located in the Willowwick Business Park where parking is limited for visitors. If necessary please park on the street rather than cheat in a spot where you're not supposed to be, which will create problems for the owners. Directions: From 680, take Concord Ave. exit east to Meridian, left on Burnett.

FRITZI FACTORY OUTLET

517 Howard Street (between 1st & 2nd), San Francisco 94105. Phone: 979-1200. Hours: M-F 10am-3:45pm, Sat 9am-4:30pm. Purchases: Cash Only.

☞ **Other Store:** 237 First Street.

When I stop by the *Fritzi* outlet I yearn for the good ol' days. Lately, I'm hard pressed to find any resemblence of the merchandise I see in the outlet to their lines sold in stores around the Bay Area. The "good stuff" just doesn't seem to make it into the outlet stores unless its irregular. What I do find is budget quality, budget priced sportswear and dresses. Yet, to be honest, their business seems to be as good as ever. I guess when you can buy a $5 blouse or a $15 dress, you're not inclined to complain about anything. *Fritzi* is popular with teens who are trying to stretch their babysitting dollars, and younger women who have limited buying power. Their styles are sometimes fairly basic, and also very trendy. Sizes fit Juniors 3-13 with discounts from 40-75% off retail. Be warned: *Fritzi* seems to play musical store, moving from one store to another with amazing frequency, but they never move more than a block away from the Fremont and Howard area, and they always leave a forwarding notice to get you from the old store to the new location.

GUNNE SAX, LTD. OUTLET, INC.
634 Second Street (Entrance at 35 Stanford, alley off Brannan & Townsend), San Francisco 94107. Phone: 495-3326. Hours: M-Sat 9am-4:30pm, Sun 11am-3pm (call first). Purchases: Cash, Check. Parking: Very limited.

In keeping with the success and volume of merchandise that *Gunne Sax* produces each year, the outlet has taken on supermarket-size proportions. *Gunne Sax* is the biggest user of lace in the country which is evident when you survey the racks of bridal dresses that are dreamy confections. Styles include delicately detailed high-necked Victorians and 18th Century satin Queen Anne gowns with layers and layers of ribbon edged lace and flounces. This is the only resource in the Bay Area for prom and party dresses which is wonderful if you're enchanted with the feminine, romantic look that Jessica Mc Clintock conveys so successfully. On a more informal note, her skirts, dresses, blouses, jumpers, and short jackets, made in voiles, dainty print cottons, velvets, and corduroys are plentiful and at prices that will make any father happy.

Except for a very limited selection of samples, and irregulars, the majority of the inventory is well past season, maybe more than a year old. *Clearance* prices in January '84 for velvet and taffeta dresses were $12-$20, prom and wedding dresses from summer '83 were $48. The prices are tempting, but care should be taken to evaluate for flaws, which are acquired easily on delicate fabrics. Some can be conveniently remedied, others are almost impossible to obscure. All sales are final, so be sure you can fix it or live with it! Sizes for Juniors: 3-13; Jeunes Filles (children): 4-6X, 7-14, PreTeen: 6-14. *Gunne Sax* has their share of leftover yardage, laces, and trims, all sold at the outlet for absolutely fantastic prices. Velvets, voiles, batistes are typically $1/yd; laces are 5 yards/$5. or 10 yards/$3; appliques, lace trims with pearls, and lace collars are equally low priced.

HOUSE OF LARGE SIZES — OUTLET STORES
207 El Portal Drive (El Portal Shopping Center), San Pablo 94806. Phone: 236-3618. Hours: M,T 9:30am-6pm, W, Th, F 9:30am-7pm, Sat 9:30-5pm. Purchases: MC, VISA. Parking: Lot.

☞ **Other Store:** Fremont Fashion Center, 39141 Civic Ctr. Dr., Fremont.

House of Large Sizes, which has ten retail stores in the Bay Area, also has two outlet stores to take all the leftovers, past season and special purchases they acquire from several manufacturers. These outlet stores are well stocked with separates, coats, sweaters and a smaller offering of dresses. Brand names include Levi, Koret, Mr. Alex, Rejoice, Catalina, Ecco Bay, Personal, and California Maker. Sizes at these stores range from 38-52 or 14 1/2-32 1/2. When the leftovers are sent to the outlet stores they're reduced by 33%. After arrival they're continuously marked down until they're sold. Get on the mailing list for their last chance sales.

JAPANESE WEEKEND

22 Isis (off 12th St., betw. Folsom and Harrison), San Francisco 94103. Phone: 621-0555. By Appointment Only M-Th 10am-5pm. Purchases: MC, VISA. Parking: Very Limited.

Japanese Weekend is an unlikely name for this manufacturer. While you might expect them to produce Futons or Shoji screens, in fact they make a line of Norma Kamali-type maternity clothes. All their clothing is made from comfortable cotton interlock knits (like sweatshirt fabrics). The styles are innovative with bubble design tops and matching drawstring pants without the traditional maternity stretch panels, along with dresses and tunics. These garments are so comfortable, so trendy and fun, that they must be a real treat for that pregnant woman who is blossoming like a souffle and lumbering like a hippo. Sizes are petite through large. At the warehouse you can buy their irregulars and discontinued styles. Prices are discounted 30%. Note: You must make an appointment before coming. Parking is a real dilemma!

KOLONAKI FACTORY OUTLET

579 Bridgeway, Sausalito 94965. Phone: 332-1275. Hours: Daily 10am-6pm. Extended hours during tourist season. Purchases: MC, VISA, AE. Parking: Street, Pay lots.

If you're shopping for clothing for a trip to Mexico, Hawaii, or a cruise, or for your 9 to 5 career apparel, give this outlet a whirl. Not only will you enjoy the charm of Sausalito, you'll be delighted with all the past season, overruns, overstocks, and missed shipments from this company. All their fashions are made in Greece of natural fibers. While they may feel the merchandise is past season, we're not likely to know the difference. Many of their career separates in raw silk are so classic, yet contemporary, they'll fit right into your wardrobe for seasons to come. The cruise, leisure and resort lines made from gauze, and crinkle cottons (wonderful for withstanding the crush of suitcases) are equally timeless while being colorful and fun to wear. The quality in this line is very nice. Sizes range from 5/6-13/14. Prices range from 20-50% retail.

LADY LIKE FACTORY OUTLET (LARGE SIZES)

425 Second St. (between Harrison & Bryant, 6th Floor), San Francisco 94107. Phone: 495-5733. Hours: M-S 10am-5pm. Purchases: Cash or Check Only. Parking: Limited.

This manufacturer for larger size ladies (36-46) maintains a small outlet room on the sixth floor of this building at the foot of the Bay Bridge. The fashions, dresses only, are designed for women in the 20-40 year age range, and are usually not appealing to LOL's with a more conventional or traditional style orientation. Past season and irregular merchandise from this moderately priced line is marked way down to wholesale or less ranging from $11-$30. Most styles are made from cotton or synthetic blends and are suitable for casual or dressy occasions and are well suited for the working gal on a limited budget. All sales final.

LILLI ANN FACTORY OUTLET
2701 16th St., San Francisco 94103. Phone: 863-2720. Hours: Sat Only 9am-1pm. Purchases: MC, VISA. Parking: Street.

This factory store for Lilli Ann and Adolf Schuman offers irregulars and seconds at wholesale prices. The styles are truly elegant, more suited to the mature woman who desires that expensive look. There are many coat and dress ensembles with exquisite design and tailoring, as well as many bright-colored all-weather coats and sophisticated sportswear. The styles are a little much for the casual, suburban way of life, but fine for more formal lifestyles. Lilli Ann sells their lines in only the most exclusive stores and shops. You probably won't find anything here for under $40, more likely $75-$150, and that's the wholesale price. Sizes are 6-16. In a separate room you'll find elegant pre-cut fabrics, clearly labeled as to fiber content and length, at wholesale prices, which again are not cheap since most fabrics are imported from Europe. All sales final.

MATERNITY OUTLET
972 Mission (5th Floor), San Francisco 94103. Phone: 543-4564. Hours: T-Fri Noon-4pm. Purchases: Cash or Check. Parking: Street, 5th & Mission garage.

So you're a career woman, over 30, having your first baby. Congratulations! Naturally, you want something more sophisticated than the cutsey maternity fashions still dominating the marketplace and you'll find them at this outlet. Featuring natural fibers, especially raw silks and cotton knits (for summer), this line is perfect for the executive suite. The past season merchandise, samples, and very few irregulars are sold for wholesale prices. There are typically 100-200 garments on the racks for customers at any one time. It's best to call ahead. There are times when factory personnel are working double time to meet a shipping order and they have no time left for customers. In fact they may request you return at a more convenient time for them. Sizes: 4-14 or S,M & L. Prices at the factory range from $30-$65.

TERRY MCHUGH OUTLET
425 Second Street (5th Floor), San Francisco 94107. Phone: 495-7590. Hours: 10am-3pm. Purchases: Cash or Check. Parking: Street or Pay Lots.

Terry McHugh manufactures a neat line of dresses that are perfect for career dressing. At the factory she has set aside the "Topaz" room to display and sell current overruns, the few irregulars, past season garments, and styles made especially for the Topaz room. Sizes are S-M-L and fit sizes 6-14. Her specialty for fall and winter fashions are the woolblend and wool jersey dresses that last from year to year with a change of accessories. When you browse through the racks, keep in mind that most of her styles must be worn to be appreciated. Do try them on for full effect. Prices at the outlet range from $30-$80.

OLGA FASHION FABRICS & OTHER THINGS

12200 Saratoga-Sunnyvale Rd., Saratoga 95070. Phone: (408) 253-2780. Hours: M-Sat 10:30am-6pm. Purchases: MC, VISA. Parking: Free Lot.

Olga, known for beautiful lingerie, undergarments and loungewear, gives sensuous savings at their outlet stores. The large selection of discontinued and irregular styles in nightgowns (petite-38), panties (4-9), bras (32-38), slips, camisoles, leotards, body slips, suits and bathrobes, is very impressive. Most garments marked irregular appear to be perfect. Garments marked as seconds have the flaws flagged with tape for easy evaluation. The discounts range from very modest to sensational. For instance, the best selling Olga bra is usually discounted a modest 20%. Average discounts are 30-40% off. *Olga* has developed a following of regulars who count on scooping up the bargains during one of their monthly sales which usually last for a week. Sometimes the Post Office doesn't cooperate and the sale announcements for private advance buying arrive after the sale — very frustrating for the devoted.

In the last year, *Olga* has carried their Christina activewear line, with leotards, leggings, camisoles, and shorts, designed to provide a dazzling appearance at your Jazzersize or aerobic exercise classes. Olga panty hose is discounted 30%.

Like outlet stores this is a self service operation, although the staff will assist with measurements and fitting if requested. The very modest will have to wait in line for the one private dressing room. Others can "bare all" in the communal dressing room.

Ladies devoted to stretch and sew will be delighted with an assortment of fabrics and laces from the *Olga* factory at great savings. The Olgalon fabric, 100% breathable polyester, cannot be purchased in most fabric stores.

THE OUTBACK FACTORY OUTLET

745 47th Street, Oakland 94609. Phone: 428-9461. Hours: M-F 9am-5pm. Occasional Sat. hours, call first. Purchases: MC, VISA. Parking: Street.

If you'd like to follow the fashion lead of Cher, Bette Midler, Stephanie Powers, and other celebrity types, then go to the *Outback*. Manufacturers of unique, trendy, elegant-funky, fun, and outrageous apparel, their garments typically do not require ironing, do not require one to worry about whether they're right side out, or inside out, (many have unfinished edges on the outside of the garment), they simply require the right state of mind. Young women are most likely to embrace the "look", yet even famous socialites (between 50-60 years old) have worn this line.

Many of their garments are over-dyed surplus apparel. Imagine being successful at buying up old T-shirts, underwear, sweat shirts, jackets, even Italian tablecloths, and with a quick dip in the dye, a slash of the scissors, the addition of a button or two, creating a sensation? Their original (from scratch) designs, are just as clever as their renovations with the use of interesting mesh fabrics, unconventional shapes, lengths, and fastenings.

The *Outback Outlet* in Oakland provides an opportunity to buy their seasonal overruns, discontinued styles, and samples at 50-80% off original retail. They also stock funky costume jewelry from several local designers, and childrens sizes in sweats and T-shirts. Sizes are S-M-L and will probably fit anyone in the 4-14 range. I had a devil of a time finding the *Outback!*. I made three trips before I successfully navigated the maze of streets and freeway onramps leading to their outlet. Directions: From 51st and Grove Sts. in Oakland (near Children's Hospital) travel west on Grove to 47th St. There is a freeway onramp right at 47th St. Stay well to the right, avoid the onramp, and turn right on 47th, go 1/2 block. The outlet is on the 2nd floor.

THE OUTLET

768 Blossom Hill Rd. (Kings Court Shopping Ctr.), Los Gatos 95030. Phone: (408) 356-5000. Hours: M-F 10am-6pm, Sat 10am-5pm. Purchases: MC, VISA. Parking: Lot.

☞ **Other Store:** 2145 Morrill Ave. (at Landress and Fwy. 680) San Jose. (408) 262-0174.

The name: Sing "26 Miles Across the Sea", fill in the blank and you'll know just who's manufacturing this great sportswear line. They've had outlets in Los Angeles for years which have been very popular. In the Bay Area they've chosen to adopt a low profile by locating in these small shopping centers. This is one place where you may want to shop as a couple because they have men and women's clothing as well as a selection of girls' swimsuits in infant sizes to 14. Prices are discounted 30-70% off

retail. Because they don't want to be in competition with their retail accounts the merchandise will be slightly past season, irregular or classified as samples. Even though the styles may be past season, the selection looks fresh and new because their line is more traditional and not given to fashion extremes. In fact, this is the reason for the enduring popularity of their line with the mature consumer.

What can you expect to find? In women's clothing: blazers, jackets, tops, blouses, sweaters, skirts, slacks, activewear, swimsuits, and cover-ups in cotton, polyester/cotton, polyester, and wool blends. Whether your needs are for the poolside, health spa, or well-made separates for the office, the stores's selection provides. Heading for the Bahama's — get all your resort fashions here. Women's sizes are 6-18, 5/6-13/14 in active wear or Junior fashions, plus sizes in 32-42 (tops) and 30-40 (bottoms). Most of the time they have a good selection of larger sizes, a rarity! Their biggest appeal for many is the wonderful selection of bathing suits for women from 8-80, particularly those hard-to-find suits for mature figures and camouflaging styles for the time-ravaged body. For Men: first, a smaller selection is available, but they have tennis apparel, shorts, swimwear, warmup suits, windbreakers, heavier jackets, sweaters and leather jackets. Men's sizes in S-XL, waist sizes 28-42.

THE OUTLET STORE

221 South Maple, South San Francisco 94118. Phone: 761-1467. Hours: T-Sat 9am-4pm. Purchases: MC, VISA. Parking: Lot.

You really have to go out of your way to find this Albee factory outlet so I'm including directions on how to get there. Take the Bayshore Fwy. south to Grand Ave., turn west, turn left on Linden, right on Victory and left on South Maple. The outlet is adjacent to the factory.

Moms and teens can shop here together if they're between sizes 6-16. Pants, skirts, sweaters and blouses predominate in the selection of samples and overruns from the factory warehouse. There is a rack at the back of the store with irregulars at super low prices. Occasionally, when people have wanted something in a different color the sales people have been able to round it up from their stockroom. Most of their fashions, made in synthetics and cottons, are seen prominently displayed in retail stores. Their quarterly warehouse sales attract hundreds of people who delve into the merchandise as if this was the last chance to buy clothes for the rest of their lives. Get on their mailing list!

PETITE WAREHOUSE SALES

Civic Auditorium, Polk Hall, 99 Grove St., San Francisco. Mailing List Address: P. O. Box 608, Temple City, Ca. 91780. Attn: San Francisco Warehouse Sale. Sales: February & August.

This manufacturer makes Petite fashions for the woman 5'3'' and under, in sizes 0-14. They have three "high class" stores in the Bay Area (plus 17 in So. Calif. and Arizona), that cater to the career woman who seeks well made, classic styles in their suits and separates. In addition to their own private label, they buy selectively from other nationally recognized manufacturers of quality Petite fashions. Twice each year, they rent a hall at the Civic Auditorium, and have a one day sale offering discounts of 50-80% on the last season's merchandise. With classic styling on garments, what is stylish one year is going to be stylish for seasons to come. They usually bring in 15,000-20,000 garments from their factory and distribution warehouse in So. Calif. for these events. To get on their mailing list for your private invitation, write to the address above. This sale is not advertised in local papers; they rely instead on their mailing lists developed from their store clientele.

RAINCOAT OUTLET

543 Howard Street (2nd Floor), San Francisco 94105. Phone: 362-2626. Hours: M-F 8am-4pm, Sat 7:30am-11:30pm. Purchases: Cash or Check. Parking: Street.

Proceed with caution when shopping at this outlet. The careless and inconsiderate shopper who throws and drapes clothing on racks and chairs is not appreciated; in fact, she'll be sharply reprimanded! You're also well advised to schedule your visits on Saturdays when there is the time and staff available to help you.

This manufacturer enjoys a good reputation for the quality and classic styling that prevails in her line of raincoats and velvet blazers and coats. Check first before you start rummaging through the racks, many are off-limits. You can choose from samples and overruns in sizes 4-24. It's obvious that some garments have been around since the beginning of time, but each season, the racks are replenished with new colors and styles. There is one small mirror and no dressing room. You can expect a 40-50% savings, but forget the service, they're simply not set up to pamper your ego.

THE SAN FRANCISCO MERCANTILE COMPANY

2915 Sacramento St., San Francisco 94115. Phone: 563-0113. Hours: M-S 10am-6pm, Sun Noon-5pm. Purchases: MC, VISA. Parking: Extremely limited street.

Owned by the makers of Queen Anne's Lace and Eileen West, this store *becomes* an outlet about every six weeks when hundreds of garments are sent over from the factory for super sales. That's the time to shop if you're after the bargains. You can call and have your name put on the mailing list for these frequent "BLOW-OUTS".

These two lines are irrepressibly feminine. The nightgowns, robes, pajamas etc. are made in 100% fine cotton or cotton flannels and are noted for their tucks and ruffles which inspire a romantic Victorian look. At retail, prices are steep! At the sales, the irregulars, discontinued styles and factory overruns are less than wholesale. Season is not a consideration for sleepwear. I can't imagine hesitating about buying a flannel nightgown in June, or a delicate batiste in December, I know I'll wear it when the season arrives. I've noted when admiring some delicate nightwear being worn by stars in soap operas or movies that often it's from Queen Ann's Lace. Eileen West dresses are contemporary, yet charmingly nostalgic of dresses from the 20's or the 1900's. Little prints in 100% cotton, corduroys, and soft challis type fabrics are often used in their fabrications. It should be said that at all times, there're a few racks of markdown merchandise in the outlet, while the rest of the inventory is current season at current prices. Good luck with parking!

S. F. O. (SPORTSWEAR FACTORY OUTLET)

10620 So. De Anza Blvd., Cupertino 95014. Phone: (408) 255-0331. Hours: Daily 10am-6pm, T Th eve till 9pm. Purchases: MC, VISA. Parking: Lot.

They'd give me till sundown to get out of town if I printed their name. Suffice it to say that this line is very popular with Juniors: very prominent in major retail stores. At retail, prices on dresses range from $30-$40, blouses $18-$24, so it's a reasonably priced line, but at the outlet store, prices are hard-to-beat. Discounts are usually 40% off original retail, with terrific end-of-season markdowns of up to 70% off. Fashions are not seconds but rather first quality overruns, overcuts, broken size lots, cancellations and samples. To even out the total inventory, they buy sweaters, and a few other lines to sell for nearly the same discounts. Younger working gals stretch dollars on their polyester, dressier blouses, gabardine pants, and trendy little dresses. You can buy a Sunday church dress as well as a New Year's eve knock out. The latest edition to their line is delightful girls sportswear in sizes 7-14. Essentially self service, the sales staff is terrific when helping moms trying to coordinate and make selections for their daughters. Caution should be exercised if you're doing this, since no returns or exchanges are allowed. Prices range from $5-$20. Dressing rooms available.

S. F. MANUFACTURING CO. OUTLET

130 Potrero (off 15th St), San Francisco 94103. Phone: 431-1178. Hours: M-Sat 9am-4pm. Purchases: Cash or Check. Parking: Limited Street.

After a few years off, the owners of this new outlet have reentered the "rag" trade. Their operation combines many facets of the trade: manufacturing, importing, distributing and liquidating. Primarily, they are providing smaller retail stores with ladies' sportswear in a moderate price range. The inevitable leftovers will be sold at wholesale prices to the public. The selection will always include a mixed bag of bargains depending on what "deals and steals" they've gleaned from the marketplace. Regular lines of merchandise include career-styled georgette blouses, very nice corduroy dress slacks and pants for women, plus wool blazers and skirts (occasionally); for men, sweaters, shirts and jeans; and for the whole family a colorful selection of activewear (sweatshirt fashions). Many of these lines are sold under private label to chain and department stores. Sizes generally fall for women between 3-15 or 4-14. Dressing rooms available. All sales final.

C. P. SHADES FACTORY OUTLET

173 Bluxome St. 2nd floor (betw. Brannan & Townsend, off 5th St.), San Francisco 94107. Phone: 777-5552. Hours: Saturday only 10am-4pm. Purchases: MC, VISA. Parking: Limited.

If you love casual carefree and fun clothing, you will love the *C. P. Shades Outlet*. When you see their fashions in retail stores, you may want to charge into the outlet to buy at bargain prices, but you won't find the current dazzlers you're after until a few months later. What you will find are the leftovers and returns from the season just ended, or current merchandise that is irregular. That's O.K. You won't be disappointed because the prices are at wholesale (ranging from $5-$40), and seconds are $2-$10 depending on the extent of damage. Most of the seconds I spotted had dye irregularities rather than construction flaws.

The street wear by *C. P. Shades* is sold in unisex sizing and is worn by both men and women. Almost everything is 100% cotton, custom dyed and pre-shrunk. Their cut is oversize on many styles. I loved their line of "wrinkled" cotton camp shirts and several styles of great pants (perfect for a little break dancin'), also their T-shirts, shorts, dresses and jumpsuits. Their fleece line of sweatshirts, cardigans, and sweat pants is very popular — but not cheap. Even as leftovers and past season, prices run $10-$20. Next year's line may be entirely different, but it will surely be at the forefront of the fashion scene. This line is not confined just to teens and the under 30 crowd. Anyone who likes to appear up-to-date will love the look and comfort, especially the working woman who wants a break from weekday career apparel. Many moms shop right along with their daughters or sons, lucky the ones who can share sizes and clothes. Sizes run Petite through X-Large in fleece lines, and Small through Large in everything else. There are no dressing rooms, so wear leotards for public try-ons (the line for the restroom is always long). There are areas in the factory that are roped off and where the merchandise is clearly off limits. Women won't want to leave the building until they've checked the third floor *Bluxome Street Outlet* for fine quality career apparel. Remember they're only open on Saturdays!

SILKY BEE
39 Grant Avenue, San Francisco 94108. Phone: 989-1138. Hours: M-Sat 10am-6pm. Purchases: MC, VISA. Parking: Pay Lots.

Silky Bee is the retail outlet for an importer of silk fashions from Hong Kong, China, and other points in the Orient. Anything that is left over, discontinued, or whatever, is sold close to wholesale under the *Silky Bee* label. Sizes range from 3/4-13/14 on silk blouses, skirts, dresses, pants and everything else in their line. The quality is better on some styles than on others and the wrinkles in some of the garments may bother you, but they will press out. Steam pressing is just not in the picture for an outlet operation like this. Prices on blouses range from $17-$30; dresses run from $47-$52. All sales final.

SOLO FACTORY OUTLET
1400 Howard (corner 10th St.), San Francisco. 94103. Phone: 864-7711. Hours: Friday 11am-3pm, Saturday 10am-3pm. Purchases: Cash, Check, (MC, VISA pending). Parking: Street.

Solo has decided to open an outlet in a corner of their factory every Friday and Saturday. Those unfamiliar with their line need only think of other well known lines like Catalina, Koret, and White Stag to get an idea of their styles and fashion orientation. Old customers will no longer find dresses in their selection since they've decided to concentrate on coordinated separates in a moderate price range for the Missy customer. Their line offers an ever dependable, no-great-surprises, but attractive and fresh looking selection of skirts, blouses, tops, jackets, shorts, culottes and T-shirts. Prices will be wholesale or less ranging from $4.90-$20. Their summer line is made from washable, permanent press poly cotton blends. Fall and winter lines are made from wool blends and gabardines with the workplace in mind. *Solo* is proud of the fact that their line is geared for Middle America, leaving the trendy, avante garde and exotic to other fashion houses. If you're one of those ladies who feels left out after checking the styles at other outlets, you're probably looking for what *Solo* has to offer. Since garments can be pulled from their factory inventory, the current overruns, samples, and discontinued styles are replenished every week. Sizes are a welcome 8-18, plus 36-46 in tops, 30-40 in bottoms. None of the ''if you're over a size 14 forget it'' frustration encountered by legions of mature women. The outlet is located on the second floor. The street parking is limited on Fridays. Don't forget to feed the meters and watch the clock!

SPRINT WHOLESALE APPAREL, INC.
453 Bryant Street (betw. 2nd & 3rd), San Francisco 94107. Phone: 957-9966. Hours: Sat Only 10am-3pm. Purchases: *Cash Only*. Parking: Limited Street.

Sprint is a jobber serving small retailers primarily; yet, they will allow the public access to their warehouse on Saturdays and allow them to buy if they can put up with the limitations. Most significant is that they will allow no try-ons under any circumstances. Their garments are ready to ship, and they're not taking any chances that garments will be damaged or tired by excessive handling. So why bother? The prices on their current merchandise will blow you away. Tailored, classic, button down styles of blouses were $8, fancy silk blouses were $19, prices on moderate quality dresses hovered at $18-$34, silk sweaters were $15, raw silk pants were $12 etc. etc. Of course in a few weeks there'll be an entirely new inventory, but chances are, prices will be in the same range. The fashion orientation is Junior Contemporary: sizes in the 3-13 range. Current styles are displayed on the walls, so a quick glance will reveal if there's reason to pick through the boxes and racks of merchandise. All sales final! *Cash Only.*

SYMBRAETTE FACTORY OUTLET

21 Janis Way, Scotts Valley 95066. Phone: 408 438-1711. Hours: M-F 9am-4pm, Closed 12:30-1pm for lunch. Purchases: Cash or Check.

Scotts Valley is a long way to drive to buy a bra, bathing suit or girdle, yet, there are several reasons why many will want to go to the trouble. First, if you have a fitting problem, you're too big, too small, uneven, or something, *Symbraette* can custom fit and design a bra that will give you support and comfort. Their regular size range is 28-46 AA-O. Bras are fancy, basic, pretty, padded, sheer, in other words, something for everyone including mastectomy, surgical, and nursing bras. Bras sold at the factory outlet are discontinued, overruns, or have been in stock too long. Prices range from $1.50-$8.00 on their standard sizes, go up to $12.50 on special sizes, and even higher for custom designed and fitted bras. Their girdles

are popular with weight lifters and bodybuilders. Bathing suit styles are typical of what you're seeing in major stores. At the factory just about everything is sold at wholesale or less. To find the outlet, from Hwy 17. take Scotts Valley Drive to El Pueblo, and turn left on Janis. The factory is at the end of the street, the outlet at the back of the parking lot. Don't hesitate to call for directions or to inquire about special sizes or fitting.

VOGUE ALLEY WAREHOUSE OUTLET

695 Veterans Blvd., Redwood City 94063. Phone: 363-1177. Hours: M-Sat 10am-5pm. Purchases: MC, VISA. Parking: Lot.

☞ **Other Stores:** 110 Town & Country Village, Palo Alto; 432 Sutter, San Francisco; Hillsdale Shopping Center, San Mateo; Stoneridge Shopping Center, Pleasanton; Sweater Connexion, 3648 The Barnyard, Carmel, Strawberry Village, Mill Valley.

Vogue Alley is for those who tend to make the "best dressed list." Quality shows on their natural fiber clothing of 100% silk, cashmere, wool, or linen and cotton fabrications. This company distributes this line (which is imported from the Orient) to fine stores throughout the country under a label that is recognized by the fashion sophisticate. In their own company owned *Vogue Alley* stores, the merchandise is sold under the *Vogue Alley* label, and is about 30% less than prices in other stores. At the warehouse store in Redwood City, the very clever carefully check the racks for irregulars that are drastically marked down. Their other stores fit innocuously into their shopping environments giving little indication to the typical shopper passing by that bargains are discreetly available. Many of my friends "fashion aesthetes" regard *Vogue Alley* as their favorite resource for silk blouses, cashmere and casual sweaters, lovely wool gabardine separates, smashing silk dresses, and knit separates (similar to St. John's). They love the consistent high quality, depth of selection, and the elegant, sophisticated, updated styles. Their spring and summer sportswear lines are more casual yet the quality is just as good. At full retail, these women would expect to pay from $75-$200 for fashions in this quality range. If the 30% discounts don't bring prices into your range, get on their mailing list for warehouse end-of-season sales, where discounts are close to 80% off. The last sale I attended, I left slightly disheveled, completely exhausted, and extremely happy with four $9 sweaters and two $16 gorgeous silk blouses! Sizes are 2-14, or Petite through Large. Men's sizes in sweaters (that's all they have for men) are S-XL.

WHITMUN'S MFG. FACTORY OUTLET

1171 North 4th Street, San Jose 95112. Phone: (408) 286-0444. Hours: W-F 10am-6pm, Sat 9am-3pm. Purchases: MC, VISA. Parking: Lot.

If you've shopped *Prestige Petites* in the Pruneyard Shopping Center in Campbell, you know the prices are not cheap on their better quality fashions. By going to their factory outlet in San Jose, there is a way to buy many of their fashions for considerably less. Most of their clothing is designed and manufactured there and all the past season, overruns, and occasional seconds are sold for 40-60% less than original retail. Their own line is essentially classic —

basic blouses, skirts, and ensembles for mature career women. The fabrics used are silks, linens, fine wools, and the best cottons. Other fashions from the store are from prestige designers of sweaters, dresses and more casual coordinated out fits. Since these are the leftovers, it's not always possible to coordinate a complete outfit, but more likely to find a great blouse or skirt that will be a wardrobe basic. Prices overall vary widely ranging from from $15-$80. Sizes on Petite fashions: 0-14. The factory store is located in a rear building of the Civic Center Business Park. Take 1st Street north from 101, look for the Hyatt Hotel, turn right on Old Bayshore Road, right again on 4th Street about 1/2 mile. You'll go under Fwy. 17 just before reaching the outlet.

CHAIN STORES

There has been tremendous growth in the chain store category with many Los Angeles and Eastern off-price chains perceiving the Bay Area as the logical place to expand. Many successful independent stores have decided to multiply by opening two or three additional stores to extend their buying power and clout. In this chain store category I have included those having at least *three* stores under the same name.

Multiple stores do not necessarily mean better stores; however, they often have greater buying power and the saving at these stores can be as substantial as those found at factory outlets. You may find a greater diversity in fashion selection since in addition to fashions from local manufacturers, they offer fashions from manufacturers around the country. These stores sell overruns, samples, close-outs, and factory irregulars. They usually take advantage of in-season buying (larger retail stores place their orders far in advance of the season) relieving the manufacturer of merchandise that is old to him, but still new to the public. The off-price buyer pays less than wholesale for their merchandise because they are taking the "leftovers", or they buy current merchandise at "inside" prices. The inside prices are given in lieu of the many perks required by traditional store buyers like advertising, markdown, and warehouse allowances. The obvious benefits to the consumer in having more local resources is no guarantee that quality choices will be available, in fact, it often seems that there is more marginal, even shoddy apparel being passed off as "quality". Don't be conned by overstated claims, instead be discriminating, and let retailers know when they're stretching the point. Many off-price chains are doing a credible job at consistently offering a good product mix and quality selection. Yet, given the growth of off-price retailers and the competition for quality goods, from time to time, even the most consistent retailers will end up with inventory that is less than desirable.

VIRGINIA ALAN

65 Town and Country Village, Palo Alto 94301. Phone: 327-2190. Hours: M-S 9:30-6pm, Sun Noon-5pm, Th eve till 9pm. Purchases: MC, VISA. Parking: Lot.

☞ **Other Stores:** 1210 Town & Country Village, Mill Valley; 414 Town & Country Village, San Jose.

Virginia Alan arrived in the Bay Area without any fanfare but with the buying power of 30 stores on the East Coast behind them. They've targeted the mature career woman as their prime customer. Accordingly, everything is geared for the office or professional environment with a lovely selection of suits, coordinated separates, dresses and blouses. Sizes are 4-16. The quality level is very gratifying especially considering their prices reflect markdowns or discounts of 40-70% off current retail. Prices on wool blend blazers hovered around $49, poly silk blouses ranged from $20-$30. Steven Barry, Samuel Blue, Nicolle, Kenneth Greene, and Liz Roberts were among the many brands consistently carried. Shopping in their stores is a real pleasure. The merchandising is so nicely done it's not evident at first that these are off-price stores until you look at the prices. Their selection makes it possible to think of investment dressing without making major investment. A word of warning . . They make no exchanges, accept no returns, issue no credits. Come prepared with your "colors" (if you have them) or give your closet a quick glimpse to fix colors and needs in mind. This store is clearly a winner for the over 30 crowd (my opinion) who want stylish, but not trendy fashions. Regulars tell me that markdowns are taken weekly to keep merchandise moving. Timing their buys for the lowest price, without missing out, is their favorite game.

CLOTHES RACK

5644 Geary Blvd., San Francisco 94121. Phone: 386-9728. Hours: M-S 10am-6pm, Sun Noon-5pm. Purchases: MC, VISA. Parking: Street.

☞ **Other Store:** Westlake Mall, Daly City; Fox Plaza, San Francisco; 20th & Broadway, Oakland; Sacramento.

Getting a fix on the *Clothes Rack* isn't easy. They've been bought and sold more times than I can count. The new owner pledges to update and upgrade their fashion merchandise mix to appeal more to the younger, updated career woman. The bubble gum fashions will be eliminated. Some "play" clothes for after work will be carried too! Discounts should fall in the 20-50% off range. Four of their stores have a high fashion shoe department that in the past was the main incentive for grown-ups' to stop by.

CLOTHES VAULT
1764 Broadway (corner 19th St.), Oakland 94607. Phone: 839-6688. Hours: M-S 10am-6pm. Purchases: MC, VISA. Parking: Lot.

☞ **Other Stores:** 225 Front St. (upstairs) San Francisco; Mc Arthur/Broadway Shopping Center, Oakland.

Take your pick! The *Clothes Vault* has three stores, and three different merchandise mixes geared to the customer group most likely to frequent a particular store. Financial District working women expect to find better quality, high fashion, career separates when they "step up" to shop at their second floor store. Here's where the Harve Bernard, Valentino, Tahari and other good lines are most prominent. In the downtown Oakland store, there's a shift towards a younger woman, with a more modest budget who likes a little more pizazz in her wardrobe. The McArthur/Broadway store leans to more casual and play apparel. There's a certain amount of crossover in each

store and in each there are wonderful prices 30-50% off retail. Sizes range from 3/4-15/16. The 19th St., Oakland store has a lovely department of large sizes in career apparel called *More the Woman*.

CLOTHESTIME
2026 El Camino Real (Mervyn's Plaza), Santa Clara 95051. Phone: (408) 984-7863. Hours: M-F 10am-9pm, Sat 10am-6pm, Sun 11am-5pm. Purchasing: MC, VISA. Parking: Lot.

☞ **Other Stores:** Concord, Dublin, Fremont, Los Gatos, Mountain View, Napa, Petaluma, Sacramento, San Jose, San Leandro, San Rafael, Santa Rosa, Vallejo.

I've stopped counting the number of *Clothestime* stores that have opened in Northern California because I have to revise my figures almost weekly. With about 125 stores, primarily in California, Arizona, Nevada and Texas and other states facing imminent invasion by this aggressive off-price chain, their buying power is considerable. They specialize in first-quality junior-sized apparel, with emphasis on moderately priced sportswear, dresses and accessories selling at prices 20-50% lower than those in conventional department and specialty stores. Approximately 70% of the merchandise is sold under recognizable brand names, and ranges from budget and moderate apparel to better sportswear and designer fashions. Teens and college students particularly love the fashions and the ambiance of the stores (fun and enervating), yet their diversity appeals to the 24-34 year old career woman as well. Their attractive stores have simple fixtures. They figure that women would rather pay for clothes than frills.

Clothestime retains a buying staff in Los Angeles and New York, who are constantly shopping the market to provide current junior fashions at discount prices. Each store receives approximately 1000 new pieces each week, with constant in-store markdowns being taken on existing merchandise to keep the inventory moving. Everything is first quality. Be sure to get on their customer mailing list to receive special discount coupons and mailers. As an off-price store you would not expect that they would take returns, make exchanges, or give cash refunds, but they do.

DIMENSIONS IN FASHIONS
700 El Camino Real (Menlo Station), Menlo Park 94025. Phone: 322-4991. Hours: M-Sat 10am-9:30pm, Sun Noon-6pm. Purchases: MC, VISA. Parking: Lot.

☞ **Other Store:** Call for new Bay Area locations.

One of the hottest new off-price chains to open in the Bay Area in 1984 was *Dimensions in Fashions*. With 56 stores nationwide they have considerable clout in bagging good buys for their stores. Their huge Menlo Park store is stocked with a smattering of everything: separates, dresses, suits, activewear, bathing suits, accessories, jackets etc., and all at fabulous prices. Their strength is the depth of selection in every category. Customers most likely to go away with arms overloaded are those desiring casual fashions for work, play or school. Although they do have career dresses and suits, I feel their selection in this area is a little anemic. Many famous brands are carried, plus some private label merchandise they use to fill in and to offer a wider price selection for their customers. Each store gets

30-50 cartons of new merchandise each day resulting in a fresh variety each time you shop. The pace is hectic, the stores are neat, and for what they do — they do it very well. Sizes for women and teens: 3-16. Prices are always discounted 40-80% off retail prices. They have a liberal return and exchange policy and provide private dressing rooms. Let's hope we get a few supersize stores (20,000 sq. ft) like those in Los Angeles that have shoe departments, kiddie play areas with video games, and food service.

DRESS BARN (FORMERLY TAGGS)
1670 So. Bascom Ave. (Hamilton Plaza), Cupertino 95008. Phone: (408) 377-7544. Hours: M-F 10am-9pm, Sat 10am-6pm, Sun Noon-5pm. Purchases: MC, VISA. Parking: Lot.

☞ **Other Stores:** Westlake Mall, Daly City; Calavares Plaza, Milpitas; 1403 N. Main, Walnut Creek.

One way for an Eastern Chain to get a toe hold in the Bay Area, is to buy out an existing chain with an established clientele. This is exactly what *Dress Barn* has done. Adding to their 100 plus stores throughout the country, they've bought the four Bay Area *Taggs* stores. Loyal customers of *Taggs* will be delighted with the new owners who have upgraded the quality of the merchandise and improved the merchandise mix. In addition to career apparel, they've strengthened the dress line, increased the activewear department, brought in better coats, bathing suits and accessories. Better brands like Larry Levine and Harve Benard are representative of the new quality emphasis. Their sizes and fashion range are targeted for both

Juniors and Misses with a decidedly updated image. Sizes range from 3/4-16. Delightful discounts will continue with most merchandise discounted 30-60%.

HARMONY & LOTUS

638 San Anselmo Ave., San Anselmo 94960. Phone: 453-0940. Hours: M-F 11:30am-5:30pm, Sat llam-5pm. Purchases: MC, VISA. Parking: Street.

☞ **Other Stores:** 513 Fourth St. & 4213 Montgomery Dr., Santa Rosa; 1541 Pacific Ave., Santa Cruz; 34 Sunnyside Ave., Mill Valley; 2286 Union St., San Francisco.

The six *Harmony & Lotus* stores are unique for their emphasis on natural fiber clothing. You can buy an outfit for a country picnic or an elegant dinner party and everything in between. The blouses, skirts, pants, sweaters, and dresses are first quality and discounted about 30-50% off the retail prices of other stores. The sweaters are suitable for men or women. Many styles are imported while others are made especially for their stores. They also carry several lines from popular manufacturers who utilize natural fibers in their clothing. All six stores have a charming boutique appearance. The clothing will appeal to those with fairly conventional taste as well as those who like a touch of the exotic. Sizes are 3-14.

LOEHMANN'S

75 Westlake Mall, Daly City 94015. Phone: 755-2424. Hours: MT&Sat 10am-5:30pm, W,Th,&F 10am-9pm. Purchases: Cash or Check. Parking: Lot.

☞ **Other Stores:** 1651 Hollenbeck Ave., Sunnyvale; 3161 Crow Canyon Pl., San Ramon.

Loehmann's has been famous for over 60 years for quality fashions at great savings. They were the *original* fashion off-price store. Their reputation was established as the purveyor of designer and couture lines at discount prices. Even with the increased competition, they still maintain this position in the marketplace.

Their stores have a no frills appearance that is in direct contrast to the exciting selection of clothing. There are all types of "mood" clothes — cocktail, dressy, fine furs, in-between, sportswear; and those of you clever enough to recognize designer clothes without a label will find fashions from Geoffrey Beene, Adele Simpson, Bill Blass, Ann Klein, Nipon and others of equal renown. Prices are guaranteed to be at least 1/3 off retail with a reliable quantity always priced at 50% off. Their end-of-season racks are almost ridiculous!

Their communal dressing rooms always seem a bit hectic, jammed with ladies, in various stages of undress, trying to keep track of their own handbag and clothes, while trying on piles of clothes. The *Back Room*, stocked with expensive (even at discount) merchandise, is restricted to women *only* since there are no dressing rooms at all! There are no returns or refunds: buy wisely. Sizes are 4-18, with a fair selection of Petites.

MARSHALL'S
(See **Family Apparel**)

PATIO SHOP

765 Broadway (next to Mervyn's), Millbrae 94030. Phone: 697-9696. Hours: M-S 10am-6pm. Purchases: MC, VISA. Parking: Lot.

☞ **Other Stores:** 532 San Mateo Ave., and 51 Bovet Rd., San Mateo; 332 Walnut Street, and 258 Woodside Plaza, Redwood City; 401 Town & Country Village, Sunnyvale.

For the Missy customer (typically a woman over 35, size 12-18, interested in fashion basics in the moderate price range at retail) the six *Patio Shops* on the Peninsula consistently offer a *good* selection at *good* bargain prices. Since they maintain such a low profile, have such a misleading name, they are easily overlooked. They don't sell mumu's as the name would suggest, rather, moderately priced brands like Campus Casual, Albee, Ardee, Rosana and many basic traditional lines that cater to the mature woman. They also carry a diverse selection that includes all weather coats, sleepwear, ski jackets, dresses and "every day" separates. This is where you can find a traditional, washable, cardigan sweater, polyester pants cut for the mature figure, plus a nice selection of leisure/jog suits. They do carry some Junior lines at equally good prices.

PATTI QUINN'S

505 Mission St., San Francisco 94105. Phone: 541-0413. Hours: M-F 10am-6pm, Sat 10am-3pm. Purchases: MC, VISA. Parking: Street or Pay Lot.

☞ **Other Stores:** 1585 No. 4th St., San Jose; 215 S. Ellsworth, San Mateo; 1139 S. Sunnyvale/Saratoga Rd., Cupertino; 218 Montgomery St., San Francisco; Clearance Center, 360 Florida St., San Francisco.

Patti Quinn's rates a high mark on the basis of their wide selection of fashion merchandise for Juniors and Women with a price range that gives everyone a chance: starting with the beginning typist right up to the department head. These are overruns and closeouts, arriving in mid-season after the retail stores have stopped buying. Additionally they belong to a large New York buying group with professional buyers scouring the market for the "very best values". Each store has a small shoe department where discounts of 15-50% prevail on current and past season's shoes. They maintain a nice leather and synthetic handbag selection of good looking copy cats of bags that cost twice as much. The Mission and Financial District stores zero in on that working gal offering more suits, silk and wools, from famous makers like Ellen Tracy, Liz Claibourne, Personal, Gloria Vanderbilt, Carol Little, Gilmore, Richard Benat and many others. The suburban stores emphasize weekend wear and clothes for the non professional woman. The final resting place for all the clothes that last too long in these locations is their Clearance Center on Florida St. in San Francisco.

PIC-A-DILLY

1847 El Camino Real, Burlingame Plaza, Burlingame 94010. Phone: 697-9846. Purchases: MC, VISA. Parking: Lot.

☞ **Other Stores:** Alameda, Berkeley, Belmont, Campbell, Concord, Capitola, Cupertino, Daly City, Dublin, El Cerrito, Fairfield, Fremont, Hayward, Los Gatos, Menlo Park, Milpitas, Modesto, Mt. View, Oakland, Petaluma, Redwood City, Richmond, Salinas, San Anselmo, San Francisco, San Jose, San Lorenzo, San Mateo, San Rafael, Santa Clara, Santa Cruz, Santa Rosa, Stockton, Sunnyvale, Terra Linda, Union City, Walnut Creek.

When you feel like shopping close to home, chances are you'll find a *Pic-A-Dilly* nearby. With more than 200 stores in their chain, they not only buy directly from major manufacturers like Calvin Klein, Polo, Jordache, Sasson, and Izod, they round out and complete their inventory by developing merchandise lines directly for their stores. Most stores have a 9 to 5 department geared just for the working woman, yet I find consistently, they serve younger women under 35 with the largest part of their inventory. Their pants, blouses, sweaters, and activewear priced at least 30% below original retail are usually up-to-date. This results from having New York buyers "in the market" every day. *Pic-A-Dilly* maintains an aggressive markdown policy to create a quick turnover, creating volume that is so essential to profits. They sell only first quality merchandise, in sizes 4-14 or 3-13. Don't take them for granted just because they're everywhere, they're definitely worth a frequent looksee!

STORK'S MATERNITY OUTLET

2048 El Camino Real (Mervyn's Plaza), Santa Clara 95050. Phone: (408) 249-8241. Hours: MTW & F 10am-7pm, Th 10am-9pm, Sat 10am-6pm. Purchases: MC, VISA. Parking: Lot.

☞ **Other Stores:** Town & Country Village, Sunnyvale; Burlingame Plaza, Burlingame.

Maternity clothes are hard to come by at discount prices which is disappointing considering the temporary nature of this type of apparel. At *Stork's Maternity Outlet*, the prices are not as low as other types of apparel discount stores, but they are the only store that is selling name brand maternity clothes at any kind of a discount. Sometimes you'll save $3-$5 on a blouse, or a pair of basic pants, maybe $2 on a maternity bra, and yet they have many garments that are almost 40% off which reflects their ability to buy these garments off price. In this instance these are usually sample garments in sizes 8-10. Their selection is typical of most maternity stores with dresses for work, party or casual needs, jumpers, pants, blouses, lingerie and nylons. Even though the discounts are smaller, their customers seem gratified to save 15-25% on the average. Sizes 4-20.

NEIGHBORHOOD STORES

These stores are frequently excellent local resources for fashion discounts. Circle those in areas where you frequently shop. The size of the stores and the depth and quality of selection varies greatly, an indication is the space I have given to each store listing. With the growth of major off-price chains, the scramble to acquire merchandise is increasingly difficult for those smaller stores that have limited buying power, who can't afford the services of a buying group or broker, or who don't have long established reliable relationships with their suppliers. In fact, many independents are being squeezed out of the marketplace, and are rapidly becoming an "endangered species".

CLOTHES CITY

861 Fourth Street, San Rafael 94901. Phone: 459-2456. Hours: M-W & Sat 10am-6pm, Th till 8pm, Fri till 9pm, Sun Noon-5pm. Purchases: MC, VISA. Parking: Street.

For the absolute latest in funky, punk, outrageous or New Wave fashions boogie right down to *Clothes City*. If you're lining up for the "Rocky Horror Show", and conventional won't do, try their spiked bracelets, bizarre T-Shirts, pants and plastic shoes. This is a fun little store for the right crowd. You'll get a kick out of their selection! Junior sizes and maximum discounts.

CLOTHES ENCOUNTER

217 Kearny Street (betw. Sutter & Bush), San Francisco 94104. Phone: 788-1747. Hours: M-F 10am-5:45pm, Sat 11am-5pm. Purchases: MC, VISA. Parking: Pay Garages.

☞ **Other Store:** 2348 Mission Street., San Francisco.

Imagine a discount store that validates! Just one block from the Stockton-O'Farrell garage they'll give you one hour's free parking with a purchase. If that isn't incentive enough consider the merchandise: Condor, Barbara-Barbara, Casadei, Pacino, and many fashion forward New York lines at 30-50% off retail. Hats, bags, belts, scarves, and jewelry are crammed in with all the clothing. Around the holidays, they bring in some elegant, dressy party dresses and ensembles. The Mission St. store has more Junior fun fashions than the downtown store.

DANDELION

250-A Magnolia Ave., Larkspur 94939. Phone: 924-6211. Hours: T-Sat 10am-5pm. Purchases: MC, VISA. Parking: Lot.

You'll get a lift just visiting this store. The merchandise speaks for itself: some of the very best classic sportswear manufacturers are found in sample sizes (8-10). Henry Grethel, Intuitions, Schraeder Sport, Emily, Patty Woodard, and John Meyer labels are the reason why many women leave their names so that they can be called when something new and just right comes into the store. Winter lines have wool skirts, pants, blazers and sweaters; and summer lines associated with the season. These samples are priced 1/3 off prevailing retail; reason alone that so many Marin value-conscious shoppers have frequented this store for the past eleven years.

DANIALS FASHIONS

278 Post Street #502, San Francisco 94108. Phone:
397-0359. Hours: M-Sat 10am-5pm. Purchases: MC,
VISA. Parking: Pay Lots.

If you find yourself around Union Square naively
looking for bargains take the elevator to *Danials* fifth floor
store. I've made many visits and find myself reacting
favorably most of the time with their selection of silk
dresses and blouses. They also carry sweaters, suits,
accessories, and an interesting selection (although small) of
fine leather and suede clothing. Depending on your timing,
the merchandise will appear well past season, or up-
to-date. Sizes 4-14. Prices are 40-50% off original prices.

DESIGNERS CLOSET

Vintage 1870, 6525 Washington St., Yountville 94599.
Phone: (707) 252-0923. Hours: M-S 10am-5pm, Sun
Noon-5pm. Purchases: MC, VISA. Parking: Lot.

The owner of *Designers Closet*, a former buyer for
Bloomingdales, is putting her years of experience and
valuable contacts to good use by keeping an intriguing
selection of merchandise well displayed in her discount
boutique. She buys for those who desire an updated image.
These are usually women from the baby boom era who
have outgrown or become too sophisticated for most Junior
lines. Sizes range from 4-14 on the dresses and separates
from well known manufacturers like Dior, Belle France, J.
G. Hook, Schrader and others. Discounts start at 20% off
and reach 40% when she can pull off a super buy. These
are very current fashions, all first quality, and selected to
"put you together . . .to set you apart." Some Petite sizes

are carried. Vintage 1870 is off Hwy. 29, Yountville exit.

THE FACTORY STORE

501 Bryant St. (at 3rd St), San Francisco 94107. Phone:
495-5940. Hours: M-Sat 10am-5pm. Purchases: MC,
VISA. Parking: Street.

☞ **Other Store:** 145 W. Santa Clara, San Jose.

The fact that they have public restrooms warms my
heart: so few stores seem to recognize the real need of
consumers for "facilities". The merchandise mix is eclectic with clothing for men, women and children. Everything
is first quality, but I'm hard pressed at times to identify the
lines they carry, but after all, there are more than 20,000
apparel makers nationwide so naturally many labels are
unknown to consumers. Ski apparel, activewear, leotards,
flannel nightgowns, and children's playclothes are jammed
on racks, along with casual and career separates for the
working woman. Prices are always discounted 40-60% off.
Children's sizes are infant to 14; women's are 3/4 to
13/14; plus blouses in sizes 36-44.

FASHION EXPRESS FACTORY OUTLET

925 Linden Ave. (1/2 mile north of West Grand Ave.),
South San Francisco 94080. Phone: 952-4556. Hours:
10am-5:30pm, Sat 10am-5pm. Purchases: MC, VISA.
Parking: Lot.

☞ **Other Store:** Garment Express, 7927 Greenback Lane,
Citrus Heights.

This discount store has joined forces with an importer of

basic polyester blouses and tops to create a new store that caters to both juniors (3-13) and women (6-18) and (36-44). Separates and dresses in a moderate price range appeal to those who want no nonsense, basic styles. If you like easy care polyester blouses and pants at a good price, you'll dive right into the racks. Some wool blazers and wool blend skirts, nicely priced, are always on hand. They keep a well stocked inventory of leather handbags during fall and winter, and canvas and nylon totes for the summer.

FASHION FACTORY

10387 San Pablo Ave., El Cerrito 94530. Phone: 525-3733. Hours: M-S 9:30am-5:30pm. Purchases: MC, VISA. Parking: Lot.

Fashion Factory features hundreds of women's garments in sizes 8-20. The styles appeal primarily to mature women and senior citizens, not much for the bubble gum crowd. The brand names are well known (Koret, Tan-Jay, Catalina, Devon, etc.) and the garments are in excellent condition, no seconds or irregulars. Of special interest to travellers is the availability of hard-to-find end of season clothing when other stores have already cleared their racks of seasonal goods. The store is clean and well organized with dressing rooms and exchange privileges. Savings average 35% and go up to 50% during "end of season" sales. What really sets this discount operation apart from most others is the quality of the sales help. They are experienced, mature, helpful and willing to give personalized service.

FASHIONS UNLIMITED

5100-5 Clayton Rd. (Vineyard Shopping Center), Concord 94511. Phone: 825-3874. Hours: M-F 9:30am-9pm, Sat 9:30am-6pm, Sun 11am-5pm. Purchases: MC, VISA. Parking: Lot.

You don't have to sweat prices at *Fashions Unlimited* with their aggressive buying, ruthless discounting, and reliable selection of sportswear from well known manufacturers. Their frequent "events" bring crowds of locals, all pushing to pick up $5 turtlenecks, and other terrific bargains that are the result of successful buying trips and dealings. Bobbie Brooks, Modern Jrs., A. Smile, Chem de Fer, Rocky Mountain, Lee, Chic, Byer, Eber, Smart Alec, Gloria Vanderbilt and Calvin Klein help provide a wide variety of styles that appeal to women and teens for the work world or campus life.

FROCKS & FINERY

118 So. Boulevard (end of 3rd St) San Mateo 94403: Phone 574-1859. Hours: Appointments preferred. M-F Noon-6pm, Sat 10-4pm, M & Th till 8pm. Purchases: MC, VISA. Parking: Street.

☞ **Other Store:** San Jose (408) 286-7085.

Frocks and Finery is a rental and consignment business for those needing formal and evening wear. What I like is that you don't have to sell your dress, you just consign it for rental, realizing a profit each time it is worn, and you retain the right to wear your garment or accessory when you have need to do so. Your garments are insured for damage or loss. Each item is cleaned following every rental, and they are returned to you cleaned and subject only to normal wear and tear. Their policy of complete privacy for consigners and renters assures a confidential and businesslike approach to all transactions. Records are kept to avoid the repeat appearance of any dress at the same event or school.

What about the PROFIT aspect? They agree to give you 30% of rental profit (after cleaning). For example, the dress that cost you $200 new would probably rent for about $45. After about $8 for cleaning the profit is $37. You receive $11.10 for each rental. If the dress is worn ten times, you'll receive $111, versus nothing if you leave it in your closet. Bridal gowns have even more profit potential. The $300 gown that rents for $100 could easily recover almost all of your original cost.

Finally, if you want to rent a gown or accessories for a prom, wedding, cocktail party, mother-of-the-bride, formal, or semi-formal occasion, call first for an appointment. At that time they'll try to determine your needs, size, and availablity of the type of garments you require. Service is private and personal. If you'd like to place a garment for rental, keep in mind, they're interested in acquiring *still-stylish* garments. They try to provide options for women and teens of varying ages, style orientations, in sizes (3-20). I'm altogether impressed with the opportunity to wear a dazzling dress for a fraction of the original cost.

JEAN HARRIS' DESIGNER DISCOUNT

1597 Botelho Dr. (Woodcreek Center), Walnut Creek 94596. Phone: 935-2044. Hours: M-Sat 10am-6pm, Th till 9pm. Purchases: MC, VISA. Parking: Lot.

☞ **Other Store:** 100 No. Hartz (corner Prospect), Danville.

Jean Harris, owner for many years of two distinctive clothing stores has converted both to discount stores with a "difference". The apparel she handpicks with discerning taste from California designers, is sometimes avante garde, usually high fashion, often one-of-a-kind, and typically expensive if purchased from Rodeo Drive in Beverly Hills, where many of her garments would typically be sold. The very chic are not disappointed with the fine textures and natural fibers of these unique fashions. There are no polyester print blouses here! You will be seduced by her selection of hand knit and hand crocheted sweaters, her marvelous selection of jewelry (20% off), and all the exotica she's acquired in her world wide travels. Prices are reduced 20-75% on her "beauties" meaning you could spend from $5-$500, depending of course, on whether you're buying a little scarf or a dramatic couture fashion. Sizes fall between 4-16. Her new Walnut Creek store is across from Simon's Hardware. One last point: if you think you lack the know-how to wear something really different, relax. Her sales staff is wonderful at helping you to create a look and an image that will impress all your friends. Service has not been discarded at *Jean Harris'*, just the prices.

INA'S SAMPLER

60 Middle Rincon Road, Santa Rosa 95405. Phone: (707) 538-0982. Hours: M-S 10am-5pm. Purchases: MC, VISA. Parking: Lot.

Look carefully for this little house set back from the street where you'll find a nice collection of better brands in ladies clothing. J. G. Hook, Evan Picone, John Meyer, Hathaway, David Smith are a few of the brands that are usually available at 30-50% discounts. There are new samples' lines in tennis and golfwear. The *samples* in sizes 8-10 usually arrive just prior to the season, giving one a chance to step out in the latest styles before everyone else. Some merchandise is available in sizes 4-12. If you cruise down Hwy. 12 stop in from time to time, since merchandise arrives weekly.

K. & E. DEPARTMENT STORE

2226 Taraval Street (Betw. 32nd & 33rd Ave.), San Francisco 94116. Phone: 731-3221. Hours: M-S 9am-6pm. Purchases: MC, VISA. Parking: Street.

☞ **Other Store:** Roger Karp's Discount Boutique, 323 West Portal Ave., San Francisco.

Golly! I used to love the hodgepodge selection and ambiance of *K & E*, and now they've gone and got fancy! They've upgraded their selection with better lines of misses and junior fashions for high rise employment and young fashion minded gals, plus nifty styles for teens. The store is still crowded with merchandise. After 39 years in business, they have developed many good connections in the trade who keep them well supplied. For *Sunset District* shopping, you won't find better prices or more variety any place else. Not only do they have square dance apparel, they also carry lingerie, loungewear, sleepwear, bathing suits, and ski apparel. This is one of my favorite "Hit and Run" stores. Whenever I'm driving out this way, I stop, take a blitz run through the store, and most often dive back out with at least one bargain under my arm. Sizes are 3-15, 6-16, or X-Large-36/38.

KATHY'S

Studio is 5 minutes from Union Square. San Francisco. Phone: 775-4210. Hours: By Appointment Only. Purchases: MC, VISA. Parking: Street.

Kathy spent her years as a corporate wife living in Hong Kong developing resources and contacts for her unique business. Operating from her studio, she sells current overruns of better womens apparel and accessories. Shopping in her studio is like going through the closet of a woman with a sizeable wardrobe. Looking at the selection, you would assume that this is a career woman working in a posh office where de rigueur dress is classic clothing in well made silks, wools and linens, but who frequently likes to step out of the mold and into more avante garde clothing to show that she knows what's hot, what's new, and what's up-to-date. Labels like Kathy Hardwick, Carole Little, Silks by Robert Haik, Jerry Sherman, 4 Seasons, DePeche of Paris, Vicky Valere of Paris, plus many major department store labels are common to her selection. Prices nestle around wholesale, with sizes in 4-14. Because of her frequent buying trips to Hong Kong and New York, regular hours are impossible to list, rather you must call and make an appointment. There's no pressure once you're there, just an opportunity to browse at leisure and chat with the other *regulars*. Be sure to get on her mailing list for announcements of new shipments and special weekend sales.

LANZ II

Ocean and Dolores, Carmel 93921. Phone: (408) 624-7472. Hours: M-Sat 10am-6pm, Sun Noon-5pm. Purchases: MC, VISA. Parking: Street.

As as teenager my idea of happiness was owning a Lanz dress and a pair of Capezio shoes. Today Lanz is enjoying renewed popularity not only with today's teens, but with their moms who never lost their love for their delightful fashions. Lanz stores today offer more than Lanz designs. The stores are stocked with quality lines selected to augment their own enduring styles and to offer a greater variety of styles. *Lanz II* in Carmel (just around the corner from their main store) is where all the bargains in Lanz fashions can be found in Northern California. Though the store is small, it is jammed with racks of everything that might have originally been sold in their other stores, but now the fashions are marked down as overruns, end of season, or irregulars. Savings range from 30-60% off original retail. The irregulars are clearly marked with a slash across the label. Bathing suits, nightgowns, suits, jackets, lingerie, dresses and sportswear are sold in sizes 4-14 or 3-13. All sales are final. Can't find your way to Carmel, then your next best bet is the wonderful sales held 2-3 times a year at local Lanz stores. Get on their mailing list.

LEOTARDS ETC.

1169 Chess Drive, Suite F (near Family Fitness Center), Foster City 94404. Phone: 573-1702. Hours: Sat Only 10am-5pm. Purchases: Cash or Check. Parking: Lot.

This enterprising woman has utilized her husband's excess warehouse space to set up shop selling leotards, tights, leg warmers and head bands to the exercise crowd. With virtually no overhead, she can pass on savings of 30-50% on fashion brands of exercise apparel. Sizes range from Petite to Large with a few gordo and maternity styles. All the leotards can be worn with bras, and although very fashionable, these are not the extreme cuts (that require a flawless figure with no saddle bags or thunder thighs) so younger and more mature women can wear them and feel good in them. Most are made from cotton lycra, many are bright solid colors or jazzy prints. Of course, the merchandising of the "outlet" is almost primitive — that keeps overhead down, but there are mirrors and private spaces for try-ons. Two piece sets that are priced around $39 in major department stores are priced at a pleasing $17. Most leotards are between $10-$20. Many of the lines are often featured in *Shape Magazine* and are frequently worn by TV fitness personalities. Please note they are only open on Saturdays. Directions: From 101, Hwy. 92 East, Foster City Blvd. North, right on Chess Dr.

MADELLE'S

1270 Newell Ave. (Newell Hill Place — behind Capwells), Walnut Creek 94596. Phone: 945-8404. Hours: M-S 9:30am-6pm. Purchases: MC, VISA. Parking: Lot.

On a scale of 1 to 10, *Madelle's* rates a 10! Their store reflects discriminating buying and a clear perception of their market. I'm amazed that other retailers don't make a greater effort to copy their success. Unlike the majority of off-price stores, they're not concerned with the bubble gum market, but rather focus on the woman over 30, who wants *quality*. They provide the basics for "investment" dressing, with lines from the makers of better suit and separates. Following the latest trend, they've strengthened their dress lines. They've covered the classic's, but for those who think classic or preppy is dullness, they supply a nice range of updated, sophisticated and casual clothing that is so well done by California manufacturers. Their Spring 84 selection contained popular ribbon sweaters, plus hand crocheted styles that sold like hot cakes. *Madelle's* just gets better every season. Contra Costa women certainly appreciate the prices that are 20-40% off in a store that is more like an expensive specialty store than an off-price store. Unlike some major chains, you don't have to weed through the rejects to find the choicest buys — everything is choice and up-to-date. *Madelle's* is tucked away in a small shopping center one block behind the *Capwell's* parking lot.

MARIKA

2020 Shattuck Ave., Berkeley 94704. Phone: 843-2100. Hours: M-S 10am-6pm. Purchases: MC, VISA. Parking: Street or Pay Lots.

☞ **Other Store:** 2308 Telegraph Ave., Berkeley.

When classes at Cal get to be too much, a popular diversion for students is a shopping sortee to Marika. These two little stores offer updated, mostly casual fashions from Esprit, Ellen Tracy, Jag, and many trendy makers of sportswear. The overall selection is eclectic, with silk blouses for Saturday nights, and oxford cloth shirts for school days. Their samples of in-season merchandise deserve the closest scrutiny for the fashion minded, while the end of season closeouts and special markdown racks fit most easily into the student's budget.

MOM'S THE WORD

2217 San Ramon Valley Blvd., San Ramon 94583. Phone: M-S 10am-5:30pm, Sun Noon-5pm. Purchases: MC, VISA. Parking: Lot.

If you're pregnant or nursing, this little shop tucked away in a small strip shopping center in San Ramon will surely please you with their prices and selection. Taking a smaller markup, the owner passes on savings of 10-30% off retail. Occasionally, special buys reflect even greater savings. Responding to a demand expressed by many nursing mothers, there is a nice selection of nursing dresses with clever openings that conceal the functional aspects of the garment. These also double as maternity dresses. Most of her lines are moderately priced and are geared for the casual lifestyle of the surrounding suburban community. Sizes range from 4-20. The store is 1/2 mile north of the Crow Canyon Rd. offramp from Fwy. 680, west side of Fwy.

MARSHALL'S
(See **Family Clothing**)

MORE THE WOMAN
3631 Piedmont Ave. (McArthur/Broadway Center), Oakland 94611. Phone: 547-6582. Hours: M-F 10am-7pm, Sat 10am-6pm, Sun 11am-5pm. Purchases: MC, VISA. Parking: Lot.

More the Woman attracts customers from all over the Bay Area, and no wonder. Off-price stores are few and far between that cater exclusively to their needs. This small shop in the MB Shopping Center is canvassed by regulars hoping to get the cream of the weekly shipments and 30-60% off retail. Tops on their "most wanted" list are the Chez dresses which are usually first quality overruns, but the wool and wool blend separates go pretty fast as well. Caftans, tops, pants and dresses in styles and quality ranging from just moderate to magnificent provide tempting bargains. Rarely there are some irregulars, but only when the prices are just too good to pass up, otherwise everything is first quality. Sizes range from 16-50.

MY FAVORITE CLOTHING & SHOE STORE
825 Francisco Blvd. West, San Rafael 94901. Phone: 453-4195. Hours: M-Sat 10am-6pm, Sun 11am-5pm. Purchases: MC, VISA.

☞ **Other Store:** 33 Drumm St., San Francisco.

I like this store because it's such an adventure to shop here. Not elegant, mind you, just racks and racks of trendy, hip, and funky fashions for the MTV crowd. When the flashdance look was hot, they had a great selection. Organically Grown, St. Germain, Gitano and The Sweater Co. were a few of their popular lines. This is not the place for the Jones of New York customer; however, women of all ages who like a contemporary look can skip right over the ultra trendy stuff, and cull and glean from the smaller selection of better quality career apparel. The shoe department, which is practically a store within a store, has a wonderful selection of boots, plus casual, dressy and high styled flats and heels from Cities, Candies, Cinema, Oceans West and others. Prices are discounted 30-60% on everything in the store!

N.A.N.C.Y'S FASHION CLEARANCE
4220 Broadway, Oakland 94611. Phone: 547-2202. Hours: M-F 10am-6pm, Sat 10am-5:30pm. Purchases: MC, VISA. Parking: Lot.

East Bay shoppers delight in the good buys and especially the merchandise that has *McCaulou's* price tags showing markdowns of 30-70% off original retail. This *McCaulou's* merchandise is always past season and has typically survived one or two sales at their retail stores before being banished to the racks at *N.A.N.C.Y.'S*. Misses, Junior and children's apparel is carried with lines representative of the fine quality associated with *McCaulou's*, and also includes special buys just for this store from local manufacturers. Many women stop by in the hopes of picking up a blouse, pair of pants, nightgown or some other wardrobe basic.

OPTIONS
(See **Men's Apparel**)

DONNA PILLER'S
(See **Shoes**)

ROSE'S BARGAIN EMPORIUM
150 No. Hartz Ave., Danville 94526. Phone: 837-1558. Hours: M-S 10am-5:30pm, Sun Noon-5pm. Purchases: MC, VISA. Parking: Street.

Rose's is reminiscent of the general stores of yesteryear. The hardwood floors, country-motif wallpaper, and the intriguing selection of merchandise is conducive to browsers. Every nook and cranny is filled with bargains of one sort or another.

The largest space is devoted to apparel in sample sizes. These fashions from Ann Klein, Willi of Calif., CW11, Hershey's and others will fit ladies in sizes 6-12 depending on the manufacturer. Discounts are 30-60%. Men are not neglected. Another room is filled with namebrand dress shirts, sport shirts, casual pants, shorts, velours and sweaters. There's a nook full of costume jewelry at 50% off,

and several rooms filled with giftshow samples priced from 30-50% off retail. The gift selection includes brass, ceramic, wood, linens, kitchen accessories, and fine art glass. There're new surprises every time you visit. P. S. This used to be the *The Sample Cell*: same owners, just innovative new merchandising.

S & R FASHION CENTER
2058 Mission St., San Francisco 94110. Phone: 626-0856. Hours: M-Sat 11am-6pm, Sun Noon-5pm. Purchases: Cash or Check. Parking: Street.

☞ **Other Store:** 960 Geneva, San Francisco.

Only the most dedicated bargain hunters will enjoy shopping at *S & R*. This is a last post outlet for many Bay Area manufacturers. You'll find out-of-season, overruns, irregulars all jammed onto racks in such a manner that few have the patience to look for that super buy amidst the clutter. The prices are an inducement to persevere: up to 70% off on their range of fashions that will suit juniors and especially matrons. Parking can be a probem at this Mission St. location. Many have acquired parking tickets when their five minute excursion lasted an hour or longer.

SECRET HANG-UPS
645 E. Blithedale (upstairs-Blithedale Plaza), Mill Valley 94941. Phone: 383-1204. Hours: M-S 10am-6pm, Sun Noon-5pm. Purchases: MC, VISA. Parking: Lot.

The atmosphere is more "boutique" than discount at this charming upstairs store in Mill Valley. It's no secret any more that you can save 30% off on the blouses, skirts, dresses, suits, etc. from manufacturers like Modern Junior, String Bean, Esprit, Collage, Carol Anderson, Sunbow, Simeon and others. Many are samples usually arriving ahead of season. Sizes range from 5-12. When new shipments arrive, the owner can hardly get the merchandise tagged before anxious customers have snatched it all up. Casual sportswear takes up most of the rack space, but there are usually some career-type fashions for ladies. Getting help is no problem, they love to help you organize a total look.

SILK & SUCH

801 A Street (at 2nd), San Rafael 94901. Phone: 454-7635. Hours: M-S 10am-6pm, Sun Noon-5pm. Purchases: MC, VISA. Parking: Street.

One of the largest selections of silk blouses and dresses is the attraction at *Silk & Such*. Many are imported directly from the same Hong Kong manufacturers that produce blouses for major designers and private label lines for our better stores. Prices range from $30-$60. They don't stop after they fill their racks with silk blouses, they scour the market for good buys on overruns and closeouts on dresses by Nipon, Liz Claiborne, Vantisse, etc.; suits by Larry Levine; separates by Daniel Caron, Anne Klein, Bijou and many others. The emphasis is on natural fibers, better quality, and all geared to the sophisticated lady. Every visit reveals a new accessory line like the Elk Skin handbags, wallets, and belts at nearly wholesale prices. Sizes range from 4-16.

SPARE CHANGES

695 3rd St. (at Townsend), San Francisco 94107. Phone: 896-0577. Hours: M-S 9:30am 5:30pm. Purchases: MC, VISA. Parking: Street.

Even though they've doubled in size *Spare Changes* has no room to spare. The store is stocked to the walls with overruns and closeouts from local manufacturers who have no outlets of their own, plus merchandise from New York, Dallas and Los Angeles. They've beefed up their career apparel section with better suits, separates and dresses in Misses, Petite and Junior sizes. While sophisticated moms are shopping, their teen daughters can check the racks of activewear, trendy Junior fashions, and school basics. Discounts rack up at 40-80% off retail. Like all off-price stores some visits will be disappointing depending upon the timing. At most times merchandise is fresh and timely, at other times, almost obsolete.

SPORTIQUE FASHIONS

2310 Homestead Road. (Foothill Plaza), Los Altos 94022. Phone: (408) 735-8660. Hours: M-F 10am-9pm, Sat 10am-6pm, Sun Noon-5pm. Purchases: MC, VISA.

Consider shopping at *Sportique* a family outing. Not only do they have a substantial selection of Juniors and Misses sportswear and career apparel, they give men, children, and teens a fair shake. They buy from approximately 300 manufacturers, local and nationally-known favorites. Their savings range up to 60% below prevailing retail and best of all they don't cut their labels. Sifting through the racks takes some time but with 21 dressing rooms there's no waiting to try on. Their efforts to upgrade the career selection for the 9-5 crowd has been well received. They offer a reasonable exchange or refund policy except on final sale merchandise. *Sportique* buys only first quality merchandise.

SUIT YOURSELF

2965 Laguna St. (at Filbert), San Francisco 95123. Phone: 931-5139. Hours: M-Sat 11am-7pm. Sun Noon-5pm. Purchases: MC, VISA. Parking: Limited Street.

It's said that the best things come in small packages; it's also true that the best bargains can come from small stores like *Suit Yourself*. Around the corner from *Perry's* on Union Street, this posh little store caters exclusively to working women with classic taste, who have aspirations of climbing the corporate ladder. The owner trys to accommodate her clientele with a price range that helps the gal who makes $25,000 look like she's making $50,000. Some of her lines are very expensive i. e. in the $150 plus range for suits even at a 20-50% discount. Yet this is just a reflection of the quality she tries to maintain. Everything is always very current, beautifully displayed, with wardrobe counseling thrown in for free to make sure you're turned out in style.

WOMEN AT LARGE

39102 Fremont Hub, Fremont 94538. Phone: 792-1292. Hours: M-F 10am-9pm, Sat 10am-5:30pm, Sun 10am-5pm. Purchases: MC, VISA. Parking: Lot.

Don't go here to buy a dress, they don't have any. However, if you need casual sportswear or separates, and you're concerned about price, you'll be pleased to discover this store. *Women at Large* is a descriptive name for the size range 36-52 in tops, and 30-40 in pants. Better yet, their clothing is geared for the younger woman and her tight budget. Most of the merchandise is discounted about 30%. These fashions are closeouts, odd lots and overruns but not old and outdated. Many popular manufacturers are well represented in the seletion.

Appliances

dazzle displays or merchandising glamour. They sell major brands of kitchen and laundry appliances plus televisions and VCR's. Their prices on General Electric, Amana, Whirlpool and RCA lines are hard to beat! Their secret for low prices is familiar: buying by the carload so they can take advantage of volume discounts. From their local warehouses they can restock their in-store inventory weekly, plus provide immediate delivery on most of the lines they carry. They will give phone quotes gladly, plus they'll really trim that discount if you can bring a pickup or van to haul your buys away. Delivery charges are assessed according to the size of your order and distance involved.

(Also see **Furniture and Accessories — Catalog Discounters, Warehouse Sales; General Merchandise — Catalog Discounters**)

A & B Premiums
(See **Cameras**)

ABC APPLIANCE SERVICE
2048 Taraval (between 30th & 31st Ave.), San Francisco 94116. Phone: 998-2906 or 800-942-1242. Hours: M-Sat 9am-5pm, Sun 10am-3pm. Purchases: MC, VISA. Parking: Street.

Marin County residents zip over the Golden Gate Bridge into Sunset District of the City for their appliance bargains. *ABC* operates a modest store completely lacking in razzle

CVB (CENTRAL VOLUME BUYERS)
1815 So. Monterey Rd. (Betw. Tully & Alma), San Jose 95112. Phone: (408) 998-2906. Hours: T-Sat 10am-6pm. Purchases: MC, VISA. Parking: Lot.

With just a few exceptions, the appliance dealers in Santa Clara County "hold the line" on prices. *CVB* is one of the exceptions. Their warehouse-type facility, low overhead location, allows them to price their appliances with a smaller markup. The game starts with the prices on their tags. If you're inclined and you think you can negotiate a lower price, give it a try. Most appliances are in the original factory crates, ready for delivery. Others are uncrated for your inspection. *CVB* offers a 30-day trade-in policy, so if you get a lemon (that can happen anywhere) they'll gladly exchange the item for you. Delivery is nominal: $29 from San Jose to Salinas. Take note — they will not quote prices over the phone.

CHERIN'S

727 Valencia Street, San Francisco 94110. Phone: 864-2111. Hours: M-F 10am-6pm, Sat 10am-5pm. Purchases: Cash or Check. Parking: Private Lot.

A great source for home appliances in every category. This store has a good selection of refrigerators, freezers, washers, dryers, TV's, microwave ovens, VCR's, sophisticated radios, even 220V major appliances for overseas use. More importantly for remodelers, they carry esoteric brands like Wolf, Sub Zero, U.S. Range, Gaggenau, plus the popular well known brands. Contractor prices prevail for everyone. They specialize in built in appliances. Their business is mostly referral since they rarely advertise their low prices that reflect only a minimal markup. Don't expect them to quote prices over the phone if they don't know you. Delivery is free within the Bay Area.

EAST WEST APPLIANCE

1057 A-E El Camino Real (behind Carl's Hamburgers, Henderson Center), Sunnyvale 94087. Phone: (408) 249-7343. Hours: Tues-Sat 10:30am-7pm. Cash or Certified bank check.

☞ **Other Store:** 1040 University Avenue, Berkeley, Phone: 549-1170.

After some sleuthing and comparison shopping, I've focused on *East West Appliance* in Sunnyvale, an unlikely looking resource for good buys on appliances, TV's and VCR's among other things. At first glance, the baby dolls, luggage, small appliances, watches, colognes, stereo equipment and housewares, stacked around the floor and counter causes one to wonder just what this business is all about. Basically, everything relates to bargains, however unconventional the merchandise mix appears. My comparisons on RCA and Sony products reveal the "best prices" in this area, and also for many other areas. (San Francisco has more than its share of price cutting dealers.)

At *East West* the merchandise is sold in factory sealed cartons. You can order home appliances from catalogues or with a model number which may require some discreet shopping elsewhere. They will not accept personal checks, and require payment by cash or certified bank check. Using MC or VISA will add 3% to the cost. If price is your bottom line, you won't be deterred by this unconventional outfit. Customers I've talked with have been more than pleased with their prices and reliability.

FILCO

1433 Fulton Ave. (Filco Plaza), Sacramento 95825. Phone: (916) 488-8484, 488-8471. Hours: M-Sat 10am-7pm. Purchases: MC, VISA. Parking: Free Lot.

In the Sacramento area *Filco's* prices are dynamite! Working with a very minimal markup, they offer an extensive selection in the camera and home appliance area. Most major brands of 35mm cameras, accessories, and instant picture cameras are in stock at terrific prices. Kodak film is sold at *cost*. This is their loss leader and certainly lures customers who often leave with more than film once they see all the other bargains. Kodak processing is always 30% off. JennAir, Kitchen Aid, Panasonic, Whirlpool, Litton, Amana, Sony and GE are a few of the major brands represented in the appliance and home entertainment divisions.

GENERAL ELECTRIC SERVICENTER
1727 No. First Street, San Jose 95112. Phone: (408) 298-4203. Hours: M-Sat 8:30am-5:30pm. Purchases: MC, VISA. Parking: Lot.

One of the very best ways to replace an old or broken General Electric small appliance is through the exchange program offered at the *General Electric Servicenter*. It is possible to trade in that old iron, coffeepot, or toaster oven for another and save approximately 30% off the suggested retail price. On price comparisons I made, the trade-in price was lower than any discount store or catalog discount house.

The reconditioned appliances on display carry the following description: "Reconditioned appliances generally represent appliances that have been used in displays or that failed in initial use. They have been carefully reconditioned by trained GE technicians using new GE replacement parts where required. They have been carefully tested to assure that they meet operating standards required of new appliances and carry the same warranty as new products." On these you can save 30-35%. If what you want isn't on display, be sure to ask — it may be on hand in the storeroom.

HOUSE OF LOUIE
1045 Bryant St. (near 9th), San Francisco 94103. Phone: 621-7100. Hours: M-Sat 10am-6pm, (closed Wed) Sun 1pm-5pm. Purchases: Cash or Check. Parking: Free lot on side of Bldg.

In this old warehouse building you can get some very good buys on appliances and home entertainment needs. Most of the items, such as refrigerators, dishwashers, dryers, VCR's, TV's, and kitchen cabinets are available on a cost plus 10% basis. You can choose from brands like Sony, RCA, GE, Maytag, Hoover, Magic Chef, etc., all in stock or extend your options with their catalogs. On special orders, all sales are final.

Their furniture resources in the low to moderate price range include sofas, chairs, formal dining room furniture, mattresses, dinettes, baby furniture, and imported Chinese Modern pieces. Savings are from 20-30%. The better goods can be ordered too, with savings of about 20%. Delivery is free within the city of San Francisco; installation is extra. Consumers from the Asian community appreciate their bi-lingual sales staff.

INTERNATIONAL HOUSEHOLD EXPORT, INC.
1169 Mission St (betw. 7th & 8th Sts), San Francisco 94103. Phone: 626-8800. Hours: M-F 10am-7pm, Sat & Sun 11am-5pm. Purchases: MC, VISA. Parking: Street, Pay Lots.

If you're being transferred overseas and you can't imagine life without your favorite appliance, check here. Not only do they sell 200 volt appliances (that they'll pack and crate for shipping) they sell most major brands of appliances for kitchen, laundry, and entertainment needs. Price competition in San Francisco is ruthless, yet this outfit seems to stay on top of the competition, consistently offering great prices on video tapes, recorders and color cameras, TV's, radios, stereos, car stereos, short wave radios and all the new telephone gadgets and equipment. Referrals are provided for installation of car stereos.

I check their ads in the *San Francisco Chronicle* every week and particularly appreciate their prices, listed with model number, that allow you to make easy comparisons with other businesses that are straight forward enough to put all the information in print. So often price claims that are not accompanied by model numbers lead to prices that are not bargains upon investigation. Their in-store inventory is quite extensive, but they can also order special merchandise they don't have in stock. Finally, buy with care. They are not likely to make exchanges unless the merchandise is defective.

L & Z PREMIUMS

1162 Saratoga Ave. (Mapleleaf Plaza), San Jose 95129. Phone: (408) 985-7918. Hours: M-F 10am-8pm, Sat 10am-6pm, Sun 11am-5pm. Purchases: MC, VISA. Parking: Lot.

L & Z is not a typical appliance store. They have some appliances on the floor but offer a greater selection from their manufacturers' catalogs. Prices reflect a very minimal markup, and delivery charges are reasonable. Most major brands of TV's, VCR's, kitchen appliances like microwaves and refrigerators, laundry appliances, car stereos and expensive radios can be ordered. Delivery is usually within a few days.

About half of their business is devoted to photographers with a complete selection of major brand cameras, accessories, dark room equipment, chemicals, papers, etc. sold for pleasing discounts. Kodak processing is 30% off and Kodak film is sold at their cost.

SUNBEAM APPLIANCE CO.

655 Mission St., San Francisco 94105. Phone: 362-7195. Hours: 8:30am-5pm. Purchases: MC, VISA. Parking: Street, Pay Lot.

It's not too exciting to have to spend good money on a new iron, mixer, or coffeepot, so bargain hunters will really appreciate the nice selection of "as is" Oster and Sunbeam merchandise available at the *Sunbeam Appliance Company*. "As is" items were once display models, salesmen's samples, discontinued models, or factory closeouts; all pieces are perfect, both mechanically and electrically, and are guaranteed to perform satisfactorily even when they may have small flaws on the finish or trim. They carry a full line of all accessories for these products. New products include air purifiers, quartz timers, quartz heaters, and electric blankets. You may also locate some hard-to-find appliances such as egg cookers, large juicers, or meat grinders. They will special order any new item for you and of course, can provide or order any Sunbeam or Oster replacement part. Ship via UPS anywhere? Of course!

Arts, Crafts, and Hobby Supplies

AMSTERDAM ART

1013 University Avenue, Berkeley 94710. Phone: 548-9663. Hours: M-Thurs 10am-7pm, Fri-Sun 10am-6pm. Purchases: VISA, MC. Parking: Street.

The long lines at the cash register must be an indication of the good prices: why else would people stand in line so long? *Amsterdam Art* is patterned after Pearl's, king of art discounts on the East Coast. In the Bay Area this is *the* resource for art supplies with virtually everything for drafting, graphic and fine arts. Discounts range from 20-40% on all major brands of fine arts tools, i.e. paints, brushes, etc.; 20% on drafting supplies and equipment; and at least 10% on graphic art supplies. If you're attempting any project you'll delight in the complete selection of merchandise that makes any professional or amateur effort a cinch. I discovered time-saving graphic supplies that I didn't even know existed, that will certainly compensate for a lack of technique and talent when undertaking a project. The next time your group, school, church, etc., asks you to make a flyer, newsletter, or invitation, don't panic. It's easy when you work with some of the new products geared for the novice that help to layout, paste-up, and design any item for printing. I loved their selection of papers in 24 colors sold by the pound, 1/2 pound, 1/4 pound, or by the piece.

Their framing department has a good selection of pre-fab frames in lucite, wood, and metal at 50% off retail; pre-cut mats, glass, and framing sections for the do-it-yourselfer are discounted, and custom frame orders that are sent out are competitively priced with other frame shops. (Custom frame services are labor intensive; therefore, it's almost impossible to think in terms of bargain prices when framing on this level.) When shopping *Amsterdam Art*, pay attention to special promotions and closeouts for super savings.

ARTISTS' CO-OPERATIVE OF SAN FRANCISCO

1407 Bush St., San Francisco 94109. Phone: 885-2052. Hours: T-Sun 11am-5pm. Purchases: MC, VISA. Parking: Street or Pay Lot.

Artist-owned and artist-operated, the gallery has exhibited the original art of Bay Area painters, sculptors, printmakers and ceramicists since 1955. The *Co-op's* founding intention was to provide an exhibiting forum for the area's new talent and offer the public works of contemporary artists at a reasonable price. Additional savings are possible because the salesman's salary and commission is eliminated by volunteer staffing of member artists. The commission structure differs from privately owned galleries and therefore the artist does not have to price his work as high to receive a fair compensation for his creative efforts. It's possible to purchase works of emerging artists and then find pleasure in watching your art appreciate as subsequent works sell for higher and higher prices.

BLUEGATE CANDLE FACTORY OUTLET
Airport Street, Moss Beach 94037. Phone: 728-3301. Hours: M-F 9:30am-4:30pm, (Weekends before Xmas). Purchases: Cash or Check. Parking: Lot.

The *Bluegate Candle Company* makes a beautiful line of candles and accessories that are sold in specialty shops and major department stores. Their reputation is based upon their own special candle techniques, painstakingly combined dyes, waxes and perfumes in great variety to achieve the highest quality, handcrafted product possible. Their colors are selected each year to coordinate with the home furnishings industry's latest color trends. Their candles are expensive at retail!

Savvy shoppers wait for their big sales which occur twice a year, before Mother's Day and before Xmas to make a big haul. In this instance, it's wise to bring boxes so your candles can be packed properly for the trip home. At the outlet you can save 30-70% on seconds which are usually just slightly off color, discontinued colors, and overstock candles. When necessary they even pull additional merchandise from their warehouse to complete your order. Along with candles they also sell a complete line of accessories, i. e. brass and wrought iron candle holders, candle wreaths, votives, etc.

The factory is difficult to find. They are located immediately west of the Half Moon Bay Airport in Moss Beach. Highway One passes along the East side of the airport. A driver, looking west across the airport, can see their building on the other side (Airport St.). One can turn West off of Highway One at the Pillar Point Harbor intersection in El Granada, or on Cypress St. at the North end of the airport. Either way one will end up crossing Airport St. which runs along the West side of the Airport.

COAST WHOLESALE DRY FLOWERS & BASKETS
149 Morris Street, San Francisco 94107. Phone: 781-3034. Hours: M-F 8am-3pm, Sat 6am-Noon. Purchases: MC, VISA. Parking: Private Lot.

One glance at the selection within the walls of this warehouse and you get the feeling that they've scoured the forests and gleaned the fields for the unusual dry flowers, wreaths, oak leaves, pine cones, etc. Garlic braids, unique baskets, potpourri, and floral supplies are also available and create a fragrant shopping environment. Prices are right in line with those at the Flower Market across the street. *Coast* is between 5th and 6th Streets, off Bryant.

FANTASTICO
559 6th Street, San Francisco 94103. Phone: 982-0680. Hours: M-F 8:30am-5:30pm, Sat 8:30am-1pm. Purchases: Cash or Check. Parking: Street, Lot.

Fantastico is the retail subsidiary of *Angray*, the wholesale supply house for nurseries and florists. Their warehouse has just about everything for all you craft-oriented people. The selection in dried and silk flowers is over-whelming. They stock all those exotic specimens you see in beautiful arrangements in fancy stores, plus all the makings to put them together: tapes, wires, ribbons, foam, etc. My favorite is florist ribbon that I buy in rolls for gift wrapping at 1/3 the cost of the Hallmark types. One roll usually lasts me about a year. For holiday decoration and ideas, this is the place to come. They also have baskets, plastic flowers and fruits, dollhouses, crates, ceramics, terrarium bottles, plant stands and many accessory items. Prices to the general public are usually 10-30% lower than anywhere else. An exception is in their paper and party supply section where retail prices prevail except on quantity purchases. Their wedding department is supported by three "specialists" who can teach you techniques for making wedding favors, and help make printing selections for wedding and party invitations.

FLAX'S WAREHOUSE

1699 Market (corner Valencia), San Francisco 94113. Phone: 874-FLAX. Hours: M-F 9am-5:30pm, Sat 10am-5pm. Purchases: MC, VISA. Parking: Free Lot.

☞ **Other Store:** 510 East El Camino Real, Sunnyvale. (408) 736-6400.

You don't have to be a starving artist to find the savings and good values at *Flax's Warehouse* appealing. They've trimmed their operating cost by using a self service approach: eliminating services like gift certificates, deliveries, store charges, etc; and they've chosen a low rent location.

Basic stocks of leading brands of fine art supplies are discounted 20-50% off the list price. Items like Grumbacher oil colors are 20% off the list price, Bellini oil colors are 30% off, brushes, pastels, watercolors, stretched canvas, pre-cut mats, plain and fancy frames, paper and other paraphernalia are discounted appreciably. Periodically, closeouts of selected merchandise are displayed with near wholesale prices. They've finally added a complete section of graphic art materials and studio furniture at discount prices.

GENERAL BEAD

1163 Mission St., San Francisco. Phone: 621-8187. Hours: M-F Noon-5pm. Sat 10am-1pm. Purchases: Cash or Check. Parking: Street.

If there's no money left in your budget to buy jewelry, even inexpensive costume jewelry, there is hope. The *General Bead* store in San Francisco sells all varieties of beads, including a large selection in all sizes of Japanese and Czechosloviakain seed and bugle beads, glass beads from all over the world, hardwood beads from the U. S. and sandalwood from India, metal beads, lucite and plastic beads, shell beads, bone and horn beads for that natural look and Austrian Strass crystal beads. The "tools and fixin's" like jewelry findings, feathers, beading needles, looms, string, nylon thread, wire and much more. Their business is both wholesale and retail. The general public can obtain quantity discounts with purchases of 10 or more of one item. Their retail prices are so low that quantity purchases are not really crucial in making some low cost jewelry.

Even if you think you're not creative, just browsing through their selection of "thousands" of beads, is inspiration enough. Pick up a copy of *Ornament* (a magazine devoted to the aesthetics of jewelry and jewelry making), buy all the components of jewelry making, and you're set. If you've been stumped trying to find the perfect color of bead to match or coordinate with a special outfit, making your own eyecatching jewelry may be the easiest solution. Their value to the average consumer is their wide selection of lower priced merchandise that is just as good for the youth group leader buying for craft projects, as it is for the budget conscious do-it-yourselfer.

Finally, if you have odds and ends of broken jewelry, (don't we all?), then you may be interested in buying repair parts. They do sell gold finished brass or steel chains, but they do not carry any "real gold" findings or chains.

JEFFREY KRIGER FRAMING

156 Russ St., San Francisco 94103. Phone: 621-4226. Hours: M-F 10:30am-5:15pm, Sat 11am-2pm. Purchases: MC, VISA. Parking: Limited Street (two spaces marked Tenant only).

This is not a do-it-yourself frame shop unless you opt to buy all the materials, i. e. mats, backing, glass and frame pieces (cut to your measurements) and then do the assembly at home with a screwdriver. This option is a consideration for artists who find that the $4.50-$7.50 assembly charge adds up when they are framing many pictures for an exhibit or sale.

Aluminum framing is the *only* framing material sold.

This might seem limiting until you see the array of colors and finishes applied to aluminum framing, and you consider the various widths and styles available. You can select budget priced materials to frame an inexpensive picture or print, or you can go first class with museum quality materials used in conservation mounting for fine works of art. Prices at this shop are often less than the do-it-yourself frame shops even when Jeffrey does all the work. This shop is practically buried south of Market. Russ Street is sandwiched between 6th & 7th Streets and Howard and Folsom.

MAC PHERSON LEATHER SUPPLY

*728 Polk St., San Francisco 94109. Phone: 771-6204. Hours: M-F 9am-5pm, Sat 10am-4pm. Purchases: MC, VISA. Parking: Street.

Leather and all related products, including dyes and tooling supplies, are the specialty items at *Mac Pherson*, which is the biggest wholesale supplier of leather in the West. Theirs is primarily a wholesale business, but they do sell to the public. Their lower-level retail store reveals only a small selection of their merchandise, but much, much more is packed away on shelves and in boxes full of rolls. Leather is available for every purpose: for shoe making, apparel making, and upholstery needs. These are the finest premium grade hides from a long-established U. S. tannery. Full or half hides are sold from 23 sq. ft. to 55 sq. ft. per skin, in the traditional leather shades plus yummy fashion shades including plums, lavenders, and blues. Modern finishes on these hides are formulated to last for years with no special care or treatment. *Mac Pherson* is not for the novice; although helpful, the salesmen are very busy and don't have time to explain all they know to amateurs. Take a class, read how-to-manuals if you need help, or do as I did, talk to other customers. I got fail proof instructions on how to make a wonderful leather skirt from a couple of ladies who have been making these skirts for years. You'll find leather lacing and remnants; kits for handbags, wallets, and belts; tools; stains and dyes. *Mac Pherson Leather Supply* will be moving to a new address in San Francisco at the corner of Keith and Evans in 1985.

SAN FRANCISCO MUSEUM OF MODERN ART RENTAL GALLERY

Fort Mason Center (Corner of Buchanan & Marina), San Francisco 94123. Phone: 441-4777. Hours: T-Sat 11:30am-5:30pm. Closed month of August. Purchases: MC, VISA. Parking: Free Lot.

The *San Francisco Museum of Modern Art* operates a rental gallery at Fort Mason, Building A, where you can rent a painting, sculpture, or photograph for a two-month period, with the option to extend the rental time for another two months. If you decide to buy the work, half the rental fee applies toward the purchase price. The rental fees are set up on a sliding scale. For example, an art work with a purchase price of from $50-$99 rents for $10 for two months. Something costing $800-$900 would rent for $50. The goal of the gallery is to give new artists exposure. Before showing at the gallery, their work is juried which indicates that the quality of the work at the gallery is high. Many of these new artists have not shown in galleries before, but they're very good. This is an excellent chance to take part in the beginning of an artist's career — at a very low cost. I particularly like the trial period option in buying a work of art that you hope to keep forever.

ABE SCHUSTER

2940 West Street, Oakland 94608. Phone: 653-3588. Hours: M-F 8am-5pm, Sat 10am-3pm. Purchases: MC, VISA. Parking: Street.

This warehouse operation, which vibrates with the noise of cutting saws, offers spectacular savings on lucite acrylic sheets for skylights, desk tops, wind breaks, picture frames, furniture, and any other do-it-yourself projects you may have in mind.

You can save 50% off on factory seconds with barely perceptible flaws. Their regular stock of plastic and plastic-related materials such as plastic letters, corrugated fiberglass, resins, and finishes are priced about 20-40% lower than at other retail stores. They cut sheets to size for a small charge. Green thumbers take note! You can purchase Filon home greenhouse panels for the lowest prices around.

STUDIO D

657 Alma Street, Palo Alto 94301. Phone: 328-1840. Hours: M-F 10am-5:30pm, Sat 10am-5pm. Purchases: MC, VISA. Parking: Street.

Studio D is the gathering place for crafty ladies on the Peninsula. Their prices on craft supplies are comparable to those at the Flower Market, with an additional 10%

discount offered to "approved" representatives of fund raising organizations buying materials for crafts and boutique items that will be sold at their special events. Their selection of baskets, ribbons, dried flowers, wreaths, florist supplies, special holiday decorative supplies, and a whole menagerie of odds'n ends appealing to do-it-yourselfers, is quite extensive. Classes and lots of how-to advice available.

SUPER YARN MART

4525 Stevens Creek Blvd., Santa Clara 95050. Phone: (408) 243-2012. Hours: M-F 9:30am-9pm, Sat 9:30am-5:30pm, Sun 11am-5pm. Purchases: MC,. VISA. Parking: Free Lot.

☞ **Other Stores:** 5200 Mowry Ave., Fremont, 793-1712; 24046 Hesperian Blvd., Hayward, 785-9384.

Super Yarn Mart operates 33 stores in the West, with another three in the Bay Area. They manufacture most of the yarns they sell in their own spinning mill and dye house in Los Angeles, the only one west of the Mississippi. Their products, sold directly through their own outlets, provide impressive savings to consumers. They also buy carload mill shipments from other manufacturers that allow them to price well below the prevailing retail of other needlecraft shops. Their stores are a maze of colors; tables piled with yarn, bins overflowing, and cones hanging neatly on the walls. Whatever kind of yarn you covet — cotton, wool, mohair, nylon, or acrylic — you'll find it in their stores. You'll also find novelty yarns, imported and domestic yarns, mill surplus yarns (still on cones), and bulk yarns sold by the pound or ounce. All for sale at reduced prices, up to 50% off the original retail price. Besides knitting and crochet supplies, they also have all the needlepoint and embroidery accessories you could wish for at discount prices. For the less adventurous there are many different kinds of kits (the same ones you see in fancy department stores) for "substantially" less.

TALLOW TUBBE

1014 Howard, San Mateo 94401. Phone: 347-0554. Hours: M-F 10am-5pm, Sat 10am-2pm (except summer). Purchases: Cash or Check. Parking: Street.

You'll be greeted by smiling faces at this informal candle shop and factory. Besides taking the seconds, off-colors and overstock from several candle manufacturers, they also make their own. You can catch glimpses of this process going on in the back room. When their own candles come out too long, or too short, or too whatever, they're sold along with the other rejects at 30-60% off. Approximately 80% of the inventory is in the "reject" category. The selection includes tapers, spirals, molded rounds, and decorative candles. Around Xmas time you can buy big blocks of candle wax to use in making your own candles or even waxing your water skis.

UNITED SURPLUS SALES

198 11th St., Oakland 94607. Phone: 863-3467. Hours: M-Sat 9am-5:30pm. Purchases: MC, VISA. Parking: Street, Free lot.

This store is well organized, spacious and airy, with a great variety of merchandise for sale. Up to 20% off retail is offered on all purchases of leading brandname artist's paints, brushes, and supplies. A large selection of frames is available, including inexpensive, unfinished raw oak frames. Stretched canvas and pre-cut mats are available at the same savings, though there's no exchange or refund on the latter.

Wall-hung rolls of upholstery yardage are sold for 50% off retail with selected seconds occasionally available at even greater savings. All sizes and quantities of foam can be found, and it will be cut to size for you (you'll appreciate this service if you've ever tried to cut a 4-inch slab of foam yourself.) They also sell camping equipment, as well as occasional bargain-priced soft goods such as camouflage pants, etc. when they can get a great buy.

UP AGAINST THE WALL

3400 Suite D, Dela Cruz Blvd., Santa Clara 95050. Phone: (408) 727-1995. Hours: 9am-5pm. Purchases: MC, VISA. Parking: Lot.

Catering to artists and interior designers, *Up Against the Wall* uses aluminum frames exclusively. These aluminum moldings are of the highest quality, come in several styles and many colors. The hardware is heavy duty, single piece metal with pre-started screws. This is a super time saver of special value to artists who may be framing a number of pieces at one time for a show or fair.

If you have works to frame you have two options: first, you can take your picture and have the job done from start to finish; second, you can opt to do the work yourself at home, after purchasing all the materials. They will cut the glass, the matts, the backing, etc. You assemble. Artists

from outside the Bay Area do all their business by mail, sending measurements, color choices for matts and receive the materials by UPS. Call for directions.

YALEY ENTERPRISES

145 Sylvester Road, South San Francisco 94080. Phone: 761-3428. Hours: M-F 7:30am-4pm, Sat 9am-3pm. Purchases: MC, VISA. Parking: Lot.

Peninsula residents do not have to travel into the Flower Mart in S. F. to find their fixin's, they can go to *Yaley Enterprises*. They are manufacturers and importers of craft items and open to the public. You'll find all general craft items like doll parts, craft books, silk and dried flowers, floral supplies, wedding and baby shower supplies, candy making supplies (including bulk chocolate), macrame, ribbons and seasonal specialities. Their Xmas selection is just what it should be and more. Prices are excellent on everything (20-50% off retail), and certainly seem to be impressive to the customers that I questioned during my visit, particularly from those scrounging the bargains in the warehouse sale room. Directions: From Bayshore Fwy.: East Grand Ave. offramp, approx. one block to Sylvester on the right.

YORK CANDLE COMPANY

21 Duffy Place (corner of Duffy Pl. & Irwin St.), San Rafael 94901. Phone: 457-3610. Hours: M-Sat 9am-5pm. Purchases: MC, VISA. Parking: Free Lot.

This candle factory is located in the industrial section of San Rafael right next to the *Bargain Box Thrift Shop*. You may find your senses overpowered with the combined fragrances of the 14 different scents used in their candle production. Because the candles are made on the premises you can buy wholesale. All their candles are made with domestic ingredients and they claim that they outburn all the imported ones they've tested. They are also dripless and smokeless. Occasionally they may have specials when a wheel runs off-color or some color proves unpopular and they slash prices to clear their inventory. A very nice accommodation is their special order department. They will make to order special anniversary, wedding or block candles.

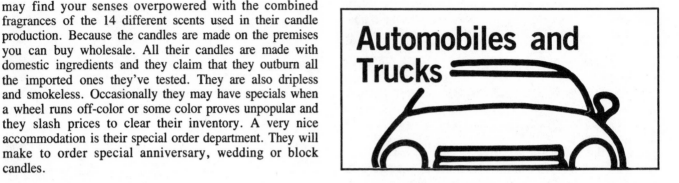

AUTO BROKERS

If you don't like to haggle or negotiate car prices, or feel that you're always being manipulated by the skillful or wily sales personnel at local dealerships, then you can avoid the whole scene by dealing with an auto broker.

In California, anyone engaging in the sale of automobiles must be licensed by the State of California, Department of Motor Vehicles. To obtain a dealer's license in California one must submit to an investigation of his background, including fingerprinting which is checked by the State and the FBI. He must have a suitable place to do business, subject to all the financial and bonding requirements of DMV, and the Board of Equalization, which is the agency collecting the retail sales tax. So, an automobile broker is a licensed automobile dealer. The primary difference is that the automobile broker handles all makes of cars, whereas the automobile dealer handles only a few makes. Automobile brokers sell brand new cars and trucks to individuals who are referred to them by personnel managers of large companies, clubs, credit unions or friends. Because of the lack of radio, TV, newspaper advertising, sales commissions and no "flooring" on inventory, the cost of doing business obviously is much lower and therefore the prices for these cars are substantially lower. Consumers obtain correct and direct information relative to the cost of new cars. Most brokers use the "Kelley Wholesale New Car Price Manual", (as do all leasing companies, banks and most credit unions) which gives the actual factory invoice cost of every new car. The factory invoice cost is the amount of money a new car dealer must pay his factory to purchase that car.

Because auto brokers do not stock cars, they suggest that you make car selections before calling for a price quote or coming to their offices. Then you can discuss the specifics, i.e. make, options, color and price. The price quoted usually includes all dealer preparation, mechanical service, polishing, etc. The price usually reflects a savings of a few hundred to a few thousand dollars depending on the make and model. Of course, if you've mastered the "strategy" of new car buying, you may get an equivalent price at a local dealer, yet few of us are gutsy and persistent enough to play those "mind games" and usually end up spending more than we need to.

Cars may be obtained from the lots of local dealers or directly from the factory. Most brokers are hooked up to computers that assist them in locating the car of your choice from a local dealer's lot, within a few hours, for delivery in a few days. Factory orders may take six weeks

to three months. Service under warranty can be performed by any factory authorized dealer. Some brokers have financing plans, others leave it all up to you.

The following list of Bay Area brokers were in good standing with the Better Business Bureau prior to publication, and come highly recommended by their customers. Finally, a comparison check on prices for an American-made, 1984 car revealed that they were very competitive with each other.

BROWN-CLARKSON INC.

365 Convention Way, Redwood City 94063. Phone: 364-7410. Hours: M-F 9am-6pm, Sat 9am-1pm. Purchases: No financing available. Parking: Street.

☞ **Other Stores:** 3368 Stevens Creek Blvd., San Jose; 14717 Catalina, San Leandro; 3600 Power Inn Rd., Sacramento.

Brown-Clarkson has racked up many years of business in the Bay Area with many repeat customers. All models and makes sold.

BUYWAY

314 South Monroe St., San Jose 95128. Phone: (408) 249-2886. Hours: M-F 9am-7pm, Sat 10am-4pm. Purchases: Bank financing available. Parking: Street.

☞ **Other Stores:** 1072 El Camino Real, Belmont 94002. 595-2886; 2645 Park Ave, Soquel 95073, (408) 475-1155.

Phone quotes welcome. Specializing in sales and leasing on any new car (domestic or import), truck, van or RV.

Optional extended warranty plan. Trades accepted.

HIBERNIA SALES AND LEASING, INC.

5918 Cutting Blvd., El Cerrito 94530. Phone: 237-6447 or 800-GET-A-CAR. Hours: M-F 9am-6pm, Sat 9am-1pm. Purchases: Financing available for leasing. Parking: Street.

☞ **Other Store:** 2766 Camino Diablo, Walnut Creek 94596, 930-0033.

All makes and models, import and domestic. Extended warranty policy available. Phone quotes. Car leasing too!

SPORT

1161 Chess Drive Suite G & H, Foster City 94404. Phone: 571-8777. Hours: M-Th 9am-7pm, Fri 9am-6:30pm, Sat 10am-6:30pm. Purchases: Assistance with financing. Parking: Lot.

Specializes in "status" imports, plus domestic cars and vans. Phone quotes, car leasing and extended warranties.

AUTOMOBILES AND TRUCKS, USED

AVIS INC.

410 So. Airport Blvd., South San Francisco 94080. Phone: 877-6763. Hours: Daily 9am-6pm. Purchases: Cash, Certified Check, Financing available. Parking: Lot.

☞ **Other Lots:** San Jose, Oakland, Sacramento.

At *Avis* they sell current-model used rental cars that have been completely reconditioned. They rent and sell primarily General Motors models. Usually cars are deluxe models with air conditioning, power brakes, power steering, and custom accessories. Since *Avis* has already made their money on rental services, you'll find lower prices than in used car lots with comparable models. Inventory changes constantly, so sooner or later they are bound to have the car you have in mind.

DOLLAR-A-DAY-RENT-A-CAR-SYSTEMS

1815 Old Bayshore Hwy., Burlingame 94010. Phone: 692-1204. Hours: M-F 9am-Midnight. Purchases: Cash, Check. Parking: Free Lot.

☞ **Other Lots:** San Francisco, San Francisco Airport; San Jose; Oakland, Oakland Airport; Palo Alto.

If you need a compact car you can save a lot of money on one here. *Dollar-A-Day* sells current model used rental cars that have been reconditioned. These are primarily Ford products whose condition is at least comparable to that of any vehicle you would find at a used car lot. All cars will have limited warranty covering engine, transmission, drive train and differential for 12 months or 12,000 miles. Since they are not out to sell cars but to dispose of capital equipment, their prices are lower than most lots. The cars are sold between October and March, according to their schedule for replacing rental stock. These cars have all been serviced regularly and are in good to excellent condition. A car will be held for you for several days while you arrange financing. If it takes longer than several days you will be asked for a small deposit, refundable if you change your mind. If you're in the market for a car, you can check on *Avis* and *Dollar-A-Day* at the same time since they're in the same vicinity.

HERTZ CAR SALES
300 E. Millbrae Ave., Millbrae 94030. Phone: 877-3737. Hours: M-F 9am-7pm, Sat & Sun 10am-6pm. Purchases: Cash, Cashier's check, Financing available. Parking: Lot.

☞ **Other Stores:** Oakland, Oakland Airport; San Jose, Airport; Hayward, Concord, Sacramento; Monterey.

Hertz selects and sells only the finer cars from its rental fleet. Every *Hertz* used car that is offered for sale has a record of service and maintenance that you can check *before you buy*. *Hertz* backs every car with a Limited Warranty covering the engine, transmission, drive shaft and differential for 12 months or 12,000 miles. All *Hertz* cars look terrific and are priced to sell. You can expect all the features you're probably looking for: air conditioning, automatic transmission, power steering and brakes, radio and radial tires. Because of their limited driving life,

rentals usually have less wear-and-tear on them. They've had more TLC too. Telephone them for more information. They are very helpful over the phone.

POLICE AUCTIONS
(See **Part II — Auctions**)

THRIFTY RENT-A-CAR
111 98th Ave. (corner Airport Dr.), Oakland 94603. Phone: 568-1220. Hours: Daily 8am-5pm. Purchases: Certified Check. Parking: Lot.

Thrifty Rent-A-Car sells their cars when they are 12-18 months old and usually have less than 24,000 miles. These American cars, compacts, full size sedans, station wagons, and occasionally vans are well maintained with service records available for your perusal. Prices are lower than at used car lots and include warranties. If you're not interested in cars, but you're going to "Fly Oakland", be advised that their rates for short or long term parking from their Park 'N' Fly lot will save you a tidy sum. Their shuttle bus is always there before you've had a chance to put your luggage down, even if you're coming in from one of World's midnight landings.

AUTO PARTS

(Also see **General Merchandise — Catalog Discounters,** **— Discount Stores**)

4-DAY TIRE STORES

390 East Gish, San Jose 95112. Phone: (408) 293-8323. Hours: W,Th,F 8:30am-8pm, Sat 8:30am-5pm. Purchases: MC, VISA.

☞ **Other Stores:** 1050 Marina Blvd., San Leandro; 2151 Marconi, No. Sacramento; 4320 Fruitridge Road, Sacramento.

4-Day has a unique but plausible merchandising approach: They are open only during the most efficient selling hours of the week, which allows them maximum sales with one-shift overhead. Their stock is large, and they say they can fit any type of car (or driver). Their weekly ad in the San Jose *Mercury* lists practically every cut-price tire they sell; it gives the regular retail price, their credit price, their cash price, their cash and carry price, and the federal excise tax on each tire (as you can imagine, it's a big ad). The brands they sell include Lee (U.S. made), Bridgestone (Japan), Dunlop, Pirelli, Veith, Semperit, Ceat, Fulda (Germany), Michelin, Metzeler and *4-Day's* own brand. They have their own special guarantee: if one of their tires fails due to workmanship or road hazards or wears out before you have received the guaranteed mileage, you can return the tire and they will give you credit (or mail you cash) for the unused miles (the percentage of unused miles multiplied by the price).

PRICE CLUB

(See **General Merchandise — Discount Stores**)

Beauty Supplies and Cosmetics

Anyone who buys beauty supplies at retail prices these days just isn't economy-minded. In most communities around the Bay Area there are stores which sell to the public name-brand retail and professional brands of bleaches, frosting supplies, permanents, hair sprays, setting lotions, conditioners, relaxers, and so forth for substantially less than retail (often at savings of as much as 40%). Many items they carry are simply not sold in your corner drug store. Some brands aren't in their usual retail store packages (complete with instructions), so it behooves you to have had some experience in this do-it-yourself approach to hair styling or to stick with brands that do have instructions. Check with the beauty supply stores in your area to see what products are available for your use.

CALIFORNIA THEATRICAL SUPPLY

747 Polk Street (off Ellis), San Francisco 94109. Phone: 925-5824. Hours: 9:30am-6pm, Sat 10am-5:30pm. Purchases: MC, VISA. Parking: Street.

Although they deal mainly with local and national television personalities, theatre, opera, and performing groups, savvy consumers often find their way through the doors to glom onto the value-priced cosmetics that they sell. The shelves are stocked with a colorful, rainbow selection of cosmetics, required for the intricate lighting requirements of the stage and studio. Geared for the pros, they're not equipped to give make-up lessons, or to spend a lot of time helping you make selections. Mirrors are practically non-existent. These mostly generic products include lipsticks, eye shadows, foundations, pancakes, powders, blushes, mascaras, pencils, and a baffling array of brushes. Professionals buy nose putty, eye lashes, mustaches, and other tricks of the trade for theatre use. Plastic surgeons refer patients for their line of camouflage make up. Planning a face painting party for kids or fundraisers? This is where you'll buy all the essential make-up/paints that are guaranteed to wash off. Prices overall are substantially less than those on comparable lines in department stores. Additionally, they have many products no longer found in the department store selections. When they're dealing with an important account, i.e. theatre or opera group, you can't expect much from them, so be patient until they're free to handle your order. While they don't have time for how-to lessons, they will refer you to a make-up artist that can transform you from a dull Diane to a dazzling Diane. That will cost you naturally!

COSMETIC AND FRAGRANCE OUTLET

318 Brannan, San Francisco 94107. Phone: 896-0989. Hours: M-Sat 10am-5pm. Purchases: Cash or Check. Parking: Limited.

If you're trying to trim the budget, consider buying your make-up at the discount *Fragrance and Cosmetic Outlet* recently opened for retail sales in San Francisco. This company does most of their business on a wholesale basis with hair and beauty salons, providing them with a "private label" line of cosmetics to sell to their clientele under their own salon label. Of course this is very profitable for salons since they may take 300-400% markups. The products: lipstick, blusher, eye shadows, pencils, mascara, and nail polish are purchased from the same "few" laboratories that supply the industry giants. Perhaps it is a measure of our gullibility that we will pay exorbitant amounts of money to buy a beautifully packaged, highly touted, advertised product, and believe that the results will be far superior to any other line. In most instances, the *only* difference between one brand and another is the name, packaging, advertising campaign targeted to a particular market and price.

At the outlet, you can buy the unbranded, naked product at a minimal markup. Lipsticks are $2.00; foundation — $3.50; nail polish — $1.00, eye shadow and blush — $2.00; and mascara — $2.00. Their holistically formulated (no frangrance, lanolin or mineral oil) skin care line with astringents, cleansers, moisture creams, etc. are modestly priced at $4-$5. Namebrand fragrances (including many of the biggies) are discounted 25% off retail. Prices on brushes are wonderful! At the outlet, you can dabble and test to your heart's delight. In keeping with their "naked"

products, the sales room is equally unadorned. Parking is difficult at most times during the week. They are near the *Gunne Sax* outlet, 1/2 block off 2nd street.

FACTORY OUTLET COSMETICS

3800 Park Boulevard (Fwy. 580 exit, 3 blocks east toward Montclair), Oakland 94602. Phone: 482-4595. Hours: M-F 9am-6pm, Sat 10am-6pm. Purchases: MC, VISA. Parking: Street.

Doing both wholesale and retail business, this company previously sold private label cosmetics to local salons and retail businesses. Women can buy at nearly wholesale prices: nail polish, nail care products, blush, lipstick, lip gloss, foundation, mascara, eyeshadow, cosmetic brushes and sponges plus lots more. Typical prices: lipsticks for $1.80; foundation for $3.60, lip liner for $2.00, etc. You won't find the extensive product selection that you would in a major department store but you won't pay their high prices either! Check the closeout table for super buys.

SOLOCO

298 Ninth Street (at Folsom), San Francisco 94103. Phone: 863-8960. Hours: M-Sat 9am-5pm. Purchases: MC, VISA. Parking: Limited street.

Soloco is a fragrant addition to Bay Area retailing and long overdue. Essentially a wholesale distributor, they've crossed over the line to sell retail to all the guys and gals who want to smell scentsational! While we can't buy at wholesale prices we are able to buy at wonderful discount prices. The reason: Their stock is made up of liquidations and closeouts, discontinued promotional products, packages and sets plus packaging changes, and bankruptcies with lines from all the *finest* perfume and cosmetic companies. Their inventory is a virtual Who's Who of the fragrance world. Prices are discounted 20-60% off the original retail value.

These were some examples of their discount prices at the time I did my research: For men — Cacharel 1.7 oz. cologne, $11 instead of $16; Givenchy Gentleman 1 oz. cologne spray, $9.50 instead of $12.50; For women — Charlie 1.7 oz. spray, $7.50 instead of $12.50; Calvin Klein 1 oz. perfume, $65 instead of $100; Chaz 2.25 oz. cologne, $8 instead of $13.50; Chloe 3 oz. ETD spray, $25 instead of $32.50; Missoni 1 oz. cologne spray, $13.50 instead of $22.50; Worth Je Reviens 2 oz. cologne spray, $10 instead of $20; Nice discounts! Anais Anais, Aramis, Bill Blass, Dior, Enjoli, Estee Lauder, Gloria Vanderbilt, Halston, John Weitz, Jovan, Lanvin, Nini Ricci, Norrell, Pierre Cardin, Rive Gauche, are other notable names in their selection and there's many more! Prices do change on fragrances according to the price *Soloco* had to pay, so the same fragrance may be priced higher or lower each time you visit.

Soloco also has cosmetics. Don't expect to find a complete Revlon line, but rather expect to find eye and makeup compacts or gift sets from the famous makers along with a limited selection of lipsticks, mascara, pencils, etc. Foundations are not in the selection initially, but that may change. There are many gift sets that would make delightful gifts especially for teen girls. Skin care products, hair care products, nail polish and nail care products are priced at 30-60% off. The selection for men is extensive.

The only hitch in the whole operation is that there are few testers — frustrating when looking at the tremendous selection of fragrances especially those that are familiar only to those who shop the salons of Paris. Plans are being considered to open additional locations in the City. Before shopping try phoning to see if a more convenient or closer location is at hand.

Building and Do-It-Yourself

(Also see **General Merchandise — Liquidators; Part II: Surplus Stores; Wrecking and Salvage Yards**)

General

BEST BLOCKS, INC.

34840 Alvarado-Niles Road., Union City 94587. Phone: 471-1966. Hours: M-F 7:30am-5pm, Sat 8am-4pm. Purchases: MC, VISA. Parking: Lot.

It's really not necessary to ripoff construction sites for building blocks because at this manufacturer's yard there are blocks for everything from hi-rise buildings to back yard barbecues. Best of all, there is always a selection of seconds and off-color blocks at savings of 15-50%. On their top quality overstock blocks you can save by buying directly from the source and on quantity purchases you can save even more. You can choose from sump blocks, stepping stones, patio tile (including seconds), garden blocks, "pavelock" concrete pavers, tree rings and decorative rock. They have over 600 sizes, styles and shapes. Whether you're building a tile patio, or installing your own fireplace or heatstove, they can tell you how to do it, what you will need, and what it will cost. Delivery service available at reasonable charge; technical and design literature available at no cost. All you need is the muscle to do the job!

S. DE BELLA BARREL CO.

1176 Harrison St., San Francisco 94103. Phone: 861-1700. Hours: M-F 8am-4pm. Purchases: Cash or Check. Parking: Street.

Salvatore De Bella is one of the biggest importers and manufacturers of barrels in the nation. When you come in you may see the coopers (barrelmakers) at their noisy work; I was fascinated by their skill and precision. The imported used barrels may have held Irish whiskey, French cognac, Kentucky bourbon, or West Indian rum. The barrels are cleaned and restored for use as planters, tables, stools, cradles, dog houses or what have you. Best of all, a used 50-gallon barrel sells for only $20., a half barrel for only $9.95. Spigots and barrel stands are also available. True, even Safeway sells barrels and half barrels during the year at similar prices, but if you need one when they're not on promotion at one of the supermarkets or building supply stores, you'll always find one here. If your taste runs to the exotic, you may be interested in the handmade, handcarved oval oak barrels, a *De Bella* specialty.

KEN'S GLASS

2905 Senter Road (at Lewis), San Jose 95111. Phone: (408) 578-5211. Hours: Daily 9am-5pm. Closed Wed & Sun. Purchases: Cash or Check. Parking: Lot.

The do-it-yourselfer will need to develop a strategy to take advantage of the cheap, cheap prices at this glass and mirror shop. Ken is able to offer these prices because he cuts corners. No secretary, virtually no overhead, no delivery, no installation, no cut-outs on glass or mirrors (although he will trim edges to size), and a cash and carry basis. Ken stocks first quality glass and mirror, also seconds with a substantial price differential, in all sizes and shapes. He always has a good selection of precut sizes of glass and mirrors for shelving, picture frames, and rounds for table tops. Check all the bargains in his 8,000 sq. ft. facility before deciding, you'll find many options pricewise (30-80% discounts) whether you're covering an entire wall with mirror or simply replacing a broken window.

LUNDY'S WOOD PRODUCTS

36 Simms, San Rafael 94901. Phone: 454-0130. Hours: M-F 7:30am-5pm, Sat 8:30am-1:30pm. Purchases: MC, VISA. Parking: Lot.

Lundy's may not be a household word mainly because they do most of their business with cabinet shops and

contractors. However, many fellows involved in various woodworking projects have reported that after extensive comparative shopping they end up at *Lundy's*. Unlike other lumber companies that advertise extensively to the consumer market offering a wide selection of woods for exterior and interior use, *Lundy's* offers a choice selection of finished products used in furniture making and cabinets. For example: Sanded fir plywood, hardwood plywood with veneers, hardwood moldings, hardwood lumber, veneers, marine plywood and softwood plywood and moldings. A friend reported saving $20 on a 4 X 8 skin of walnut! Exterior siding is available by special order as are the Andersen Window Walls (the double insulated wooden sash windows). They also carry oversized 5 X 9 plywoods for ping pong table tops and 4 X 10 sizes in fir plywood. Where their prices on woods are substantially less you can assume that they have been able to buy "right" from their suppliers. *Lundy's* is directly across the street from Marin Surplus.

McINTYRE TILE CO.

55 West Grant, Healdsburg 95448. Phone: (707) 433-8866. Hours: M-F 9am-5pm, Sat 10am-5pm. Purchases: Cash or Check.

McIntyre Tile is not displayed in any Bay Area distributors' showrooms, but rather, sold directly through architects and interior designers. It is expensive, about $7 a sq. ft., and is handmade, high-fired stoneware. It is very appealing for it's natural look and many neutral shades. Before making a trip to Healdsburg, call first and request a selection of samples in your color range. If you see one you like, then inquire about their seconds, which are 1/2 price and may be off color, slightly warped, but otherwise structurally sound. The "thirds" are $5.00 per box. They prefer that you make an appointment, before coming in to see them; many days their production schedule is so heavy they don't have time to spend with customers who want to pick and poke through the seconds selection.

NISSAN TILE

697 Veterans Blvd., Redwood City 94063. Phone: 364-6547. Hours: M-F 8am-5pm, Sat 9am-4:30pm. Purchases: MC, VISA. Parking: Lot.

☞ **Other Store:** 1226 So. Bascom Ave., San Jose. (408) 298-9766.

You can't possibly imagine the potential for beauty, design and interest in your home until you contemplate the selection of tile at *Nissan*. Their showroom floor is a patchwork of exotic and different tile patterns; in fact I could hardly bring myself to walk across. *Nissan* claims they are the biggest importer of ceramic tile in the Bay Area. They distribute to tile contractors and retail stores. They have Italian, Japanese and domestic tiles. You can save 30% on the tile sold under the Nissan label and particularly on odd lots left over from custom jobs. They have supplies for do-it-yourselfers and all the free advice you need.

REED SUPPLY

1328 Fruitvale Avenue, Oakland 94601. Phone: 436-7171. Hours: T-Sat 10am-5pm. Purchases: Cash or Check. Parking: Street Lot.

The outward appearance of this salmon pink drab-looking warehouse is deceptive. People who are involved in remodeling projects will make many visits if they appreciate good prices. Displayed with restaurant lighting the appliances, kitchen cabinets, bathroom vanities, custom countertops (including Corian, marble and maple), Greenhouse windows, waterheaters, central heating sheet metal products, flexible piping (used from the wallboard to hook up fixtures and appliances), special plumbing fixtures, shower doors, wall and baseboard heaters, Cadilliac lines of faucets, etc. etc., are stocked, ready to be checked off your list and carted home. Something really esoteric on your list? Chances are they'll find it in one of their catalogs and special order for you. Working on a low markup, they essentially sell at contractor's prices to *everyone*. In fact, most of their business during the week is done with the trade. It should also be noted that they represent many major brands of appliances, including the less well known "super status brands", popular with architects and kitchen planners, for very good prices! Delivery charges relate to distance involved. Legions of satisfied customers forsake the typical, slick merchandising of other large chain stores to scoop the bargains at *Reed's*.

SKY LIGHT & SUN

2019 Blake St., Berkeley 94704. Phone: 841-2323. Hours: M-F 9am-5pm. Closed between Noon-1pm. Purchases: Cash or Check. Parking: Limited Street Parking.

If you're building or remodeling and contemplating a passive solar system design for energy savings, chances are you may need insulated tempered glass. *Sky Light & Sun* stocks and sells tempered glass in three sizes. These panels of glass are available in single panes of glass or in sealed insulated units. This material is best described as factory-seconds, or factory surplus glass, a designation that refers to minor, nonstructural, cosmetic scratches or blemishes. Intelligent design work utilizing these three sizes can greatly reduce the cost of a greenhouse, solar collector, or other building project. Your savings: about 50%. It is important to know building code restrictions regarding installations, so it is sometimes better to have your contractor do the buying for you. In any case, check the availability before framing. They sell tremendous quantities of these seconds, but occasionally a contractor will buy their entire inventory leaving their cupboards bare until the next shipment.

STONELIGHT TILE

1651 Pomona Ave., San Jose 95110. Phone: (408) 292-7424. Hours: M-F 8am-4:30pm, Sat 8am-4pm. Purchases: MC, VISA. Parking: Lot.

Stonelight Tile is a glazed tile with an unusually dense body like those made for centuries in Europe. The fact that it is made chiefly of natural clays instead of talc, as is most commercial tile, means that *Stonelight Tile* will have

a "natural" look and contributes to its great popularity among architects and designers. Made locally in San Jose, their outdoor yard has stacks of tiles that are left over from custom jobs or have been judged as seconds because of surface irregularities, color imperfections, or have chips. People are welcome to browse and handpick those tiles that they need for their own remodeling projects. The savings are considerable. Seconds sell for $2.25/sq. ft. and overruns are $3.00/sq. ft. Normal retail for these tiles is in the neighborhood of $4.80-$6.00/sq. ft. You may have to pay a full price for trim pieces if they are not in the seconds or overrun selection. The best time for shopping is during the week, when the selection is the best, and preferably in dry weather. Boxes for packing are provided. This is a friendly place, they will give you instructions, and can sell you the mastic, grout, coloring agents, and spreaders necessary for installation. There's nothing like getting the best for less!

Tools

BLACK AND DECKER MANUFACTURING CO.

15206 E. 14th, San Leandro 94577. Phone: 276-1610. Hours: M-F 8am-5pm, Sat 9am-1pm. Purchases: MC, VISA. Parking: Street.

☞ **Other Stores:** San Jose, South San Francisco.

If your husband is a "Handy Andy" and loves to buy new tools for his own garage workshop, make sure he checks *Black and Decker* before investing any money in tools. The reason is simple: there are many "reconditioned" tools available here at great savings, such as sanders, saws, drills, even lawn edgers, and lawn mowers. These reconditioned tools may have been returned by their owner within 90 days because of performance failures. They have had a trip back to the factory and are now provided with all new parts and the same one-year guarantee as new tools. Some other tools are box damaged or were once salesmen's samples.

The savings range from 20-30% off regular retail. Because the supply and availability of these tools may vary, you should call them about what you want; they'll gladly take your name and notify you when your tool is available.

PORTER-CABLE TOOL CENTER

3029 Teagarden Street, San Leandro 94577. Phone: 357-9762. Hours: M-F 8am-4:30pm. Purchases: MC, VISA.

☞ **Other Store:** 2305 De La Cruz Blvd., Santa Clara.

The Rockwell line has become Porter-Cable. The name may be different but the product is the same. Like other service centers you can buy reconditioned portable electric tools for about half the retail cost.

POST TOOL & SUPPLY

328 12th Street, Oakland 94607. Phone: 893-1212. Hours: M-Sat 8am-5pm. Purchases: MC, VISA. Parking: Street.

☞ **Other Stores:** 915 Piner Rd., Santa Rosa; 2935 Arden Way, Sacramento; 1038 Mc Henry Blvd., Modesto; 7277 Pacific Ave., Stockton.

Buying in tremendous quantities from major tool manufacturers, both American and foreign, and buying up liquidated merchandise and government surplus, allows *Post* to offer great discounts for tools and supplies that people require for their projects. You will usually find drill presses, bench grinders, hand tools, jacks, vises, wrenches, socket sets, electric tools, air tools, electric saws, lathes, and tool boxes. Everything is fully guaranteed and comes in the original factory packaging. In addition to the tool selection they have an eclectic assortment of miscellaneous merchandise like cutlery sets, camping knives, starter cables, etc. The only drawbacks are the stores cramped quarters that lends itself to a slightly disordered feeling.

SKIL POWER TOOL SERVICE CENTER

1170 Burnett Ave., Suite D, Concord 94520. Phone: 827-1427. Hours: M-F 8am-5pm. Purchases: MC, VISA. Parking: Lot.

☞ **Other Store:** 2130 De La Cruz Blvd., Santa Clara.

If you have a broken electric home shop tool, you're lucky if it's made by *Skil Power Tools*, for you can probably trade it in for a new one if reconditioning is too expensive. On a trade-in you save about 30% on the less expensive and up to 50% on the more expensive tools. (Not every tool in the Skil line is included in their exchange program, however.)

There are three categories of tools available with savings up to 25%. All are specifically labeled with special tags which state: ''To assure the controlled high quality required for sale at a *Skil Service Center,* Rebuilt Power Tools, Discontinued Models, and Factory Appearance Rejects are tested for conformance to original equipment standards. Factory Trained Repair Technicians have performed a complete Detectron diagnostic examination of the tool. All repairs and/or parts replacement have been made as required to effect a like-new operative condition. Each of these tools is guaranteed against defects caused by faulty materials or workmanship.'' These tools carry the same guarantee as their other retail tools.

The Skil line includes weedeaters, sanders, drills, jig saws, hand saws, and Recipro saws. Occasionally they have discontinued industrial tools. You can call in advance for information on the availability of a special tool.

TOOLS-R-US

10251 So. De Anza Blvd., Cupertino 95014. Phone: (408) 725-8300. Hours: M-F 9am-9pm, Sat 9am-6pm, Sun 10am-5pm. Purchases: MC, VISA. Parking: Lot.

☞ **Other Stores:** Alum Rock & Capitol Ave., San Jose; 2255 The Alameda, Santa Clara; 2265 41st Ave., Capitola.

In the South Bay the advertising circulars from *Tools-R-Us* are given close scrutiny by gals/guys in search of good buys on automotive and carpentry tools. They won't

have any measuring cups or flower pots in their ads, they stick to business! They sell the better brands of tools like Black & Decker, Stanley, Makita, etc., most with industrial ratings. They have a clearance center in Santa Clara, yet, it's very small and does not have a significant inventory of special bargains. You might find a damaged piece marked way down and odds'n ends of super discounted leftovers, but the inventories at their other stores are better and prices are best for the area. Occasionally, on a hot item they will give rain checks.

UNITED TOOL CENTER

854 Ellis (betw. Van Ness & Polk), San Francisco 94109. Phone: 673-8841. Hours: M-F 9am-5:30pm, Sat 10am-5pm. Purchases: MC, VISA. Parking: Street.

☞ **Other Store:** 10585 San Pablo Ave., El Cerrito. Phone: 524-0979.

I confess. I know practically nothing about tools! But I can compare prices, and even better I know some pros. My friends, Paco and Jose, who race stock cars, and when bored take their engines apart and put them back together, are well qualified to make a recommendation since they've canvassed the area for best prices. Their source: *United Tool Center* where *professional* rated tools (vs. consumer rated) are sold at lower prices every day. As the owner said ''we carry some cheap tools too at bargain prices, mainly for the gal/guy who tightens a screw once a year.''

Their prices reflect volume buys directly from the manufacturer, and low overhead locations. Their stores are not fancy, but the serious consumer doesn't seem to mind. They appear to carry all the basics in tools and equipment for automotive and carpentry needs. According to the owner, competitive stores never sell at the manufacturer's list price. An example: a heavy duty 800 lb. capacity engine stand lists for $159, sells at most stores for around $99, and at *United* for $74; or a Waterloo tool chest and roller cabinet lists for $220, typically sells for $169, at *United* for $119. Consistently, they trim their prices 25-30% below their toughest competitors, and even more when compared to others. Serious do-it-yourselfers and professionals appreciate the selection of quality lines for their rigorous requirements.

WESTERN HARDWARE & TOOL COMPANY
1947 Carroll Ave., San Francisco 94124. Phone: 468-4530. Hours: M-F 8am-5pm, Sat 9am-4pm. Purchases: MC, VISA. Parking: Street.

This is truly handyman's heaven! If you have a heavy duty job and need a heavy duty tool, this company is for you. They are a major industrial supplier of tools for linemen, electricians, auto mechanics, carpenters, iron and steel workers, as well as manufacturing and industrial plants in Northern California. These are not always the same products that you will find in the neighborhood hardware or building supply store. They have industrial ratings and sometimes may cost a bit more, even at discount, than a home rated product. Even so, the prices on their tools are substantially discounted from the manufacturer's published price list. On products that serve for both the industrial and home shop market, like Stanley tapes, vice grip sets, block sanders, saws, hammers, and other hand tools your savings may range from 15-40% off prevailing retail prices.

Don't be concerned when you walk in the door and don't see any tools, they're in the back warehouse where you're welcome to browse. They have no sales gimmicks, loss leaders, etc., just low dealer prices everyday. Don't plan on a lunch hour visit, they close down.

Cameras

(Also see **General Merchandise — Catalog Discounters — Discount Stores**)

A & B PREMIUMS PHOTO & APPLIANCE CENTER

4375-D Clayton Road, Concord 94521. Phone: 827-3373. Hours: M-F 9am-8:30pm, Sat 9am-6pm. Purchases: MC, VISA. Parking: Lot.

The value conscious "aspiring" photographers that I know in this area all shop for their photo needs at this unlikely store. All Kodak processing is done for a 25% discount all year long. To be sure, Kodak processing is quite expensive, but for those who want superior quality and assurances of good results, their prices are about the best. Kodak film is sold for cost! (This is their loss leader to create traffic, good idea.) Additionally, cameras, accessories such as lenses, filters, flashes, tripods, etc. plus darkroom equipment, papers and chemicals are sold at super discount prices. Another aspect of their business is related to small and large home appliances and entertainment needs. Washers, dryers, dishwashers, compacters, refrigerators, TV's, and radios are sold for a minimal markup.

ALAMEDA CAMERA SWAP

2540 Santa Clara Ave., Alameda 94501. Phone Information: 521-2177. Hours: Sundays 8am-1pm. Purchases: Cash or Check. Parking: Street.

The *Alameda Camera Swap* is held each Sunday in the Grand Ballroom of the Alameda Hotel, at the corner of Santa Clara and Broadway. Anything photographic is fair game in this indoor flea market that always has a good selection of cameras, camera accessories, books, images, lenses, darkroom gear and paper prints, merchandise that appeals to both the collector and the photographer. At the camera swap there are no dealers for new merchandise, no stores represented. The average Sunday swap has approximately 45 dealers with tables of merchandise. Many dealers have been coming regularly for years and enjoy a reliable reputation. This is a very legitimate operation, all items with serial numbers are checked out by the Alameda Police Department. Most of the dealers will guarantee their equipment. Be sure to ask for a guarantee and a receipt for your purchase.

If you have equipment you'd like to sell, you should go to the swap on Sunday morning between 7:30-8:30am to reserve your table; the charge is $15. There is a $1.00 admission charge to the public, children under twelve are free. The swap is a great place to meet and talk with photographers, collectors and others seriously interested in all aspects of photography or photograhic collectibles. Most dealers are very willing to give you the benefit of their expertise.

FILCO, L & Z PREMIUMS
(See **Appliances**)

OSAKA-YA CAMERA
1581 Webster (Japan Center-West Bldg.) San Francisco. Phone: 563-5556 or 567-1160. Hours: M-Sat 10am-5pm, Sun Noon-5pm. Purchases: MC, VISA. Parking: Garage.

Osaka Ya consistenly offers low prices in San Francisco on a wide variety of cameras representing most major brands. They're pretty good about providing advice, will accept phone orders, and will even give you validation for free parking in the Japan Center Garage with purchase. Watch for their ads in the *Chronicle* for super sale prices.

PHOTOGRAPHER'S SUPPLY
576 Folsom St., San Francisco 94103. Phone: 495-8640. Hours: M-F 8:30am-6pm, Sat 9:30am-5pm. Purchases: MC, VISA. Parking: Very limited street.

If you're a novice, bring a friend. This is for serious photographers (professional or amateurs) who buy film, paper, and chemicals in quantity and willingly relinquish seminars at the cash register in favor of the 25% discounts. They supply the 35mm camera market with 25% discounts on Kodak film; everything for the darkroom; a nice array of background paper; and equipment for the professional studio. If you're into the esoterics of lighting, check downstairs at *Studio Equipment Supply* where greater service and TLC is provided along with decent discounts of 15-20%.

SAN JOSE CAMERA
1600 Winchester Blvd., Campbell 95008. Phone: (408) 374-1880. Hours: M-Sat 10am-6pm, Thurs till 8pm. Purchases: MC, VISA. Parking: Lot.

Photo buffs who are interested in the more sophisticated, exotic and usually more expensive cameras and accessories will feel right at home in this camera shop. Most major brands are carried: Leica, Cannon, Nikon, Olympus, Vivitar, Rollei, Minolta, Pentax, Hasselbald, Mamiya, Konica, Beseler enlargers, Kodak carousel projectors, Gossen exposure meters and Halliburton cases. In keeping with new trends in the market they've added the latest products in video cameras and recorders from Sony, Pentax, Hitachi, and Panasonic.

I would suggest that you do some research regarding your needs and selections before coming here because their staff is very busy. They simply don't have the time to give you lengthy demonstrations or sales seminars if you're a novice with a thousand questions. If you can tell them what you want, they'll probably be giving you the lowest price in the Bay Area. Do some armchair shopping by perusing their ads that are plastered all over the *Mercury* and *Chronicle* almost weekly. They are very good about standing behind their merchandise or handling any problems; however, they have a *strict* policy regarding exchanges, all sales are final! Save gas if you're out of the area by placing your order by phone using your MC or Visa and having it shipped UPS. *San Jose Camera* is located at Hamilton & Winchester, take Hamilton offramp from Fwy. 17.

Carpets and Floor Coverings

(Also see **Furniture — Catalog Discounters, Warehouse Sales**)

Comparison shopping is essential when bargain hunting for carpeting and other floor covering. Shop only at stores that do not substitute their private label for the manufacturer's label. This practice is legal but confusing if you are comparison shopping (which is what they're trying to obstruct). Some stores give you a lower price on the carpet but make up for it with their installation and padding costs, while others charge a slightly higher price for the carpeting but toss in the installation and padding for free. The variance in the price is the only constant. Always remember to price the carpet and padding separately, since there are different weights and quality to consider in padding. When comparing the total cost among the stores, be sure you're comparing the same quality carpeting, padding and installation. Ask how they plan to arrange the carpet seams and how they will be joined. Have the area measured by at least two carpet dealers to insure a correct measure. Be sure that the bids are complete and that they include *all* extras such as take up of the old rug, disposal of same, furniture moving and all metal (door bars), etc. These extras can really add up, so avoid surprises, make sure bid is complete. Ask also what kind of stripping will be used when soft and hardcover floor coverings meet. Be sure to tell the salesman what you expect of the carpet (how long you expect it to last, the kind of traffic it will bear, its exposure to strong sunlight, etc.) He will be better able to advise you. Finally, do not make up your mind in a hurry, never get pushed into signing a contract the same day regardless of the pretext; special offer, last day of sale, one of a kind, etc., etc. This is often the single biggest investment you'll make in furnishing your home, buy wisely.

The cunning and expertise of the retail carpet store buyer will greatly effect the price you pay. One carpet store may pull a coup in a big buy, enabling them to sell that stock at a lower price than its competitors. Two months later a different store may make the best buy, and then sell at a lower price. Carpet "wholesalers" abound throughout the Bay Area, and they are able to offer good buys because of their different business styles. On the other hand, some use these buying techniques to gain a larger profit margin without necessarily passing the savings on to the consumer. Some stores specialize in buying overstocks and closeout patterns and colors. Others buy room-size remnants or pieces in off-color dye lots. Some specialize in bankrupt stocks. For these many reasons you can save on your carpeting dollar. Remember that it's a changing market. Always take your time, comparison

shop, and consider all the factors. Be sure to check the listings for furniture catalog discounters. These resources come through with exceptional prices on carpeting as well as home furnishings.

General

CAMEO CARPET CO.

1590 El Camino Real, San Bruno 94066. Phone: 873-4050. Hours: M-Sat 10am-5pm. Purchases: MC, VISA. Parking: Street.

If you want to deal with carpet professionals that provide quality installations combined with good service and prices be sure to visit *Cameo Carpet*. They carry many of the better lines plus commercial and moderate carpet lines with samples you can borrow for trial matching at home. They can also acquire other lines if you can give them the manufacturer's name and carpet number. Their installation charge is a modest $2.25/sq. ft. which includes take up of carpet, removal of same, furniture moving, etc. Keep in mind the more carpet you buy, the better the price. Their prices are always better when compared to the high profile carpet dealers and home furnishings departments of major stores.

LAWRENCE CONTRACT FURNISHERS

470-B Vandell Way, Campbell 95008. Phone: (408) 374-7590. Hours: M-F 8am-5:30pm. Purchases: Cash or Check. Parking: Lot.

For South Bay shoppers *Lawrence's* is one of the best resources for carpeting, vinyl floor coverings, hardwood flooring kits, draperies, wallpapers and many fine furniture lines. The showroom is stocked with wallpaper books, carpet and flooring samples and furniture samples. It's almost too much to take in all at once. Installation of flooring and carpeting will be provided (of course you pay for it) but I've found their prices to be lower than most other places. They can't provide decorator services at these prices, but they enjoy a reliable reputation. Three times a year they have a clearance sale on showroom samples with prices ranging from 40-70% off retail. To find this out-of-the-way showroom from the San Thomas Expressway, take the Winchester offramp in Campbell, go East to Hacienda, turn left, and turn right on Dell. *Lawrence* is on the corner of Vandell and Dell.

MONROE SCHNEIDER ASSOCIATES

274 Wattis Way, South San Francisco 94080. Phone: 871-6276. Hours: M-F 8am-5pm by appt. Evenings & Weekends by appt. Purchases: Cash or Check. Parking: Lot.

This firm specializes in working with developers to design and furnish the interiors for model homes, and then works with the new home buyers who are making selections of carpeting, flooring, wallpaper, and window coverings that will go into their new homes. With all these resources they're willing to provide the same service to the general public at considerable savings. Their carpeting prices are excellent; the installation and padding is also arranged. One nice extra is the design assistance provided by their staff. It's important to make an appointment before coming in so a member of the staff will be free to help you. Along with carpeting, you can order other home furnishings from their catalogs at noteworthy savings.

S & G DISCOUNT OUTLET INC.

505 So. Market Street, San Jose 95113. Phone: (408) 292-8971. Hours: M-F 9am-6pm, 9am-3pm. Th eve till 9pm. Purchases: MC, VISA. Parking: Street.

10-30% discounts are extended on their extensive selection of linoleum. *S & G* carries Armstrong, Mannington, Congoleum, and other brands of floor coverings. Indoor-outdoor carpeting is by special order only.

S & G supplies the trade, and the pace is sometimes pretty busy. When you go, know what you want covered (for one thing, you might find just what you need among their remnants). They had a fairly large selection when I was there, but turnover is brisk.

TRADEWAY STORES WAREHOUSE

350 Carlson Blvd., Richmond 94804. Phone: 233-0841. Hours: M-Sat 10am-5:30pm, Sun Noon-5pm. Purchases: MC, VISA. Parking: Free Lot.

☞ **Other Store:** 10680 San Pablo Avenue, El Cerrito.

If you're looking for good deals on carpeting, this warehouse for the *Tradeway Stores* offers a selection of carpeting that has been written off as an insurance loss. Namebrand carpet mills also dispose of overruns, excess inventories, seconds, and off-color carpeting here. Carpeting is stacked in rolls 20 feet high and higher — conveying a feeling of walking through a mini Grand Canyon. If you want to see a particular piece fifteen feet up, they pull it out presto using a special forklift that delights the kiddies.

Savings are usually about 30%, though on unusual or novelty carpeting you may save as much as 60-70% off the original price. This is strictly a case of "what you see is what you get." There are no special or custom orders. Padding is sometimes available at below wholesale prices. They do not install, but will refer you to installers. All carpet is ready for immediate delivery, though you'll save more if you haul it home yourself, or have your installer pick it up.

Their second and third floors are filled with furniture representing manufacturers' fire and insurance losses. Other, new furniture in a moderate and budget price range is nicely discounted.

Remnants

CARPET CENTER
921 Parker Street, Berkeley 94710. Phone: 549-1100. Hours: M-Sat 9am-5:30pm, M & Th eve till 8:30pm. Purchases: MC, VISA. Parking: Street.

Located in the low rent industrial district of Berkeley, this huge warehouse has one of the best selections of carpet remnants and area rugs in the East Bay. Even better, they have an accommodating price range in carpets to choose from, from budget to best! They can provide the padding and installation at extra charge. Parker is off 7th St., one mile No. of Ashby.

CARPET UNLIMITED
1145 Jordan Lane, Napa 94588. Phone: (707) 252-6695. Hours: M-Sat 9am-5pm. Purchases: MC, VISA. Parking: Street.

Discontinued patterns from Walter's Carpet Mills, Atlas, Mohawk and others are sold in remnants, full rolls, or off the roll. Prices range from $5-$13 a yard, a hefty savings most of the time when you consider many of these carpets sell in the neighborhood of $15-$30 a yard. Their commercial carpets are perfect for the businessman doing a small office on the cheap. Some of their rolls are large enough to carpet a whole house. They won't do the installation, but will refer you to installers they feel do a reliable job.

FLOORCRAFT

470 Bayshore Blvd., San Francisco 94124. Phone: 824-4056. Hours: M 8am-9pm, TWThF 8am-5:30pm, Sat 8am-5pm, Sun 10am-5pm. Purchases: MC, VISA. Parking: Street.

They always have about 400 remnants in stock priced from $3.99-$8.50/yard. Your best prices are always on the "weird" sizes, because it's harder to sell a piece 7' X 20', than a standard 10' X 12'. Installation is provided, keep in mind the cost for a small room is disproportionately high when compared to doing a whole house or several rooms. Watch for their ads in the *Examiner* and *Chronicle*.

MACY'S FURNITURE CLEARANCE PLACE
(See **Furniture and Accessories**)

REMNANT WORLD CARPETS

5160 Stevens Creek Blvd. (at Lawrence Expressway), San Jose 95129. Phone: (408) 984-1965. Hours: M-F 10am-9pm, Sat 9am-6pm, Sun Noon-5pm. Purchases: MC, VISA. Parking: Lot.

☞ **Other Stores:** 2730 Story Rd., San Jose; 3058 Almaden Expressway, San Jose.

They're really set up for the do-it-yourselfer. If you buy your carpet from them they'll lend you a tool box with all the tools necessary, including the knee-kicker (carpet stretcher), and give you plenty of free advice. Their remnants come from the leading mills. Over 5,000 remnants in stock for one room or the whole house. Their prices are good and if you lack the fortitude to lay it yourself, they'll install it for you.

Most people are at once intrigued and intimidated by computers and computer jargon. Entering the fascinating world of these wizard-like little machines can be an enjoyable experience with the right support, or a jungle without it. When considering the potential listings I had prepared for this edition, it soon became evident that it was impossible to provide accurate and up-to-date information about *who* is selling a particular computer at *what* price. Like hot tubs a few years ago, every shopping center and office complex has acquired at least one or two tenants selling computers. Many are too new to boast a track record, nor is there any assurance that in this competitive market, they'll still be there a year from now. Furthermore, I felt that when considering the purchase of equipment that can easily run into the thousands (when all costs are computed for the first year of ownership) it is inappropriate and unwise to think in terms of price as your basic consideration.

Getting information about which are the best computer software programs or the best computer system for you doesn't necessarily come from a computer store, where typically they carry three brands or less. Do a lot of research before buying. More important than anything else, take time. The easiest resource right now is the growing collection of magazines devoted to the personal computer industry. Some magazines are very technical — geared primarily for sophisticated users, while others are perfect for the non-technical, completely ignorant neophyte. You can receive a good pre-purchase orientation reading several months of *Popular Computing* and *Personal Computing* plus several introductory books on computers.

Once you've made the software and hardware system choices, you'll find that magazines are particularly valuable for the advertising that shows you what's for sale and at what price. Use these ads as a reference point for what kind of competitive pricing you should look for in your market area. Generally the prices at retail computer stores are likely to be 15-35% higher than mail order discount prices. Retailers justify their higher prices by assurances of post-purchase support, installation services, and repair services. On the other hand, mail order software and computer companies do not offer or expect to provide that level of support. That's fine, if you're unlikely to need support, but most first time buyers who have no previous experience with computers will need lots of TLC and support. Initially, it's frustrating, sometimes even frightening when you encounter a glitch, problem, or other obstacle in usage, and must rely on a dealer that's 60 miles away, or even worse a company that feels no obligation to sort out your problem.

I recommend narrowing your choices to those local dealers that offer the best prices on the system you want to buy — then be prepared to negotiate. If you know mail order prices, you can demand extras for the higher price the dealer is asking, or you can even end up negotiating a lower price. This is a buyers' market, and if you're buying a complete system you're in a great position to haggle. Finding a dealer in the Bay Area is not difficult. Bargain priced resources for software and add-on hardware (memory, modems, boards, etc.) after you've passed the novice stage are located all over the Bay Area but particularly in Silicon Valley. Sometimes it seems as if, when it comes to owning a home computer, the costs never end. Screening the ads in magazines, attending computer shows and networking with user groups will lead you to these businesses.

A valuable Bay Area publication for resource information on microcomputers is *Computer Currents*. It provides practical computer information for businesses, professionals and serious home users. They have question and answer columns, let you know what's available in the Bay Area — where to find services and products, the event or class you want to attend, the organization or user group you want to join. *Computer Currents* is disributed in well over 1,000 locations in seven counties around the Bay. You're most likely to find it in local libraries, colleges, adult-education facilities, record stores, video and electronic stores, and anyplace where hi-tech people are likely to hang out. Don't expect to find it in all your local computer stores, many are reluctant to have customers peruse the competitors' ads when they're trying to make a sale. If you can't find one — call their office between 9am-5pm.

COMPUTER CURRENTS

Phone Information: (415) 848-6860 to find a local distribution point.

■ ■ ■ ■ ■

Finally, this edition of *Bargain Hunting in the Bay Area* was written on an IBM-PC using WordStar, a feat that takes on miraculous proportions when considering my state of techni-phobia relating to all machines and things technical!

Dinnerware and Accessories

(Also see **Furniture and Accessories — Catalog Discounters; General Merchandise — Catalog Discounters; Giftwares; Jewelry and Diamonds**)

General

CHAR CREWS CO.

1212 W. Hillsdale Blvd., Laurelwood Shopping Center, San Mateo 94403. Phone: 573-0345. Hours: M-Sat 10am-5pm. Purchases: MC, VISA. Parking: Lot.

☞ **Other Store:** 55-A Bellam Blvd., San Rafael, 454-7658.

Char Crews Co. has an unusual approach to serving their customers. They're committed to selling fine china, silver and holloware, fine quality stainless, crystal and other table top items at the lowest prices. Therefore, when you come in to buy, they'll advise you when the manufacturers will be offering promotional sales, to which they'll add a 20% discount to the manufacturer's sale price. If you insist or you can't wait, of course, they'll sell you whatever you want that day for a 20% discount. Most manufacturers of sterling have sale periods that extend over approximately six months during a year. Usually this is when department stores run huge sale ads with 30-50% discounts on settings, etc. Fine china has a smaller sale period during a year, usually one month in spring and one month in the fall. By checking with *Char Crews* and having your name put on their mailing list, you'll be notified when the optimum time to buy occurs. Brides can take advantage of the bridal stock maintenance program that involves reserving a number of place settings with a deposit for their gift giving guests that insures that their guests will be able to buy at maximum discounts. (The bride is obligated to buy all the remaining reserved stock in her name that is not purchased for her.) *Char Crews* carries most of the best lines, typically considered more high-end like Villeroy & Boch, Royal Worcester, Haviland, Rosenthal, Royal Doulton, Minton, etc. With 13 trained sales people they offer excellent service and advice (important when buying long term family heirlooms), bridal registry, telephone ordering, UPS shipping and gift wrapping. For important occasions like weddings, you'll save money, and if the family grapevine is in good working order, so will gift givers.

S. CHRISTIAN OF COPENHAGEN, INC.

225 Post Street, San Francisco 94108. Phone: 392-3394.
Hours: M-Sat 9:30am-6pm. Purchases: MC, AE, VISA.
Parking: Pay Lots.

☞ **Other Stores:** 1001 Front, San Francisco; Town &
Country Village, Palo Alto; Town & Country Village, San
Jose.

Make a beeline for the best buy in the store — the
crystal table with Rosenthal seconds and irregulars priced
at least 60% below retail. The flaws are very slight — tiny
bubbles in the glass, size differences among pieces of a
set, a few swirl marks. They do not in my estimation
effect the magnificence of this marvelous handblown glassware in the least. You're not limited to the pieces of
stemware, vases and bowls on the table, they have much
more in the back room. You can buy one piece or often a
complete set of stemware. You might want to consider the
special prices on their Collector's plates and dining room
sets while you're looking around.

COST PLUS IMPORTERS

(see **General Merchandise — Discount Stores**)

DANSK FACTORY OUTLET

801 Main St. (Dansk Square), St. Helena 94574. Phone:
(707) 963-4273. Hours: Daily 9am-6pm. Purchases: Cash
or Check. Parking: Lot.

☞ **Other Store:** Ocean Ave., & San Carlos, Carmel
Phone: (408) 625-1600.

Dansk's new store in St. Helena is a showcase for all
their fine quality products. Originally known for their
Kobenstyle Cookware and nonconforming items, teakwood
trays and salad bowls, china, stemware and bar glasses,
colorful plastics in dinnerware and accessories, stainless
steel items, candles and candle holders, they've expanded
their line with many new products including fine china and
casual dinnerware. Their line is particularly appealing for
the clean contemporary lines they manifest and the functional aspects of all their products. Prices are typically
discounted 30-60% on discontinued merchandise and factory overruns. Their stores are fun to visit, beautifully
merchandised and brimming with colorful, well-priced bargains.

HEATH CERAMICS INC. — FACTORY STORE

400 Gate 5 Road, Sausalito 94965. Phone: 332-3732.
Hours: Daily 10am-5pm. Purchases: MC, VISA. Parking:
Lot.

A visit to Sausalito is a *must* for the tourist, an outing
for Bay Area residents. The *Heath Factory Store* in
Sausalito could well be the focal point of the trip. Bargain
hunting in this pleasant environment is a unique experience. Overruns and seconds of tile for flooring, counters,
and walls are available in extraordinary colors and textures
at very worthwhile savings. Their dishes and heat-tempered
cookware that do not pass their high standards during
inspection are sold for 40% below retail prices. This does
not mean that they're chipped or cracked, just little flaws

that the untrained eye can hardly discern. If you haven't visited in a while, you'll find a new line of whiteware (dinnerware) in all shapes and special one-of-a-kind decorated plates. With these savings from regular retail prices, you are apt to find yourself returning, to round out your dinnerware set, to buy gifts, to purchase tile for a remodeling project or just to introduce a friend to the experience.

MARJORIE LUMM'S WINE GLASSES

112 Pine St., San Anselmo 94960. Phone: 454-0660. Hours: M-F 10am-4:30pm. Weekends by appt. Purchases: MC, VISA. Parking: Municpal Lot.

Marjorie Lumm runs a nationwide mail order wine glass business, carrying probably the most extensive selection of classic wine glasses to be found anywhere. Tables of seconds in her warehouse/store attract savvy shoppers with 50% discounts. Marjorie's wine glasses are handblown, good quality glasses of medium weight. The glasses are made in West Virginia, the center for fine glassmaking in the United States. Wine enthusiasts prefer glasses that are made from clear glass, with no color or cut designs to impede the evaluation of color and clarity. Her all purpose wine glass sells for $6.15 in her catalog and is reduced to $3.05 as a second. These glasses are not chipped but may have small bubbles or swirl effects in the glass which you can barely discern. Certainly your guests will never spot the flaws. You can obtain one of her catalogs by writing to P. O. Box 1544, San Anselmo, Ca. 94960, and then determine from the pictures if these glasses are in keeping with your tastes and whether a visit is warranted. You can buy two or twenty, suit yourself. Sometimes they may not have just the pieces you want or in the quantities you need, so you might call ahead first. For a special occasion, you might consider having your glasses engraved. On some days, it's possible to have it done while you wait.

MASLACH ART GLASS STUDIO & SECONDS STORE

44 Industrial Way, Greenbrae 94904. Phone: 924-2310. Hours: T-Sat 11am-5pm. Purchases: MC, VISA. Parking: Street.

Original glassware, where each piece is handblown into contemporary designs, is perfect for people who are looking for something just a little different. You'll save 50% off on their pieces of stemware, bowls, bud vases, hurricane lamps and egg shaped paperweights. Marble collectors will love rummaging through their seconds and will surely find a choice original. While browsing you can watch their master glassblowers at work. A goblet classed as a second, which may have minute cosmetic flaws, sells for about $15-$30. There are good quantities of many pieces. You can buy a whole set or just a few. New glass designs are added on a yearly basis as well as the popular designs being produced on an ongoing basis. Many people start with a pair of goblets and add to their collection each time they visit. Great wedding presents! The store is located 1 block north of *Cost Plus*.

TABLE TOPICS

521 Main St. (left off of San Mateo Blvd.), Half Moon Bay 94019. Phone: 726-3799. Hours: Tues-Sat 10am-5pm, Sun Noon-5pm. Purchases: MC, VISA. Parking: Street.

Table Topics is a special source for bargain prices on the Mikasa line. Utilizing special connections in the table top business the owners buy discontinued lines, open stock lines, take advantage of stock reductions, special purchases and any other good deal they can wangle to stock their charming, beautiful little store. Everything is sold for at least 10% below recognized sale prices. (Sale prices are usually 20-30% below the manufacturer's suggested retail price when advertised by major stores.) Even better are the special purchases where reductions are as much as 50% off. For instance during my visit heavy lead crystal barware regularly $17.95 was $6.95 a piece, a Mikasa semi-porcelain 5 piece placesetting regularly $44.95 was just $31.95. Oneida stainless flatware is frequently on sale for 50% off by the place setting or the set. On open stock patterns, special orders will be placed at sale prices.

I was particularly impressed with the beautiful vases, platters, and bowls designed by Larry Laslo for Mikasa. The colors in this line are simply beautiful! These pieces would make beautiful and distinctive gifts. While no giftwrapping services are offered, boxes are provided. The store offers a good selection of everything in table top catagories. Fine quality placemats and napkins, crystal stemware, glass serveware, cookware, bone china, semi-porcelain, stoneware will allow you to buy for the needs and lifestyles of just about everyone. Not all Mikasa patterns are on display, so be sure to know the name of the one you admire. You can order by phone with UPS delivery. For those who have never gone over the hill to Half Moon Bay, keep in mind that from the intersection of Fwy. 92 and Fwy. 280 the store is just 10-15 minutes away depending on traffic. During the summer plan your trip for a hot day and bring your suntan lotion and bathing suit and head for Frances Beach before or after shopping. *Other locations may be opening in the Bay Area in 1985, so call first.

WS II (WILLIAMS-SONOMA OUTLET)

Vallco Fashion Park, 10123 West Wolfe Rd. (next to Penney's — upper level), Cupertino 95014. Phone: (408) 257-9044. Hours: M-F 10am-9pm, Sat 10am-6pm, Sun Noon-5pm. Purchases: Cash or Check Only on outlet mdse. Parking: Lot.

Williams-Sonoma of catalog fame (they mail 16 million gourmet cookware catalogs a year) has finally opened an outlet. This outlet takes up a corner of their dazzling store in the Vallco Fashion Park. It is a separate entity, with all sales kept separate from their full service retail operaton. Unlike the other part of the store, you can't have purchases gift wrapped or mailed, neither can you return them. The outlet section contains their slightly damaged goods, discontinued merchandise, and leftovers. Prices are reduced 30-60% off the original retail price. The selection changes constantly. One day you may see racks of chili bowls, and then you may never see them again. Gourmet foods (one of their specialties) are completely safe and wholesome, but may have a slightly dented container or soiled label. It's possible to find the most esoteric gourmet foods or cookwares in *SW II*, along with the most basic kinds of merchandise, i.e. pots, pans, baking sheets and kitchen linens.

Restaurant Supply Stores

COMMERCIAL FOOD EQUIPMENT CO.

501 E. 12th St., Oakland 94606. Phone: 893-2736. Hours: M-F 8:30am-5pm, Sat 8:30am-Noon. Purchases: Cash or Check. Parking: Street.

Restaurant supply stores are truly a boon for families with fumbly-fingered young children (or couples who fight a lot). There are stacks of sturdy dishes in the back room of this establishment that may not have the graceful look of your regular china, but they will probably last a lot longer. Both new and used dishes are priced by the dozen here; for quantities of less than a dozen, 10% is added to the price. On used dishes, savings are about 50%, and all they need is a little soap and water to become useful additons to your kitchen.

FOOD SERVICE EQUIPMENT INC.

710 E. 14th St., San Leandro 94577. Phone: 568-2922. Hours: M-F 8am-5pm, Sat 9am-2pm. Purchases: MC, VISA. Parking: Street.

Although there are many restaurant supply stores around the Bay Area, most are unwilling to deal with the consumer who is only interested in buying odds 'n ends of *dinnerware. Food Service Equipment* is a welcome exception. Consumers can inspect the specials on the first floor that are discontinued merchandise, or one-of-a-kind items. Then they can take advantage of the bargains in the upstairs back room which is stacked high with sturdy restaurant dishes in many colors or patterns. Here there are used dishes and kitchenware at savings of about 50%, discontinued lines of dishes, and new dishes that have been returned to the store. Dishes are priced by the dozen.

Draperies

American Draperies makes draperies for homes and apartment houses. Twice a year they clear out their warehouse of miscellaneous stock, discontinued fabrics, production overruns, and odd sizes, most priced between $12 and $35. Bring your rod sizes and lengths required. The draperies are on hangers in panels or pairs. Their sales are announced in Bay Area newspapers and usually occur on the first weekend in May and November. All sales are final. For the best selection be there when the doors open; however, at 2:30 in the afternoon, an additional 20% discount is applied to the sale merchandise. If you really don't want to miss this sale, call and ask to be put on their mailing list. Directions: 1 mile east of Hwy 17 at Whipple, left on Medallion, right on San Luis Obispo.

Fabrics

(Also see **Fabrics — Drapery and Upholstery Yardage and Supplies**)

Ready Made

AMERICAN DRAPERIES

1168 San Luis Obispo, Hayward 94544. Phone: 489-4760. Hours: Usually last weekend in May and November. Purchases: MC, VISA. Parking: Lot.

FOOTHILL DRAPERIES

3121 Story Road, San Jose 95127. Phone: (408) 258-7599. Hours: M-Sat 9am-5:30pm. Purchases: MC, VISA. Parking: Private Lot.

This custom drapery store has found a way to cut losses and keep their overhead down. They utilize all leftover fabrics by making up ready-made draperies in standard window sizes. They have hundreds of these leftovers in their showroom. Most are one-of-a-kind and there are some customer returns. You can buy custom quality at 25-35% off. Bring your measurements and choose from satins, brocades, open weaves, linens, patterns and sheers.

THE YARDSTICK

2110 S. Bascom Ave., Campbell 95008. Phone: 377-1401.
Hours: M-F 9am-8:30pm, Sat 9am-6pm, Sun 10:30-5pm.
Purchases: MC, VISA. Parking: Lot.

If you need draperies right away or you want luxury window treatments at budget prices, check the mezzanine at the *The Yardstick*. They usually have about 3,000 readymades (guaranteed 2 1/2 fullness) from their own workrooms ready for you to take home and hang. Bring your measurements and in no time at all you'll be walking out the door with your selections. The fabrics used in their draperies are suitable for windows in a cabin or at the other extreme, in a formal dining room. The *Yardstick* also has a large dress yardage department. Check their ads in the San Jose *Mercury* for your dress, drapery or upholstery needs.

Custom Draperies

(See **Furniture and Accessories — Catalog Discounters**)

DRUG BARN

150 E. El Camino Real (next to Pak'n Save), Sunnyvale, 94087. Phone: Store (408) 733-3011. Pharmacy (408) 733-4553. Hours: M-Sat 9am-9pm, Sun 10am-6pm. Purchases: Cash or Check. Parking: Lot.

A major development for Bay Area bargain hunters was the opening of the first truly discount drug store in Sunnyvale. Common to other areas of the country, stores like the *Drug Barn* are likened to the growth of super warehouse grocery stores. The appeal is the brand-name-value orientation these retailers project. To obtain the price/quality equation, the "deep" discounter buys brand name merchandise usually for cash "on deal" from the manufacturer, getting a healthy discount. He passes 25-50% savings off suggested retail prices to the customer, and makes profits by minimal use of advertising, eliminating fancy decors and displays, and carefully controlling payrolls. In return for low prices and a supermarket atmosphere, customers at *Drug Barn* have to put up with no delivery, no service (except prescriptions) and no MC or VISA.

What to expect: everyday at *Drug Barn* American Greetings cards are 40% off list price; Foster Grant sunglasses are 50% off; Goody hair care accessories are 40% off; cosmetic items from Revlon, Max Factor, Almay, Maybelline, Coty, Cover Girl, etc. are at least 20% off; Amity wallets are 50% off; and Timex watches are 25% off. If you eliminate popular loss leaders from the list that are used by other heavily promotional chain stores you find that "consistently" *Drug Barn* saves you money on almost every purchase. I saved $9 on my first trip buying two contact lense products ($3) and a pair of reading glasses ($6). You can always find a cheap price on toilet paper and paper towels. It's all the other toiletries and beauty aids that decimate my budget, the ones to buy at *Drug Barn*.

Prescription drugs are a bit more complicated. Most chain drug stores select 15-20 commonly prescribed drugs (like birth control pills etc.) and sell them near cost to convey the image that they are low priced in the pharmacy department. They take far greater markups on all the rest! It's in the "all the rest" category that *Drug Barn's* prices are significant. Anyone with health problems who requires several prescriptions filled on a regular basis, should check their prices. A survey using the prescriptions of a senior citizen with major health problems showed a savings of $43/month. With Medicare coverage what it is today, that was good news for this senior who typically spends $200 a month on prescriptions, a lot for someone on a limited retirement income.

H & J PRODUCTS
2547 San Carlos Avenue, Castro Valley 94546. Phone: 582-1806. Hours: M-F 9am-5pm. Occasional Saturday. Purchases: Cash or Check. Parking: Street.

I'm not about to make any claims about food supplements, vitamins or minerals. For those of you who regularly use these products you might be interested in checking the prices at the *H & J Products* Factory Outlet. This company manufacturers food supplements, i.e. Vitamin C-1000mg, Super Stress Formula B-Complex with Vitamin C, Bee Pollen, Pure Spirulina, A-D Chewable, and various Hi Protein tablets and powders, plus a full page of other products that are pure, safe, and fresh, but may have a crooked label, label change, or they are just surplus products. These are discounted 40-50% but a few are discounted a modest 20%.

H & J sells their products to Bay Area and nationwide wholesale distributors who in turn sell to local retail nutrition stores. Their products are sold under their own label and they also have private label products for special accounts. Finally, *H & J* sells DMSO. If you have been wary of buying this product in some of the unconventional retail outlets that advertise this product, you'll probably feel more confident buying here. If you would like a complete discount price list, send a self-addressed stamped envelope to the address above. They will ship anywhere in any amount, but of course you pay the shipping.

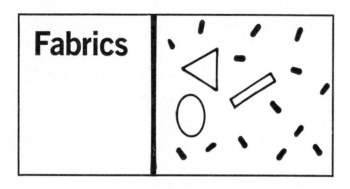

Fabrics

General

BOLTS END

15980 East 14th St., San Leandro 94578. Phone: 481-1090. Hours: M-Sat 10am-5pm. Purchases: Cash or Check. Parking: Lot.

A tiny little shop absolutely crammed with fabrics, trims, buttons, linings and other paraphernalia. The owner buys mill ends, fabrics from apparel manufacturers, or in other words, leftovers. Prices are very good, the selection is always interesting even though somewhat eclectic. Plans are being made to move to larger quarters, so do call to verify location.

JEANNE MARC FABRICS

262 Sutter St., San Francisco 94108. Phone: 362-1121. Hours: M-Sat 10am-5pm. Purchases: MC, AE, VISA. Parking: Pay Lots.

Jeanne Marc offers fabrics at wholesale and below wholesale prices. Fabrics are featured from the preceding season's collections, including everything from terry cloth to silk, quilted and pleated fabrics, cotton prints, broadcloths, batistes, wools and silks. All textiles are first rate and many are imports from Paris or printed exclusively for them. Some of the fabrics match the samples and discontinued apparel from their line that is on their clearance racks at this store. These fashions are expensive at retail, sought by women who are fashion forward and typically up-to-date on what's new in the fashion world. New fabrics arrive weekly, apparel markdowns are ongoing.

CARY FACTORY OUTLET
(See **Apparel — Children's**)

EXOTIC SILKS

252 State St., Los Altos 94022. Phone: 948-8611. Hours: M-Sat 9am-5:30pm. Purchases: MC, VISA. Parking: Street.

Exotic Silks is a wholesale business with a small retail store to clear out excess inventory. The company buyers scour the Orient in search of beautiful silks to import. These silks are used by artists, decorators, lampshade manufacturers, fashion designers, smaller yardage shops and individual sewers. The silks available to the public are the "leftovers" in plain or print silk crepe de chine, silk satin, raw noil silk, silk corduroy, handwoven Thai silks in vibrant colors, taffeta, pongee, and brocade silks. Yardage may be limited to a few remaining yards on a bolt or up to 40-50 yards. But when it's gone, your chances of finding a particular fabric again are nil. So buy as much as you need the first time around.

Unlike other yardage shops, *Exotic Silks* sells no patterns, threads, zippers or other notions. However, they always have several racks of silk apparel that are well priced. Silk scarves, cotton and fine linen handkerchiefs, beautifully embroidered tablecloth and napkin sets are usually available when they've found them at a good price on their buying trips. The silk yardage may be discounted 20-40% off retail prices. Catch their ads in *Vogue* pattern magazine if you would like to order sample fabrics.

FABRICLAND-MILL OUTLET

Mervyn's Plaza, 2042 El Camino Real, Santa Clara 95050. Phone: (408) 246-6977. Hours: M-Sat 10am-6pm, Th eve till 9pm, Sun Noon-5pm. Purchases: MC, VISA. Parking: Lot.

Every manufacturer of apparel uses thousands of yards of fabric each season. Byer, headquartered in San Francisco is no exception. Leftovers cost money, so Byer has opened a fabric outlet store and stocked it with fabrics from their cutting rooms. Additional fabrics have been purchased from major mills to round out their selection. Prices are reduced at least 30-50% off the retail prices of other fabric stores.

The clever seamstress can make exact copies of current Byer fashions in the stores. Prices on some popular fabrics are as follows: At $2.97/yard, 100% cotton calico, 60" cotton knits, and wool/blends; at $1.97/yd., plaid shirting, 60" 100% cotton sheeting (used in Byer skirts and pants), and many types of polyester silk-type fabrics. 90% of the fabric selection is under $4/yard. Exceptions are the double sided quilteds at $6.97/yard, and single side quilteds at $4.97/yd. If these prices are not enough to entice you, consider the notions. Threads, zippers, scissors, quilting hoops etc. are discounted 25% off retail. *FabricLand* is only lacking in finer quality wools, but their remnant prices more than make up for this.

FABRIC WAREHOUSE

2327 Mc Kee Road, San Jose 95116 . Phone: (408) 926-3203. Hours: M-F 10am-9pm, Sat 10am-6pm, Sun 10am-5pm. Purchases: MC, VISA. Parking: Lot.

☞ **Other Stores:** 3690 El Camino Real, Santa Clara; 898 Blossom Hill Road, San Jose; 651 W. Hamilton, Campbell.

Picture a supermarket-sized store filled with fabrics and you can understand how overwhelmed you'll feel on your first visit to these warehouse stores, located next to *K-Mart*. Most of these fabrics are purchased directly from Eastern mills, and all are first quality. Except for wools, their selection is very extensive in all categories.

Prices on all upholstery and drapery fabrics are low enough to lure upholsterers into the store to buy fabrics for their customers; they're often 50-60% off retail. Everyday regular prices reflect savings of 20-50% off established retail prices on all their goods, greater reductions are on fabrics advertised in their special weekly promotions.

They have an interesting dual pricing policy based on full bolt purchases vs. cut to order. The full bolt lower price refers to any amount of yardage remaining on a bolt, whether its 3 yds. or 40 yds. All notions are discounted 15-25% off manufacturer's list price and all patterns are discounted 15%.

FARR WEST DESIGNS
(See **Apparel — Women's Factory Outlets**)

GUNNE SAX OUTLET
(See **Apparel — Women's Factory Outlets**)

HARAN'S
2853 Mission, San Francisco 94110. Phone: 647-7746. Hours: M-Sat 9:30am-6pm, Sun Noon-5pm. Purchases: MC, VISA. Parking: Lot.

☞ **Other Store:** 820 Clement, San Francisco.

Haran's offers all kinds of fabrics at fantastically reduced prices — some fabrics here are for sale elsewhere at twice the price. Almost everything in the store is specially purchased from mills in other states. Good buys are plentiful, but be alert for second-quality merchandise; check the fabric for flaws before purchasing. This store will make exchanges, but you will save time if you're careful before you buy. This is not the resource for finding fabric for couture patterns.

IMPORO
149 10th St. (upstairs), San Francisco 94103. Phone: 552-0132. Hours: M-Sat 9am-5:30pm. Purchases: MC, VISA. Parking: Street.

Located between Mission and Howard, *Imporo* offers a wide selection of fabrics at bargain hunters' prices. Most of their loyal customers are garment workers from the City's apparel industry. There are many synthetics and natural fibers (including wools) that make sewing your own clothes a real money saver.

LILLI ANN FACTORY OUTLET
(See **Apparel — Women's Factory Outlets**)

OLGA FASHIONS AND FABRIC OUTLET
(See **Apparel — Women's Factory Outlets**)

THE SEW HELP YOU SHOP
540 Florida St., San Francisco 94110. Phone: 626-9426. Hours: M-F 9am-4pm. Sat. call first. Purchases: Cash or Check. Parking: Limited Street.

The *Sew Help You Shop* works closely with apparel manufacturers as a special contractor. They do quilting, cording, and cut bindings on fabrics that will be made into garments. They opened an outlet at their plant where leftover fabrics, both quilted and unquilted, linings, threads, lace, bias tapes, cordage, spaghetti cording and batting are sold for discount prices. Prices on quilted fabrics are approximately 40% below retail prices. 4 oz.

poly/cotton batting is just $.75/yd. If you're a quilter you may be interested in the nice selection of mini-print fabrics in 100% cotton at $2.49/yd., or their poly/cotton blends at $2.35/yd. If you're creative, you can make placemats of your own or anything quilted in the way of apparel. 8 oz. polarguard is just $2.25/yd. and wonderful for making ski or other cold weather apparel. Parking is limited but the owners suggest that customers park in their freight driveways on the side of the building.

STONEMOUNTAIN & DAUGHTER

2516 Shattuck Avenue, Berkeley 94705. Phone: 845-6106. Hours: M-F 10am-6:30pm, Sat 10am-6pm, Sun ll:30am-5pm. Purchases: MC, VISA. Parking: Street.

The owner of this small shop has long established connections with the apparel industry in Los Angeles. He attempts to combine quality with low price in making his purchases so that he can pass on worthwhile savings to consumers. Often I've spotted a fabric that I've just seen on a garment in a department store. Along with some ordinary fabrics, he has the best selection of fine quality bargain priced wools, silks, cottons and rayon blends that are really quite special. In fact, the fabrics are much more elegant than his modest little store. Bring your patterns, he doesn't sell patterns or any notions.

Drapery and Upholstery Yardage and Supplies

(Also see **Furniture and Accessories — Catalog Discounters; Draperies — Ready Made**)

ALAMEDA UPHOLSTERY SHOP

863 W. San Carlos, San Jose 95126. Phone: (408) 295-7885. Hours: M-F 9am-5:30pm, Sat 9am-4pm. Purchases: MC, VISA. Parking: Street.

Whether you need supplies for reupholstering a piece of furniture or just advice about doing it, this shop can help you. They cater to do-it-yourselfers, with some nice fringe benefits. For example, they make up a small beginners' kit that includes most of the tools needed to start reupholstering on your own, and they usually have a few books on the subject as well. Their selection of upholstery fabrics is huge, and they can order from almost any major manufacturer in the country, including Van Waters & Rogers, Waverly, S. Harris, Schumacher, and many others at savings of 25%. (Students can get another 10% discount). Draperies, woven woods, and mini-blinds are sold for a 25% discount when the customer measures and hangs their own. They will also cut to order foam rubber that comes in 30 sizes, 1/4" to 6".

ANN'S FABRIQUE

160-C Alamo Plaza (Fwy. 680, Alamo offramp to Danville Blvd, turn left) Alamo 94507. Phone: 837-8579. Hours: M-F 10am-6pm, Sat 10am-5pm. Purchases: MC, VISA. Parking: Lot.

If you'd like to buy a charming 100% cotton print fabric for your home decorating project that retails at $18.95 for just $6.99, you'll love going to *Ann's Fabrique* in Alamo. That's a fairly typical price and discount on the lovely selection of quality seconds, factory overruns, and first quality goods. Better yet, these are very up to date fabrics. Most can be coordinated with current wallpaper patterns from well-known wallpaper books and manufacturers. They have wallpaper books in the store so that you can do all the coordinating, even order wallpaper at a 20% discount. The seconds are carefully unrolled for your inspection before purchase so that you can verify the flaws. Most of the time, you can't even find them.

The selection is slanted towards country charm, but there are velvet upholstery fabrics, plaids, contemporary-styled Marimekko-type prints, solids, florals, chintz, and other upholstery and drapery fabrics. Discounts range from 25-70% off retail. The smaller discounts apply to first quality fabrics purchased to provide a good well rounded selection of decorating fabrics. They gladly cut swatches and allow you to take fabric home on approval.

For those who can buy but not sew, they provide referrals for labor and workrooms to have upholstery, slipcover, drapery, bed and pillow treatments made up. Additionally, the sales staff can assist with fabric estimates and plenty of free advice. The store is immaculate, the selection fresh, and prices are wonderful. It's already popular with the local craft/boutique makers and antique dealers that are always looking for a good source for fabrics for their upholstery renovations.

BERESSI, S. FABRIC SALES

1504 Bryant St., San Francisco 94103. Phone: 861-5001. Dates: Fall and Spring. Hours: Daily during sale. Purchases: MC, VISA. Parking: Lot.

For two months each year, *S. Beressi*, a bedspread manufacturer popular with interior designers and local stores, opens its doors to the public and gives everyone a chance to buy fabrics, threads, polyester fiberfill and bedspreads from its upstairs warehouse. Prices on the huge assortment of *leftovers* are less than wholesale to encourage fast sales and speedy removal. Most of the fabrics sold are first quality, discontinued patterns and colors from their regular line. These fabrics are used not only for bed-spreads, but for draperies, upholstery, slipcovers, costumes, apparel, crafts and theatre set decorations. Added to the selection are fabrics purchased from mills on buying trips around the world to supply the many wholesale upholstery and drapery studios he keeps supplied with fabrics. These may be exquisite velvets from Italy, 120 in. drapery sheers, or silk damasks from Europe. Regulars at these sales will always recognize the small selection of practically pre-historic fabrics that seem to last from sale to sale, but they get cheaper and cheaper every year. Mr. Beressi can help determine the amount of yardage required for your project and also give a lot of how-to information, plus referrals to reliable workrooms where you can have the draperies, upholstery, etc. made up. Call the office for specific dates and times. This is one sale you don't want to miss for budget decorating needs.

CALICO CORNERS

2700 El Camino Real, Redwood City 94061. Phone: 368-1610. Hours: M-Sat 9:30am-5:30pm, Sun Noon-5pm. Purchases: MC, VISA. Parking: Free Lot.

☞ **Other Stores:** 5764 Paradise Dr., Corte Madera; 39A Almaden Plaza at 5353 Almaden Expry., San Jose; 5753 Pacheco Blvd., Pacheco.

The real bargains are not calico, actually, but beautiful imported and domestic upholstery fabrics — some of the finest upholstery fabrics, drapery and slipcover fabrics I have seen, for 35-50% off regular retail. Hanging rools neatly display beautiful fabrics whose only fault are tiny minute flaws that can easily be worked around (some weren't even visible to the unprofessional eye), plus many fabrics that are first quality at super bargain prices. Each piece is tagged with fiber content, width, price and place of manufacture. This store is an absolute pleasure to shop in, not only for its extraordinarily low prices, but also for its neat arrangement and its helpful clerks, who will refer you to a custom upholsterer, or slipcover expert. Draperies are sent out to be made by the store with the wholesale labor price being passed on to the customer. They will allow customers to borrow a bolt of yardage for home evaluation.

FIELD'S FABRICS

1229 Park St., Alameda 94501. Phone: 865-7171. Hours: M-Sat 9:30am-5pm. Purchases: MC, VISA. Parking: Street.

This small shop offers a complete stock of beautiful home decorating fabrics at 40-60% off retail. The reason: these are seconds, discontinued patterns, and mill over-runs. The ladies who work here couldn't be more helpful in giving suggestions and assistance to the novice.

(Also see **General Merchandise — Discount Stores**)

ARCHITECTURAL CERAMICS WEEKEND SALES

1940 Union St. (1 1/2 blocks off Grand Ave.), Oakland 94607. Phone: 893-5314. Hours: Occasional Weekends. Purchases: Cash or Check. Parking: Street.

The pots and containers manufactured by this outfit are usually seen accommodating large plants and indoor trees in lobbies and office buildings. Their smallest container is a one gallon 8'' X 7''. They make low 6'' X 17'' pots for color spots or succulent containers, while their largest container accommodates a 15 gallon plant and is 17'' X 20''. The public is allowed to come to the factory every few months on weekends to buy their seconds. Prices are 50-65% off retail depending on the flaws in the glaze or

the size of the chip. If you're interested in these bargains which will range from $4.50-$30, be sure to call ahead to verify that they will be open, or watch for their ads in the *Chronicle* or Oakland *Tribune*.

CAPE COD NURSERY

29216 Taylor Ave., Hayward 94544. Phone: 785-3378. Hours: M-Fri 7:30am-5pm. Sat till Noon. Closed daily between Noon and 1pm for lunch. Cash preferred, checks with I. D. Parking: Lot.

For major landscaping projects, make careful plans especially if you'd like to buy bargains at the *Cape Cod Nursery*. This outfit is a wholesale nursery that supplies general landscape contractors with plants, shrubs, trees, etc. Most of these contractors are working on city, county, and state jobs or on private commercial sites. If you're willing to do your homework, make out a list, and find your way to this offbeat location, you can buy for the same wholesale prices.

This is not the place to pick up a pony pak of petunias, for that go to PayLess. This is ideal for a major landscaping project where you'll need flats of ground covers or annuals, shrubs, and trees. An example of spring'84 prices: Most varieties of bedding plants — $6.75; most flats of ground covers — $9.50 (examples — Vinca Minor, African Daisy, Ajuga); one gallon shrubs — $1.95 to $2.10 (Pittosporum, Raphiolepis, Nandina, Abelia, Oleander); most 5 gallon shrubs — $6.50-7.25; most 15 gallon trees-$33 (ex.-Chinese Elm, Liquidamber, White Birch, Camphor). Bedding plants and ground covers must be ordered three days in advance with a 20% deposit. Most other varieties of popular plants, shrubs, and trees are in stock, or if not, they can also be special ordered. If you're placing a large order, delivery may be free depending on where you live.

The owner emphasizes that he does not have the time or staff to give advice, recommendations, or planting suggestions for the novice. You are expected to navigate through the yard by yourself, pick out your own plants, bring them to the office and pay. He will help load them in your car or truck. He recommends *waiting* until mid-March for spring planting. During the winter months the yard is a little bleak. Directions: From Fwy. 17, take the Industrial Pkwy. offramp East. Go about 1 mile to Taylor, turn left, drive to end of street. The nursery is set back from the road and one house from the end of street. It's right across the street from a rabbit farm. (Psst, a tip from the owner I can't wait to try. Planting the shrub Euphorbia Lathyris which has a scent that repels moles and gophers.)

FANTASTICO
(See **Arts, Crafts, Hobby Supplies**)

FLOWER TERMINAL
6th and Brannan, San Francisco 94103. Hours: M-F 2am-11am, Sat. hours for a few vendors 8am-Noon. Purchases: Cash or Check. Parking: Street or Lot.

Several wholesale nurseries are located within this block of buildings. Retail sales of house plants are made to the public at wholesale prices. Because these businesses are basically wholesale operations, this is certainly not the place to shop with your children or to expect information on plant maintenance or other advice. The quick cash sale is appreciated but there is neither time nor personnel for retail services. You are required to pay sales tax unless you have a resale number. Only people with resale numbers are allowed to park within their lot and street parking can be a real problem! For the best service and selection on indoor plants I recommend shopping on Tuesdays and Thursdays. Several dealers in the complex sell dried flowers, ribbons, papers, and other craft essentials. I would not say that prices are "wholesale" on anything, however many items are simply not sold at the retail level. From October through Xmas these dealers are crowded with shoppers anxious to get a head start on their holiday decorations.

MAINLY SECONDS
15715 Hesperian Blvd., San Lorenzo 94580. Phone: 481-1902. Hours: M-Sat 9am-6pm, Sun 10am-6pm. Purchases: MC, VISA. Parking: Street and Lot.

☞ **Other Store:** 701 San Pablo Ave., Albany. Phone: 527-2493.

When warm weather rolls around and you're in a potting mood, you'll find good buys on pots and planters at these two stores. Both are stocked with a wide array of planters and pots to suit almost any style of interior and exterior decor. True to their name, much of the merchandise is classified as seconds, with small flaws or irregularities that will not deter the bargain hunter. I've brightened up my patio with several of their terra cotta hen-shaped pots and strawberry planters at 30-40% discounts. The ceramic pots suitable for small trees made by Architectural Ceramics are always 50% off. Handthrown stoneware pots are 40-50% off. I spotted one for $7.99 that sold elsewhere for $15. Unrelated to their other merchandise, they display tables laden with ceramic bathroom accessories like toothbrush holders, tissue holders and soap dishes at approximately 70% off. These must be checked carefully for flaws. Closeouts of terra cotta gourmet cookware are 50% off and great for microwave cooking. Of course all these pots are surrounded by plants, dried flowers, silk flowers and macrame holders to provide a complete selection. Everything is discounted!

PAYLESS DRUG STORES GARDEN CENTERS

2130 Contra Costa Blvd., Pleasant Hill 94523. Phone: 685-2450. Hours: M-F 9:30am-9pm, Sat 9am-8pm, Sun 9am-7pm. Purchases: MC, VISA. Parking: Free Lot.

☞ **Other Stores:** Castro Valley, Dublin, Fremont, Hayward, Oakland, San Mateo, San Pablo, San Rafael, Santa Rosa, Vallejo.

For garden plants it's hard to find better prices than the ones at *PayLess Drug Store's Garden Centers*. Their secret is volume buying and quick turnover. Each store does its own buying to suit the special climate and soil conditions of its area. Since this is a selfservice store, you won't get the attention you might get at a nursery.

Prices are 30-50% below those of independent nurseries during their seasonal sales. Usually garden department sales are held every three weeks throughout the year; these are advertised in local papers. During spring and fall, the peak gardening season, sales occur weekly. Even without the sales, prices are 25-35% less than you'll find almost anywhere else.

PayLess will accept exchanges on plants that do not thrive or aren't satisfactory if you have your sales slip (otherwise at the discretion of the garden center manager).

PRICE CLUB
(See **General Merchandise — Discount Stores**)

POTTERY OUTLET

1793 Lafayette St., Santa Clara 95050. Phone: (408) 984-0467. Hours: Daily 9am-5pm. Purchases: MC, VISA. Parking: Lot.

You'll find some of the bargains out in the yard and some inside the two story yellow building at the back of the lot. They distribute pottery containers of all types (from basic red clay to fancy glazed) and sell discontinued styles plus pottery seconds for 20% above wholesale. They buy inventories from other manufacturers when they go out of business to produce an everchanging selecton. Badly damaged pots are priced very low — they need to be, since some seem barely usable.

Food and Drink

(Also see **General Merchandise — Discount Stores, — Liquidators**)

BAKERY THRIFT SHOPS

It would take three pages to list all the bakery thrift shops that exist in the Bay Area. Truly, it's worth your while to check the yellow pages of your phone directory to spot those close to you then try to include a stop on your way around town. *Parisian, Orowheat, Langendorf, Kilpatrick* plus many other smaller bakeries maintain thrift stores to sell their day-old bread, baker's mistakes (odd shaped, undercooked, overcooked etc.), plus freshly baked surplus. Savings range anywhere from 20-75% off retail depending on the category. Depending on the company you may find cakes, cookies, donuts, sweet rolls, loaves of bread, bread crumbs, Pannatone, dinner rolls, sandwich rolls etc., etc. Buy a lot at one time — you can freeze whatever you don't use right away.

Groceries

ALUM ROCK CHEESE CO.
215 E. Alma Ave., San Jose 95110. Phone: (408) 293-9400. Hours: Sat Only 9am-3pm. Purchases: Cash or Check. Parking: Lot.

Saturdays are bargain days at this cheese company. Drive around to the back of the building to find their retail store. Ricotta, mozzarella, cheddar, Swiss, American and processed cheeses are sold for considerably less than at your neighborhood deli. There's no minimum purchase required. If you're planning a pizza party, take the easy way out. Buy their thick or thin prepared pizza crusts, sauce, diced blended cheeses and meats that will keep your efforts to a minimum.

BACK DOOR MEAT & FOOD CO.

850 Sycamore (at Mission), Hayward. Phone: 889-1133. Hours: M-F l0am-7pm, Sat 9am-5pm, Sun llam-5pm. Purchases: Checks & Cash. Parking: Lot.

☞ **Other Store:** 1111 West El Camino, (Cala Ctr.), Sunnyvale. Phone: (408) 773-1953.

First, let me say that I'm not promoting the consumption of more meat in your diet, rather trying to provide options and the opportunity to save money. The story: *Back Door Meat* buys their meats in carcass form, processes the meat from A to Z and sells directly to the public from their plant. Their meat is federally inspected daily! All their meats are hermetically sealed in vacuum packages. All air is removed from around the meat and as a result, bacterial growth is slowed. The meat will stay fresh in a vacuum package for up to 2 weeks as long as the seal remains tight. Once the seal is broken, the meat must either be eaten or frozen within 3-5 days. The lack of air makes the meat look darker temporarily while the vacuum seal is in place, bright red color returns minutes after the seal is broken.

Their meat is from range-fed (grass-fed) beef, not feed-lot fed beef. Range-fed beef is leaner and considered healthier due to the lower cholesterol concentration, and has less waste — making it less expensive than grocery store meats. Some of their meats are tenderized mechanically without the use of any chemicals or enzymes. The mechanical tenderizer uses a set of long thin knives to penetrate deep within the meat and works to physically break down the internal tissues and renders the meat more tender. All meat items are guaranteed to customer satisfac-

tion or your money will be refunded.

About prices (spring 1984): Their ground beef with 18-20% fat was $1.39/lb. (it's also used by several fast food franchises in their hamburgers). The pre-Cut Steaks like New York in a 20 steak box (5 packages of 4 steaks) were $2.69/lb. Filet Mignon was $3.98/lb.; and rib eye was $2.89/lb. You may continue to age the meat to your taste in the vacuum packaging and then freeze to halt the aging. Even better prices are found on their bulk packages like top sirloin 8-10 lbs. for $1.59/lb. In addition to their own processed meats, they also sell chicken, pork, fish, deli items and cheeses at very good prices.

BEST FRIEND FOODS PET NUTRITION CENTER

1455 E. Francisco Blvd., San Rafael. Phone: 459-3505. Hours: T-Sat 9am-5pm. Purchases: Cash or Check. MC, VISA (San Rafael Only). Parking: Lot.

☞ **Other Store:** 71 Monument Plaza, Pleasant Hill. Phone: 798-1327.

For those who must treat their pets like royalty, you may pay royal prices, but not at *Best Friend Foods*. Carrying only the very best dog and cat foods, they'll save you at least 10% and usually more like 20% on these "gourmet nutrition products." Science Diet, Iams, Kasco, Wayne, Nutro, Breeders Choice, and other favorites for the kennel set are sold in bulk sizes with solid information from their trained staff thrown in for free. Regulars buy all their supplies, food supplements, collars, leashes, vitamins, flea control products and animal carriers at princely discounts. A #100 Vari Kennel sold for $31 versus $52 at a local pet shop.

BETTER BUYS
(See **General Merchandise**)

CALIFORNIA CHEESE CO.

1451 Sunny Ct., San Jose 95116. Phone: (408) 288-5151. Hours: M-S 8:30am-5pm. Purchases: Cash or Check. Parking: Lot.

Don't go on an empty stomach or you'll be tormented by the aroma of fresh cheeses, deli meats and pizza products. Although they have a wide variety of cheeses, their speciality is mozzarella and ricotta which is made in their own factory. Their prices on all products are discounted $.50-75 /lb from supermarket prices. They're at the end of a dead end street, but it's easier to call for directions if you're not familiar with the area.

CANDY OUTLET

209 Utah, South San Francisco 94080. Phone: 871-1800. Hours: M-F 8:30am-4pm. Purchases: Cash or Check. Parking: Street.

You may rue the day you set foot in this store especially when you step on your scale. This is the Bay Area distribution center for Blum's candies. Theoretically, everything that comes in should go out with mathematical precision. Of course, reality is quite different. All the candies and Blum's products that are leftovers are sold for 25% off minimum and daily specials may go for 40-50% off. All the candies are sold in packages, boxes, bags or clever promotional containers. In the selection you'll choose from mints, fudge, peanut brittle, mixed creams, nuts and chews, also ice cream toppings, cookies and fruit cakes. You won't leave empty-handed!

CANNED FOODS INC.

1717 Harrison (14th St., entrance), San Francisco 94103. Phone: 552-9680. Hours: M-F 9am-7pm, Sat 8am-6pm. Purchases: Cash, Check, Food Stamps. Parking: Lot.

☞ **Other Stores:** Berkeley, Redwood City, San Jose, Sacramento, Stockton.

These are the quiet guys in town. They don't advertise for two reasons: (1) the items they stock change in quantity and variety from day to day, and (2) not advertising helps to lower their overhead and prices. *Canned Foods* specializes in buying carload shipments straight from packers and canners. They also buy overstocks, label-change goods, odd lots and some cannery dents. But they buy wholesome food and stand behind their products 100% with a money back guarantee. To save money, they do not carry a full line of groceries but whatever you buy is usually priced below the competitions' regular prices. Your success at *Canned Foods* depends on your ability to spot super values, so it's important to know the food prices of items you consistently buy. Don't shop *Canned Foods* with a prepared list, shop instead with an eye towards exceptional values that you can stock up on and bypass the marginal ones you can easily buy at local stores. Some of the labels that are unfamiliar are from Eastern companies, or have been repackaged to protect the identity of the regular manufacturer. Best buys often include seasonal items like Halloween candy, summer drink mixes, or Xmas labeled items.

CASH & CARRY WAREHOUSE

452 Dubois St., San Rafael 94901. Phone: 457-1040. Hours: M-F 9am-5pm, Sat 9am-1pm. Purchases: Cash or Check. Parking: Lot.

☞ **Other Store:** 3440 Vincent Rd., Pleasant Hill. Phone: 932-1414.

If you're cooking for a crowd, the swim team, your church, or just plannning a big party, the *Cash and Carry Warehouse* may have some products that will not only save you money, but make your preparations easier. These are for the most part institutional products used by restaurants, catering services, schools etc. Their frozen foods, like shrimp, crab, chicken parts, hamburger patties, vegetables, berries all come in large packages geared for quantity cooking. All canned goods are choice grade. The paper products are particularly appealing for group gatherings. Individual tablecloths, banquet rolls of table cloths, doilies, napkins, cups, plates, etc. are always in stock in a good selection at better than supermarket prices. The warehouses are immaculately maintained, service is excellent, and any chairperson burdened with buying the essentials for the group function will be happy to find this outfit. The warehouse is on the West side of Francisco Blvd., call for directions.

CITADEL'S CANNERY WAREHOUSE

405 East Taylor (Betw. 9th & 10th), San Jose 95112. Phone: (408)275-0410. Hours: M-Sat 9:30am-6pm, Sun 11am-5pm. Purchases: Cash or Check. Parking: Lot.

The selection of dented cans and odd lots for sale here covers the whole warehouse floor. Prices on canned goods are low enough (when compared to major supermarkets) to entice residents of East San Jose and the downtown area to make frequent stops. Both institutional and regular sizes are carried, but not every size in every item. They carry national brands as well as *Citadel's* own brand. Everything is guaranteed.

COUNTRY CHEESE

2101 San Pablo Ave., Berkeley 94702. Phone: 841-0752. Hours: M-Sat 10am-6pm. Purchases: Cash or Check. Parking: Street.

Domestic and imported cheeses, meat products, dried fruits, nuts and seeds, grains, spices by the ounce, and health food items at wonderful prices keep Berkeley residents happy. If you're in the East Bay and haven't checked them out, you don't know what you're missing. Inquire about their discounts for co-ops and volume orders.

COUNTRY STORE

2070 So. Seventh St., San Jose 95112. Phone: (408) 280-2349. Hours: M-F 8:30am-4:30pm. Purchases: Cash or Check. Parking: Street.

This is the retail outlet for the *Mayfair Packing Co.*, a packager of many kinds of nuts, primarily walnuts, but with an appetizing selection of dried fruits. Prices on items like walnuts and apricots depend largely on size (whole, diced, halves, etc.) and grade. Prices are very good, far less than supermarket prices.

CREATIVE CONCEPTS

3218 Whipple Rd., Union City 94587. Phone: 471-4956 or 471-4957. Hours: M-Fri 8am-4:30pm. Purchases: Cash or Check. Parking: Lot.

Creative Concepts does most of their business on a word of mouth basis. Even those who consider themselves to be good cooks find that the demands of a busy schedule often force them to take shortcuts and to rely on quick mixes. *Creative Concepts* are specialists who formulate their own products; specifically spices, seasonings, gravies, salad dressings, and assorted products for sale to schools, restaurants and consumers who buy in quantity. Their bulk packages, (16 oz.) for puddings, etc., are packaged with labels and recipes for making smaller quantities.

On most purchases, the prices are considerably less than the supermarket's. Their Italian salad dressing is $3.27 for 16 oz. This is equivalent to 26 packages of a well known brand at a total cost of $16.30. Supermarket cinnamon is about four times the cost of their 16 oz. pack. Because of the 8 & 16 oz. packaging on most of their products,

buying with a friend, or friends, helps defray costs and gives you a reasonable quantity.

Creative Concepts appreciates when you're prepared to order everything from the front office. Otherwise, you'll be sent back to the warehouse to make your choices in the midst of the hustle and bustle of packing, shipping, etc. For really efficient service write for their free catalog and price list, and phone in your order. They will ship UPS anywhere. They are located in a warehouse complex at the corner of Whipple and Union City Blvd.

HOOPERS CONFECTIONS INC.

4632 Telegraph Ave., Oakland 94609. Phone: 654-3373. Hours: M-Sat 9:30-6pm, Sun 10am-4pm. Purchases: Cash or Check. Parking: Lot.

Just because you don't see their seconds (*Hoopers* Bloopers), don't think they're not here. Just ask and they'll sell you whatever they have on hand in their stockroom. *Hooper's* chocolates retail from $5.95-$7.95/lb. The Bloopers are sweetly priced at $3.98/lb. just because they're imperfectly formed pieces discovered through *Hooper's* careful screening before chocolates are packed into boxes. They usually include most all varieties of creams, chews, chips, nut roll, mints and truffles. *Hooper's* chocolates are made with 92 score dairy butter, whipping cream, fresh nutmeats, natural flavors such as black raspberry puree, Vermont maple syrup and fine imported chocolate. You have to buy a 50 cent minimum, but that's not hard as you contemplate all the Deeeee-licious sweets!

JANA'S SUPER BUYS

22224 Redwood Road, Castro Valley 94546. Phone: 582-6770. Hours: Daily 10am-6pm. Purchases: Cash, Check, Food Stamps. Parking: Lot.

The owners of this store will sell anything from A-Z if they can get a good buy on it. Primarily they're selling grocery items and food products. Prices on meat and cheese are super. Institutional size cans, salvage canned goods, promotional items and just plain grocery items are all discounted. The constant arrival of such a disparate collection of products defies any attempt at immaculate displays, however, their loyal customers don't complain.

LE MOULIN INC.

2170-Q Commerce Ave., Concord 94520. Phone: 676-2770. Hours: M-F 8:30am-5pm. Purchases: Cash or Check. Parking: Lot.

If you're not able to make perfectly shaped golden brown croissants then cheat!! *Le Moulin Inc*. in Concord supplies many caterers, deli's, restaurants and bakeries with several different types of croissants. All their products are sold frozen, by the case. You can buy hand rolled frozen dough croissants that require thawing, rising, and baking; or even easier, pre-risen frozen croissants, just thaw and bake for a fast uniform product; or pre-baked and frozen croissants, simply heat and serve. Consumers seem to prefer their 3 oz. frozen hand rolled croissants, 36/case for $13.94 (spring 1984 price). Creative cooks can turn these into elegant entrees using the same types of fillings called for in crepe dishes; or add spices, nuts, raisins, jams, etc. for a sweet dessert; there's really no limit to the possibilities. They have a sheet of recipe and baking suggestions for the novice. Their croissants are as good as any I've tasted anywhere. With so many luncheons, parties, and celebrations occurring throughout the year, I'm sure that hostesses will want to consider the addition of croissants to their menus.

Their location in Concord is just one mile East of Fwy. 680, (Concord Blvd. offramp to Commerce Ave.). Look for their offices and bakery on the side of this building. You must place your order at the front office and within a few minutes your case is brought from the back rooms. It's possible (sometimes) to arrange during the week for a Saturday pickup, otherwise there are no regular Saturday hours. By all means call if you would like more information about their product line; they're very happy to do business with the general public as long as it's understood that you *buy by the case*, and you have to come pick it up! Your incentive is the 50-60% you'll be saving off bakery prices!

MOORE MEAT

1068 Kiley Blvd., Santa Clara 95051. Phone: (408) 249-4545. Hours: Daily 9am-6pm. Purchases: Cash or Check. Parking: Lot.

☞ **Other Stores:** 55 No. Milpitas Blvd., Milpitas; 6918 Almaden Expressway and 2809 So. White Rd., San Jose.

If you're a master planner, and if you're willing to take butcher knife in hand to whittle down these subprimal cuts into manageable portions for your family, you can really save on your beef purchases at *Moore's Meats*. Most of their meats are U.S. Choice (harder to find in most supermarkets these days), or Midwestern cuts (no roll-equivalent to most supermarket private grades). Prices on expensive steaks are at least a dollar off per pound on choice cuts, even more when compared to no roll. The biggest psychological obstacle is shelling out $30-$40 for a large subprimal cut at one time. These cuts are vacuum sealed to preserve freshness, but you will probably want to cut them into family sized portions or steaks before rewrapping and freezing. The fella's at *Moore's* are very helpful when dealing with the novice, they're nice about getting you started as an amateur butcher so you can become a regular customer. *Moore's Meats* also has good prices on cheese, salami, deli meats, pork, veal, chicken parts, etc., etc.

NORTHSIDE WALNUT SHELLING CO.

590 North 5th St., San Jose 95112. Phone: (408) 294-0336. Hours: Oct thru Dec M-F 8am-5pm, Sat 10am-2pm. Jan thru Sept M-F 8am-3pm. Purchases: Cash or Check Only. Parking: Street.

Sweets and snacks filled with dried fruits and nuts are not only tasty and sometimes nutritious, they are also expensive. To trim those costs, consider the good buys on walnuts, pecans, pistachios, almonds, as well as the dried apricots, peaches, pears, prunes, and raisins that are sold at this processing plant. The walnuts from the Patterson and Modesto area are shelled and processed for several namebrand food companies right here. You may purchase fresh nuts and dried fruits in quantity from their office. They have sample packages on display to give you an idea of quantities and size of the nut meat in each package.

When you order, fresh shelled nuts are pulled from their back warehouse. Walnuts are sold in 5 pound boxes for $10.00 and 25 lb. boxes for $43.95. Refrigerated or frozen they will keep for several months. There is no shipping so your best bet is to take orders from several friends, split the gas and make one big haul.

OLD WORLD CHEESE COMPANY

107 Monument Plaza, Pleasant Hill 94523. Phone: 789-9107. Hours: M-Sat 9am-5pm. Purchases: Cash, Check, Food Stamps. Parking: Lot.

Rather barnlike in appearance, the customers seem to appreciate the savings more than the decor. This is a good place for No. Contra Costa residents to stock up on cheeses and other goodies for their pantry. Bulk pastas, cases of canned goods, and other bulk grocery items are bargain priced. One item popular with mothers is the fresh pizza crusts, spread with sauce and cheese — they're ready for the oven.

PAK N' SAVE

762 Sunnyvale/Saratoga Rd., Sunnyvale 94087. Phone: (408) 720-0244. Hours: MTW 9am-9pm, Th & F 9am-10pm, Sat 8am-9pm, Sun 9am-7pm. Purchases: Cash, Check, Food Stamps. Parking: Lot.

☞ **Other Stores:** 255 "D" Street (next to Serra Bowl), Colma; 4950 Almaden Expressway, San Jose; 6525 Florin Rd., 3400 Arden Way, and 7301 Greenback Lane, Sacramento.

One measure of the success of *Pak N' Save* is that they were bought by *Safeway Inc.* in 1983. (That's one way to deal with your competition!) However, they remain a separate entity free to continue with their successful merchandising which has proven popular with consumers across the board. Basically, they are a super warehouse "supermarket", eliminating nonessential frills, and service. Unlike your friendly Safeway store, they will not be your neighborhood banker, instead they'll cash a check for the amount only, and only then with proper I. D. On a checklist of 50 grocery products that I compared to prices at two local supermarkets, I found items to be 4 cents to 70 cents cheaper. This list did not include easy loss leaders typically on sale, but rather the items you must buy, but rarely offered at loss leader prices.

The key to their low prices rests with the reduction in overhead gained by not shelving the merchandise in traditional fashion, but rather in cut-away cartons piled canyon high in their wide aisles, also the use of computer checkout and absence of individual prices marked on each product. Overall, I feel that if you consistently shopped at a *Pak N' Save*, you'd probably save 15-20% off your annual grocery bill, a lot when you realize that a family of five can easily spend $5,000 per year on food. I found their stores to be well stocked with major brands, many specialty and ethnic foods, an abundant produce department, and meat counters practically overflowing. My one complaint: not enough parking spaces.

PRICE CLUB
(See **General Merchandise — Discounters**)

PRICE RITE CHEESE
1385 North Main, Walnut Creek 94596. Phone: 933-2983. Hours: M-Sat 9:30am-6pm. Purchases: Cash or Check. Parking: Street or Lot.

Buy 2 pounds of cheese — save plenty, buy 10 pounds — save even more. Serving local restaurants and caterers as well as the public, *Price Rite* offers both low priced (yet high quality) jack, cheddar, mozzarella and a tremendous assortment of all the fancy cheeses, pates, and specialty meats, at discount prices. Top it off with a bottle of wine, or coffee fresh roasted on the premises, for a delicious "encounter of gourmet kind".

SUGARIPE FARMS
2070 South Seventh St., San Jose 95150. Phone: (408) 280-2349. Hours: M-F 8:30am-4:30pm, Sat-Xmas season only). Purchases: Cash or Check. Parking: Lot.

To buy nuts and dried fruits, you don't have to go all the way to San Jose to take advantage of the bargains at this packer's warehouse store. You can do it over the phone. They'll ship anywhere as long as you pay the freight. If you do go into the store you'll find their own *Sugaripe* brand prunes, dried apricots, dried peaches, dried pears, dried apples, walnuts in their traditional shell (or, walnuts already shelled); also raisins, dates, almonds, cashews, filberts and brazil nuts. These are all sold for lower than supermarket prices. For gifts at holiday time inquire about their holiday gift packs, pre-made to your specifications.

VALLEY CHEESE SHOP

20573 Santa Maria, Castro Valley 94546. Phone: 886-8627. Hours: M-F 9:30am-6pm, Sat 9:30-5pm. Purchases: Cash or Check. Parking: Lot.

Another fragrant, tantalizing cheese shop! Fresh shipments are received four times a week. Prices are competitive with all the other cheese shops listed, but they're particularly appealing to all the local residents who appreciate good prices without having to get on the freeway. Their basic cheeses, i.e. mozzarella, mild cheddar, Monterey Jack hover consistently at $2/lb., while prices on imported Jarlsberg, Harvarti, Roquefort, Gouda, etc. are the lowest in the Castro Valley/Hayward area. Discounts are extended to churches, food co-ops, and youth groups.

PRODUCE

FARMERS MARKET

100 Alemany Blvd., San Francisco 94110. Phone: 647-9423. Hours: T-Sat 7am-5pm. Purchases: Cash Only. Parking: Free Lot.

There is something about openair markets and fresh produce that appeals to everyone. *The Farmers Market*, owned and operated by the City and County of San Francisco for 40 years, attracts growers from 28 counties who truck in their produce to sell. The numbers of growers arriving each week or day depends on the harvest season of their crops. Saturday is the best shopping day. During the summer months all 120 selling stalls are abundant with fresh fruits and vegetables. Consumers can buy by the box or bag. Prices are reasonable, and there's a wonderful comraderie about the whole place. Some of the vendors are real characters. (I noticed that some of the sellers are quite willing to let you sample before you buy, but ominous signs above other stalls read ''no tasting''). Shop early because it gets quite crowded after 11am. On very rainy days, sellers often close early.

GOLDEN GATE PRODUCE TERMINAL

Produce Ave., South San Francisco. Hours: M-F 1:30am-10am. Purchases: Cash or Check. Parking: Street.

Just look for the long row of buildings and then try to find a parking place. Although they will do business with co-ops, you'll not find the service of your friendly neighborhood grocery store.

OAKLAND PRODUCE MART

Dealers located at 2nd & Franklin (near Jack London Square), Oakland. Hours: M-F 1:30am-approx. 11am. Purchases: Cash or Check. Parking: Street.

The *Oakland Produce Mart* handles 90% of the produce sold to independent retailers in the East Bay. The 15 wholesalers buy and sell from a cavernous open stall divided by high wooden walls and floor-to-ceiling wire mesh. They start work about 1:30am, trading peaks early in the morning, and they begin to close at 11am. For housewives seeking escape from high retail food costs, this source is about the best way I know to save money on vegetables, fruit, beans, rice, even peanuts. All the produce is sold by the crate, dozen, or sack.

Co-op shoppers are welcome, as well as individuals willing to buy in bulk quantities. The sellers at the *Produce Mart* prefer selling to the public during the middle of the week. On Mondays, Fridays, and days before and after holidays, they're just too busy.

This is one of the few businesses left that operates by supply and demand. Prices vary according to the quality and kind of food, time of day, and how well the sales are going. You can usually count on savings of at least 25-50%.

Starting a co-op is not difficult and it behooves every bargain hunter to consider the effort and try to round up friends and neighbors to share in the benefits of co-op shopping. Typically, a 12 member/family co-op will delegate 2 members to take a grocery list and "do the shopping". By going early in the morning (about 6:30am), they can make selections, have the car or wagon loaded, and be back home by 7:30am, just in time to get everybody off to school. The buyer's rotation comes about once every three months.

SAN FRANCISCO PRODUCE TERMINAL

2000 block of Jerrold Ave., San Francisco. Hours: 1:30-9:30am. Purchases: Cash or Check. Parking: Street.

This large complex is overwhelming with its high loading docks and vast selection of produce. When I went to shop I felt very insignificant moving around between huge trucks and busy, busy men.

Produce "Down on the Farm"

One way to save money is to go to the source — the grower — and eliminate all those middleman expenses in between. Many farmers and ranchers seasonally set up fruit stands on or near their farms and sell to the public. You benefit in two ways: first, you'll save money; second, you'll be buying really fresh, farm ripened, flavorful produce. It's well worth the drive into the country, especially if you buy in quantity or if you have a talent for home canning. Some farmers invite people to pick their own for even greater savings.

Many farms do not advertise, but the word is spread by satisfied customers who return year after year during the harvest season. The San Jose *Mercury* and San Jose *News* have a classified section entitled "Good Things to Eat", with listings of local growers.

Following is a list of Growers' Associations who print brochures complete with maps pinpointing the growers who sell to the public, the foods they harvest and harvest times. Send a *self-addressed stamped envelope* to the addresses below to get a copy, then plan your summer excursions.

Contra Costa County:
HARVEST TIME
P. O. Box O
Brentwood, Ca. 94513

El Dorado County:
APPLE HILL GROWERS
P. O. Box 494
Camino, Ca. 95709

Sonoma County:
SONOMA COUNTY FARM TRAILS
P. O. Box 6043
Santa Rosa, Ca. 95406.

Yolo and Solano Counties:
YOLANO HARVEST TRAILS
P. O. Box 484
Winters, Ca. 95694.

Furniture and Accessories

General

A. C. GRAPHICS

79 Belvedere Street #12 (1 block East of Francisco Blvd. East.), San Rafael 94901. Phone: 456-0363. Hours: M-F 9am-5pm, Sat 9am-Noon. Purchase: Cash, Check. Parking: Lot.

Seconds on stretched handscreened printed cotton graphics are 50% off the wholesale price. These fine graphics are frequently seen on walls in lobbies and business offices around the Bay. You can buy one or combine two or more to fill a wide expanse of bare wall. Photographs are mounted on masonite and protected with a clear lacquer finish. Available in 16'' x 20'' and 30'' x 40'', they're reduced 75% as seconds. They also sell 2nds and 3rds of fabric for do-it-yourselfers at prices that are hard to beat anywhere. Metal picture frames, cut to size are sold at wholesale prices to the public. Many quiltmakers find *A. C. Graphic's* quality fabrics and prices easy on the wallet. *A. C.* has a space in an industrial complex so be sure to look for door #12 down the side of the building.

A.S.I.D. DESIGNERS SALE

The Galleria, 101 Henry Adams St., (formerly Kansas), San Francisco 94103. Phone: 983-5363 (For sale dates and information check local newspapers). Hours: 10am-4pm. Purchases: VISA MC. Parking: Pay Lots.

For the past several years the *ASID* (American Society of Interior Designers) has sponsored two sales a year to benefit their educational fund. There is a certain mystique regarding this showplace because unless you are a designer, a decorator or working with one it is unlikely that you will have access to the treasures within. These beautiful facilities are the resource centers for designers. The showrooms inside are the repository for some of the finest furnishings in home decorating. Many lines are not displayed through retail furniture stores which makes the prospect of seeing them first hand and having the chance to buy the showroom samples and rejects particularly appealing.

Members of *ASID* staff the sale and receive a percentage of the profits for their fund. They also charge $1.00 for admission. If you are interested in buying living room, dining room and bedroom furniture, outdoor furnishings, antiques and exotic and unusual one-of-a-kind items, consider trekking into the City for the big event. It's advisable to bring carpet, paint, and fabric samples of existing furnishings that figure in your decorating scheme. The designers staffing the sale are very willing to help you with your selections so it's to your benefit to come prepared. Because the showrooms are attempting to clear out the old to make way for the new, prices are reduced 25-60%. Delivery arrangements can be made for you. Watch for announcements in local newspapers for these semi-annual sales. Scheduled dates for 1984-1985 are: Nov. 3rd, 4th, 1984; June 15th & 17th, 1985: and Nov. 16th & 17th, 1985. Information on touring the wholesale showrooms of Showplace Square may be obtained by calling the Showplace Square Tours office at (415) 621-TOUR.

ABBEY RENTS . . . AND SELLS

1314 Post St., San Francisco 94109. Phone: 673-5050. Hours: M-F 8am-5pm. Purchases: MC, VISA. Parking: Street.

We all think of *Abbey Rents* as the best-known renter of all kinds of furniture and equipment. However, are you aware that they have a new name, *"Abbey Rents . . . and Sells,"* and that the same merchandise is also for sale at any one of the stores in the Bay Area? Periodically, certain goods are judged obsolete and put on special sale at each office-warehouse. You can buy furniture, party paraphernalia (in San Francisco store only), sickroom equipment, and reducing gear. The condition of these items ranges from slightly to very used, with prices corresponding. Most are reduced about 40-60% from their original price at the discretion of each individual manager. Occasionally sales are announced in local papers, but it's best to call and inquire at the store nearest you.

ANGELES DISCOUNT FURNITURE

55 4th St (off Oak St.), Oakland 94607. Phone: Pending. Hours: Wed-Sun 10am-6pm. Purchases: MC, VISA, CREDIT PLAN. Parking: Lot.

Angeles has an out-of-the-way location in the East Bay near Jack London Square close to the Nimitz Freeway. Their ads state that they buy closeouts and current lines of furniture from major manufacturers at substantial discounts. They are then able to sell these furnishings at great discounts to the public from their no-frills warehouse store. The selection and quality of furnishings runs the gamut from budget to best with brands like Lane, Broyhill, Bernhardt, Burlington, Basset, Thomasville, American of Martinsville, Hibriten and Mt. Airy in living, dining, bedroom and occasional furniture. Their best selection is in the case goods category i. e. bedroom, casual and formal dining room furniture. This is a terrific place to pick up odds 'n ends like end tables, headboards, mirrors, framed posters, dining room servers, wall units, etc. Their upholstered furniture is well priced and many pieces can be special ordered with 25-35% discounts. The furniture styles include contemporary, traditional, oriental (with many lacquered pieces), and a little bit of everything else found in today's market. The selection changes all the time so one visit is just the beginning. To find what you want you may stop by several times and then *VOILA!* Delivery is provided at an additional charge. Their new warehouse is a cut above the previous one by the Oakland Coliseum that burned down in a spectacular fire in Fall '83.

BREUNERS RENTS CLEARANCE CENTER

1600 Duane Ave., Santa Clara. Phone: (408) 727-7365. Hours: T-Sat 10am-6pm. Purchases: MC, VISA, Store charge. Parking: Lot.

☞ **Other Store:** 3254 Pierce St., Richmond (Albany area).

Breuners has two clearance operations. The first in Santa Clara is geared towards liquidating all their rental returns at prices that must surely appeal to starving artists or students trying to furnish their apartments on small change. Not everything is used, old or tired, occasionally they include new discontinued rental lines at substantial discounts. At their Albany/Richmond store a large section of the store is devoted to clearing out all the leftovers, floor samples, discontinueds, cancelled orders, slightly damaged or distressed furniture and accessory pieces from *Breuners* retail stores at 30-50% off original prices. Each item is tagged with the original price and the as-is clearance price. Delivery is extra and varies according to the size of the item and delivery distance. You may go around in circles trying to find the Santa Clara outlet which is located right next to Fwy. 101, off the San Tomas Expressway.

BUSVAN FOR BARGAINS

900 Battery St., San Francisco 94111. Phone: 981-1405. Hours: M-Sat 9:30am-6pm, Sun Noon-6pm. Purchases: MC VISA and financing. Parking: Validated & pay lots.

☞ **Other Store:** 244 Clement, San Francisco.

Although not your typical furniture store, *Busvan for Bargains* offers real possibilities. Almost anything can be purchased from their huge three-story warehouse: furniture, appliances, rugs, pianos, antiques, paintings, books, bric-a-brac and office furniture. The basement features used furniture that has seen better days, but the prices are rock-bottom. The main floor is filled with furniture from Art Deco through traditional mahogany and walnut pieces. The selection is always changing; it pays to stop by often.

The top floor is crowded with budget-priced and namebrand new furniture at substantial savings over regular retail. Other good values are the large number of floor samples and factory closeouts that *Busvan for Bargains* offers. Although the staff is friendly and helpful, the sheer size of the store makes it primarily selfservice. All sales are final. A 20% deposit will hold merchandise for 30 days. Bring your own station wagon or van; *Busvan* will pad your furniture and tie it on your vehicle for free. The minimum delivery charge is $24.50.

CALIFORNIA FURNITURE RENTAL AND SALES

3021 Kenneth St., Santa Clara 95050. Phone: (408) 727-RENT. Hours: M-F 9:30am-6pm, Sat 10am-6pm. Purchases: MC, VISA. Parking: Lot.

☞ **Other Stores:** 351 Foster City Blvd., Foster City: 2001 Van Ness Ave., San Francisco, 1984 Stevens Creek, San Jose.

If you don't have the time to scout the garage sales, this is the place to go for budget-priced home furnishings. This furniture rental company always has a good selection of used home and office furniture. Some pieces, well — you know they've been used — but they're still usable; sofas for $50-$150 are good values. Then there are many pieces that were on display in apartment or condominium models. They look like new but truly can't be sold as new furniture or for new prices. You'll save 20-40%. Their styles go right down the middle, conventional or traditional — the type that appeals to the majority of people. You can also pick up tables, chairs, lamps, pictures, mattresses, bedroom and dining sets, and accessories. Check their prices on the new furniture too: I saw some good buys.

CHAIR STORE WAREHOUSE OUTLET

701 Bayshore Blvd., San Francisco 94124. Phone: 468-5540. Hours: M-Sat 10am-5pm, Sun Noon-5pm. Purchases: MC, VISA. Parking: Lot.

The *Chair Store* has designated about 25% of the floor space at the San Francisco warehouse store as a clearance department of odds 'n' ends, returns, showroom samples, damaged pieces, and special purchases. Most of this merchandise is marked down 40-50% off the original price. Of course they always have chairs in reproductions of popular traditional styles, classic modern (such as the Breur chair), also bar stools. There's no guarantee you'll find a complete set, on the other hand, occasionally they'll have 20 of the same style. Tables for informal dining in butcher block, oak, or beechwood are always available, plus chopping blocks and work tables. Twice a year there is a super sale at the warehouse where all the stores clean house, send discontinued styles, leftovers, etc. to the warehouse for the big event. This is worth catching just for the bigger selection of bargains. Delivery is extra.

COTTAGE TABLES

101 Brannan (betw. 1st St. & the Embarcadero), San Francisco 94107. Phone: 957-1760. Hours: Tues-Sat Noon-6pm. Purchases: VISA MC. Parking: Lot.

Tony Cowan, the owner of *Cottage Tables*, is a craftsman of the old school. His trademark is the pine table, suitable for kitchen, dining or office environments, that is completely hand made from solid wood using dowel and glue construction. There are no nails, screws or staples in his designs. His tables are then given a handrubbed Varathane finish resulting in a soft sheen that is deceptively durable. The quality and timelessness of design of all of his tables provide the consumer with a 100 year table that can withstand the rigors of family use, and will no doubt be handed down from this generation to the next. When buying tables from his shop, you can see construction in progress, finished products waiting for delivery, and stacks of wood waiting to be used. In addition to his basic 3' by 5' pine table that sells for $300 (the same in oak is $450), he will take orders for tables to suit your dimensions, add turned legs, drawers, etc., and offer a choice of pine, oak, ash, maple or walnut. Delivery is usually made within a month's time. If you need chairs of classic design to go with your tables he sells a line of compatible chairs for a 20% discount off retail prices at other stores. This is an opportunity to get a superbly made table to suit your size requirements at a price that is at least half of what comparable tables sell for in designer showrooms.

DESIGN INNOVATIONS

3349 Sacramento St., San Francisco 94118. Phone: 346-5188. Toll Free: 800-233-5039. Hours: M-Sat 10am-6pm, Sun Noon-5pm. Purchases: MC, VISA. Parking: Street.

In San Francisco the easiest way to see a good selection of brass beds at affordable prices is at this classy store. Their brass "heirlooms" that can be passed from generation to generation are discounted all the time, with extra discounts on selected styles (featured in newspaper and local print ads) offered almost monthly. Pricing on brass beds at retail is generally inflated at most conventional stores (this allows the stores to give the appearance of providing good sale prices when they do advertise a sale); however, *Design Innovations* offers discount pricing on a day in, day out basis. They carry well known lines, and have a good instock inventory for immediate delivery. If you're visiting the area, you can still take advantage of their good prices and have the bed shipped to your home anywhere in the U. S.

EMPORIUM CAPWELL HOME CLEARANCE CENTER

1789 Hillsdale Ave., San Jose, 95124. Phone: (408) 265-1111 ext. 305. Hours: M-F 10am-9pm, Sat 10am-6pm, Sun Noon-5pm. Purchases: Capwell, Broadway, Weinstocks cards or AE. Parking: Lot.

The really sharp consumer will watch the San Jose *Mercury* ads for the frequent 4-day specials when the bargains become "super buys". With 28,000 sq. ft. of floor space you'll have a good selection of furniture for every room in the house, plus area rugs, accessories and household linens. The merchandise is sent to the clearance center from all the stores in Northern California. These are floor samples, some slightly damaged, some discontinued, etc. You can be sure of getting more than your dollars' worth, with discounts of 30-60% off retail all the time. Delivery costs extra. In 1983 *The Good Buy* shop was incorporated into the clearance center. This is where all the leftover apparel from their stores end up for final clearance. This is one of the largest clearance centers in the Bay Area.

FOSS ANNEX

1326 E. 12th St., Oakland 94601. Phone: 534-4133. Hours: M-F 9:30am-5pm. Purchases: Cash or Check. Parking: Street.

The *Foss Annex* is located right next to the *Foss Factory*, a company that has been in business for 65 years making some of the finest lampshades you can buy. Their customers are usually interior decorators (shopping for their clients), hotels, restaurants, and prestige home furnishings stores. They've been entrusted with the job of restoring and replacing shades for places as famous as the Hearst Castle.

Occasionally something goes wrong in the factory; an imperfection in fabric, finishing, construction, or patterns becomes evident on the final inspection. These "misfits" are sent to the annex, where less fickle people like you or me will delight at marked-down prices. Since all Foss shades are handmade, even outlet prices may seem high until you consider the level of craftsmanship and original pricing. You can spend from $6 to $50. Be sure to bring your lamp in with you (you wouldn't buy a hat without trying it on). On floor lamps just bring in the measurements of the reflector bowl. Pick up a simple basic shade, then jazz it up with some of their trims.

ERIC FREY, W.

1618 Fourth St., San Rafael 94901. Phone: 459-6666. Hours: M-Sat 11am-6pm, Sun & Eve. by appt. Purchases: MC VISA. Parking: Street.

Buying a brass bed is a timeless purchase, but finding it at a reasonable price is something else. *W. Eric Frey* specializes in selling several name brands of brass and iron beds, solid oak reproduction lines of rolltop desks, and leather chairs and sofas. He trims his prices (35-50% off retail) by taking a smaller markup, operating essentially a one man business, and buying right from the source. Depending upon whether you're buying a complete set (headboard, endboard and rails), or the size of your order, delivery may or may not be included. He sells both uncoated and coated styles. He has a good showroom selection available for immediate delivery but additionally he can special order many other styles from several catalogues. Special orders may take from one to eight weeks for delivery. I particularly appreciate his low key approach in selling. He can't provide the same big discount on other merchandise he sells, like brass lamps, hand quilted bedspreads and comforters, mattresses and boxsprings, but he does very well offering about 30-50% off prevailing retail. If you've shopped around, there is little more he needs to say, because his prices say it all. Directions: Central San Rafael exit off Hwy. 101 from North or South, then west on 5th St. about 10 blocks to "G" St. Turn left, go 1 block to 4th and "G" (corner).

FRELLEN'S

2095 San Ramon Blvd., San Ramon 94583. Phone: 837-7787. Hours: T-Sat 9:30am-5:30pm, Sun 11:30am-4:30pm. Purchases: MC, VISA. Parking: Lot.

Prices on patio furniture are rarely sold for the manufacturer's list price. Most competitive stores sell for less, but *Frellen's* consistently trims their prices just a little bit more than all the others. They're lucky to own their own building, reducing overhead, and after many years in the business they've established a solid following resulting in volume purchasing power. One sure way to offer good prices is to buy right, taking advantage of special incentive programs offered by manufacturers during off-season or pre-season periods, and then passing on these discounts to customers. At *Frellen's* the best buys are from Washington's birthday through March, and from mid-August to mid-October. The selection is not necessarily best at these times, but prices are reduced 35-50% off original list prices, while during the season prices are discounted 25-35% with even lower prices on selected lines during special promotions. Even better, they have a wonderful and extensive inventory of many fine lines, from moderately priced to the Cadillac lines, ready to be delivered. If they don't have every piece in a line you want, they can always special order. The styles, finishes, fabrics, and colors available in patio furniture (including umbrellas) are a far cry from the redwood tables prevalent from my childhood days. Now most manufacturers offer matching chaises, end tables, gliders, glass tops, etc. all designed to create a patio that is as elegant and classy as many living rooms.

Frellen's maintains their sales during the off-season by stocking a large inventory of rattan and fireplace furnishings. The rattan, geared for the family room and informal life styles, is discounted 30-35% all the time. Just minimal savings are available on the fireplace accessories. Delivery to local customers is free, out of the area rates are very reasonable.

GIORGI FURNITURE

212 Baden Ave., South San Francisco. Phone: 588-4621 or 872-1311. Hours: M-Sat 9am-6pm, Fri eve till 9pm. Purchases: Cash, Check, Financing arranged. Parking: Street.

If you would like to shop where you can buy for immediate delivery and at a good discount price, *Giorgi Furniture* in South San Francisco has a very large furniture selection for every room in your home. Their tags have one price which is their discount price (usually 33% off prevailing retail), plus mfg.'s name and model #. A very popular kitchen set made from solid oak (42" with one leaf), 4 chairs with castors and fabric seats, priced at $850 in most stores, $749 on sale, is always $600.60 at *Giorgi*.

When you're ready for living room sofas they'll have about 100 on the floor, about 60 dining room and bedroom sets, grandfather clocks for every budget, carpeting, mattresses, appliances, chairs, occasional tables etc. etc. If you live on the Peninsula delivery will be free if you spend over $600. Like most places with good prices, it follows that parking is lousy, but that may improve in a few months. *Giorgi* is not an elegant store although many of their furnishings are. Medium to higher priced fine quality brands are found in their store along with a few modestly priced brands. Of course, they can special order if their vast selection does not provide what you want.

HOMESTORE

1115 S. Saratoga-Sunnyvale Road, San Jose 95129. Phone: (408) 255-5900. Hours: M-Sat 10am-6pm. Thurs Noon-9pm, Sun Noon-5pm. Purchases: MC, VISA.

Scandinavian design (contemporary) furniture is often a better buy than the more traditional, higherpriced fine quality lines for the young or beginning householder, especially college students who may move in and out every year to a new apartment. The natural or lacquered finishes are easy to maintain and knock down (known in the industry as k.d.). This construction makes it easy to carry the boxed items out of the store and less expensive to move them from one place to another.

There are two basic reasons for the lower price of Scandinavian designed and manufactured furnishings. The first is that the knocked down pieces are shipped to the United States in large containers, which helps to keep transportation costs down. The second is that the continued strength of the U.S. dollar has enabled furniture buyers to make better deals with overseas manufacturers. In the Bay Area the *Homestore* applies this concept to their business.

Their new location in San Jose is stocked with an impressive selection of furniture for the bedroom, living room, dining room, and office. In keeping with the times, they also have a good selection of computer tables and desks.

Their youth or teen lines of bedroom furnishings, that help organize and create an efficient storage system for clothing, toys and student needs, are very popular. These lines also do double duty in guest rooms or second homes. For young families with modest budgets, it's possible to start with a few basic pieces and expand as the need and funds arrive. Their sofas and other upholstered lines, that are made in Southern California, are sold on a shorter markup reflecting a 25% discount from other retail sources.

Unless otherwise stated, all exposed surfaces are in genuine wood, veneers and solids. Prices on the showroom samples at the *Homestore* reflect the k.d. price (sold in cartons, unassembled). This applies not only to the case goods, but also to many upholstered pieces. Delivery is left to you. By loading the cartons in your car or truck, you save considerably. For those without means of delivery, referrals to delivery services will be made by the store, payment and arrangements are your responsibility. If you think assembling k.d. furniture requires special skill, relax, it's about as difficult as Lincoln Logs, Legos or Tinkertoys. If it's been awhile since you considered Scandinavian or European contemporary furniture, it's time for a second look.

LAWRENCE CONTRACT FURNISHERS
(See **Carpeting**)

MACY'S FURNITURE CLEARANCE PLACE
5160 Stevens Creek Blvd. San Jose 95129. Phone: 248-6343. Hours: M-F 10am-9pm, Sat 9:30am-6pm, Sun Noon-5pm. Purchases: Cash, Check, Macy's charge. Parking: Lot.

☞ **Other Store:** 567 Floresta Blvd., San Leandro.

Macy's Furniture Clearance Place is where you'll find furniture for 20-50% off. Some pieces are purchased just for *Clearance Place* (budget lines never found in *Macy's* regular stores); others are buyers' mistakes, distressed or damaged goods, department store overstocks, and discontinued models or lines. You can shop for almost any room in your home for furnishings, appliances and entertainment needs. Delivery is extra and you'll want to look your selection over carefully, since all sales are final. You can use your *Macy's* charge account to arrange special terms.

Their linen department, which occupies a space at the back of the store, is where I have found good buys on sheets, towels, comforters, bedspreads, bath rugs, etc. When all these discontinued lines, broken lots and leftovers arrive here from the 16 other stores, they are priced below cost. By this time *Macy's* wants them sold and out of their warehouses where space is always in demand.

In the last year, consumers have been beating a path to the clearance centers just to buy apparel sent there after surviving several sales and interim markdowns. This leaves many garments a little "tired". The irresistible bargains have orange tags which means that the last marked price is further reduced 50% at the cash register. Merchandise comes in every Tuesday and Thursday; markdowns are ongoing. Be sure to check every rack, and every garment. There're treasures buried in the midst of less appealing merchandise. Expect to find apparel from any of *Macy's* departments in all price ranges and qualities, for men, women and children.

NATIONAL SOFA BED AND MATTRESS CO.
2328 Telegraph Ave., Oakland 94612. Phone: 444-2112. Hours: M-Sat 9am-6pm, Sun 11:30am-4:30pm. Purchases: VISA, MC. Parking: Street, free lot.

You'll find good values in furniture and appliances at *National*. To start with, here is a great way to get a good quality Simmons mattress at savings up to 50% off. There are usually many slightly irregular factory seconds of mismatched sets to choose from. The defects or flaws are carefully explained to you when you are making a selection. They also have first-quality mattresses, as well as an extensive selection of sofabeds.

Savings on nationally advertised namebrand sofabeds are 25% off. I recognized some truly worthwhile savings on this good quality name brand furniture. Each piece has two prices, the lowest representing the special values offered by this company. If you have shopped around you will recognize the savings available. Most sales will include free delivery. *National* has a complete G. E. appliance department, all with gratifying discount prices. Finally, they are an excellent resource for carpeting from namebrand manufacturers.

NIGEL'S
1450 Franklin Street, San Francisco 94109. Phone: 776-5490. Hours: M-F 10am-5:30pm, Sat 10am-4pm. Purchases: MC, VISA. Parking: Validated, Sutter Place Garage.

It's rather hard to comparison shop imported oriental furniture but I feel *Nigel's* offers far better values, dollar for dollar, than stores selling comparable quality furniture in the Chinatown and downtown areas that cater to the tourist trade. The showroom has a beautiful selection of dining, living, and bedroom furniture, standing Coromandel screens, as well as occasional pieces in a choice of natural or dark rosewood. All sofas and chairs are offered in a choice of fabrics. I was particularly impressed that the backs of all cabinet pieces are finished and need not be set up against the wall. I also found the owners to be very knowledgeable and helpful!

PACIFIC FURNITURE RENTAL
600 50th Ave., Oakland 94601. Phone: 533-3700. Hours: M-F 9:30am-5:30pm. Purchases: MC, VISA. Parking: Lot.

☞ **Other Store:** 124 Belvedere St., San Rafael, 456-9130.

You can't complain about the prices on the used rental furniture for sale in the back room. Club chairs for $69.95, sofas for $129, and loveseat combinations in herculon plaids for $359, roll-away beds for $59.95, $99 for a kitchen table with four chairs and on and on. Some furniture looks a little worse for the wear, but is priced accordingly. The conventional image of rental furniture has changed dramatically in the last 20 years. At one time it was perceived as being only of the Danish modern period. Today, you'll find the same furniture styles for rent that you see for sale in most retail stores.

SEARS FURNITURE OUTLET
1963 West Ave-140th St., San Leandro 94577. Phone: 357-6622. Hours: M-Sat 9:30am-5:30pm, Sat 9am-4:30pm. Purchases: Cash, check, Sears charge. Parking: Lot.

☞ **Other Store:** Florin Rd., Sacramento

Sears warehouse in San Leandro has a showroom which has (slightly) freight-damaged and returned furniture for sale at reduced prices. The customer returns have been reconditioned, and all bedding has been sterilized. There is usually a selection of more than 50 large appliances and televisions (your best buys here), and a smaller group of furniture, upholstered pieces, and mattresses. There are also accessory items, such as tables, also building supplies (doors, heaters, central air conditioners, and fencing). The *Sears* warranty applies to all appliances purchased. You must pay for delivery — so, if you can, bring a truck.

THE SLEEPER
2172-C San Ramon Valley Blvd. (off Hwy. 680 & West Crow Canyon Rd.), San Ramon 94583. Phone: 831-1011. Purchases: MC VISA. Parking: Lot.

Overhead is a key factor in establishing pricing for any retail business. A visit to *The Sleeper* in San Ramon will convince you that their prices, 35-50% off retail, are due in part to the absence of gracious amenities and decor. Their service, however, is accommodating and friendly, in keeping with their desire to be a successful family-owned and operated bargain resource. If you're shopping for moderately priced lines of sofa beds, trundle beds, adjustable beds, day beds, roll-a-way beds, mattresses etc., you'll love their minimal markups. Additionally, their prices on brass and iron bed frames are excellent! Delivery is additional ranging from $20-$40 depending on the distance from the store. You can borrow sample fabrics and special order any item at the same discount as in-store merchandise. Watch for the Brass Door restaurant, then drive to the back of the parking area where their modest store is located.

SOFA BEDS LTD.

7190 Regional Street, Dublin 94566. Phone: 828-2401. Hours: M-F 10am-9pm, Sat 10am-6pm, Sun Noon-5pm. Purchases: MC, VISA. Parking: Lot.

There's no fancy merchandising evident here, instead their aim is to provide as extensive a selection as possible in the space allowed. Their basic concept is to make a profit through volume sales rather than high markups. Therefore, you can expect to save 25-40% on sofabeds from approximately twelve major manufacturers including Simmons, Serta and Michael Kaye. The best buys are on sofabed and loveseat combinations and sectional sleeper combinations. They concentrate on offering a wide selection in fabrics and styles on medium priced pieces that become terrific bargains when the discount is applied. The average price is somewhere around $500, with many good buys for far less and a smaller selection of higher end goods often acquired through special purchases from the *Furniture Mart* showrooms. Some pieces are just right in the anonymity of the back bedroom, others formal enough for the living room, and most are perfect for the casual living and heavy use in a family room. For a really custom selection they will special order and extend a discount that may not be as great as in-stock merchandise, but is still worthwhile. Their name doesn't indicate that they also sell a diverse selection of beds (trundle, brass, flotation systems, electric, etc.) and box springs and mattresses at the same solid discount prices, but they do. Delivery charges are minimal.

WELLS INTERIORS INC.

10065 East Estates Rd., Brentwood Shopping Ctr., Cupertino 95014. Phone: (408) 252-6650, or (toll free 1-800-546-8982). Hours: M-F 10am-6pm, Sat 10am-5pm. Purchases: MC, VISA. Parking: Lot.

☞ **Other Stores:** 801 Third St. (at Lincoln) San Rafael, 459-1355; 1983 No. Main (corner Ygnacio), Walnut Creek, 930-9631; 7171 Amador Plaza, Dublin, 829-2121; 7357 Greenback Ln., Sacramento, (916) 723-3500.

Almost daily you can spot an ad for a discount price on mini blinds or similar window coverings in your local newspapers, sometimes offering discounts as much as 40-50% off retail. Occasionally these discounts are taken from inflated price lists. I have found that *Wells Interiors Inc.* consistently offers 50% off the manufacturer's list price on major brands and types of window coverings. They are able to offer these tempting discounts because of the tremendous volume of business they do nationwide from ads placed in leading home publications. Because of this volume they are extended a distributor's discount and can therefore discount 50% and still make a reasonable profit. Their 50% discounts apply to Levolor 1'' Mini Blinds (available in three different qualities), Levolor Vertical Blinds in cloth or fabric, Verosol (energy efficient) pleated shades, Bali Mini Blinds, Louver Drape Vertical Blinds, private label wood blinds, and finished or unfinished wood shutters. You receive a 40% discount on all Kirsch and Del Mar window coverings. The discount price includes UPS shipping charges, but doesn't include installation or measuring services. If merchandise is too big to ship by UPS, a freight charge will be added. Installation of most window coverings can be done by anyone with the ability to read instructions and use a screwdriver.

You can order directly by visiting their stores, or you can use their toll free phone service. If you're wary about ordering over the phone, bear in mind that the *Wells* people are pros. They will first send you a complete package of product information, including samples and measuring instructions. Next, they will clarify any questions you may have over the phone. Through experience they've learned how to avoid mistakes. Finally, if your windows are taken care of, you might want to check their prices on namebrand carpeting, vinyl flooring and Bruce Hardwood flooring kits that are discounted 20 — 30% off retail.

Baby Furniture New & Used

BABYLANDIA
6340 Mission St., Daly City 94014. Phone: 992-1750. Hours: M-Sat 10am-6pm. Purchases: MC, VISA. Parking: Street.

Babylandia has a smaller selection of new furniture when compared to the quantity of "mature" used furniture and baby equipment. Many people recycle their new and used furniture year after year as their needs change. I'd suggest calling ahead to check availability on specific types of items, because the choicest used pieces move fast. Their clothing category has grown with predominately used, budget priced clothing and a smaller selection of new at 20% discounts. Sizes are 0-14.

BABY FURNITURE UNLIMITED
Paradise Shopping Center, 5627 Paradise Dr., Corte Madera 94925. Phone: 924-3764. Hours: M-Sat 10am-5pm, Sun Noon-4pm. Purchases: Cash, Check and trade.

☞ **Other Store:** 1029 First St, Novato, 892-2644.

Eventhough they've expanded, there is still hardly room to navigate around the crowded floor which is jammed with "quality" reusable baby furniture and equipment. Starting with very basic needs, i.e. cribs, playpens, high chairs, strollers, etc., they also have some unusual items like wicker bassinets, baby carriers, and snuggle pouches. Recently, they've started carrying and selling (at a good discount price) major lines of infant furniture and equipment. They can also special order from catalogs. You don't have to be "truly needy" to appreciate the racks of clothing (mostly used) for infants and children. They have both new and used maternity clothing plus children's shoes. Keep in mind that while they're primarily interested in selling goods, in order to do this they are buying all the time: so if you're not interested in buying, maybe you've got something to sell. Of special interest to baby's relatives is their new rental policy on all baby furniture and equipment.

BABYWEAR OUTLET
(See **Children's Apparel**)

BABY SUPER DISCOUNT
522 So. Bascom Ave., San Jose 95128. Phone: 293-0358. Hours: M-Sat 9:30-5:30pm, Thurs eve till 9pm. Purchases: VISA, MC, Lay-a-way. Parking: Lot.

☞ **Other Store:** 536 So. Bascom Ave., San Jose.

It's not easy to keep prices low when competing with catalog discount firms like *Best Products* and *Consumers Distributing*. *Baby Super Discount* often beats their prices and offers more by way of selection both in quality and merchandise. Prospective parents can completely prepare for the coming "event" in purchasing anything that a baby would require for the first 18 months. This includes infant clothing, diapers, blankets, plus cribs, high chairs, car seats, etc. The owners are pros. If you're overwhelmed with choices, they can help you determine your needs and also keep you within your budget. It helps that they offer a

six month no interest lay-a-way period. Occasionally they take advantage of manufacturers' overruns or overproduction, and irregulars, because then they can discount even more. Make sure you canvas both of their stores (which are just six doors apart). At the 536 address, they display all the wood furniture and coordinating case goods plus mattresses, soft goods to dress the cribs etc. They also show juvenile furniture, i.e. bunk beds, trundle beds, and dressers. At their main store they show all the layette goods, clothing, strollers, car seats, high chairs, porta-cribs etc. In deference to the car seat safety leglislation, there is an entire room devoted to car seats.

LOU'S BABY FURNITURE
221 Willow Ave. (from A Street, take Princeton to Willow), Hayward 94541. Phone: 581-6082. Hours: TWFS 9:30am-5:30pm. Th 9:30am-9pm. Purchases: MC, VISA. Parking: Lot.

This is a most unconventional store. Years ago when this family wanted to get started in business they didn't rent a store downtown; instead they cleared out their garage and put up a sign. Their garage is now a small warehouse located behind the family home. Low overhead, no frills, and no advertising account for the low, low prices. All the major brands of fine-quality furniture are available — everything for babies' needs except clothing and toys. Simmons, Strollee, Peterson, Childcraft and Hedstrom are among the brands represented in cribs, playpens, high chairs, dressers, infant seats, etc. All those hard-to-find repair parts will keep your furniture going through several children. They also have good values on used furniture. They accept trade-ins and lay-a-ways and also rent furniture. If you're not in any great rush, put your name on their mailing list and catch their super sales 2-3 times a year.

PORTIGOL'S

5424 Geary Blvd., San Francisco 94121. Phone: 752-0989. Hours: M-Sat 9:30am-6pm. Purchases: MC, VISA. Parking: Street.

Portigol's has a wonderful selection of children's clothing, layette goodies, baby and infant equipment plus accessories at fairly typical retail prices, but they really shine in the furniture department in terms of price. Their upstairs room is well stocked with bunk beds, chest beds, dressers, matching sets, headboards, canopies, bookcases, and desks all priced at 25% off retail. The have modestly priced lines and better ones including the latest "made-to-last" lines of modular oak and pine units that can be ordered finished or unfinished. These sturdy, functional, well designed lines have become very popular with parents for their durability and clean lines. A 20% deposit is required for special orders (if they don't have just the exact item you want), otherwise deliveries can be made in a few days. Set up and delivery charges are modest.

Warehouse Sales

Major stores like *Emporium-Capwells* and *Macy's* have major warehouse sales 2-3 times a year. The reason is obvious. Space is a problem in their warehouses just like it is in your closet at home. These sales are well advertised in all major Bay Area newspapers, usually accompanied with maps to lead you directly to these sites, far removed from the retail stores, most often located in some obscure industrial area. At these sales the major emphasis is on clearing out the hard lines of merchandise, i.e. furniture, appliances, and boxsprings, etc. However, accessories, remnant rugs, linens, and housewares are usually sold too.

If you want first crack at the sale merchandise you'd better bounce out of bed early on those weekend mornings. There are so many one-of-a-kind items, priced so low, that you can't afford to dally. All sales are final. Usually delivery is extra, so if you want to save even more, borrow a pickup from a friend and forget the delivery charges.

Catalog Discounters

When it comes to buying new furniture for your home or office, the catalog discounters offer the best alternative to high retail prices. The businesses I have listed are all similar in that they take a lower markup, eliminate costly services, and usually don't advertise. Since their businesses are maintained on referrals and reputation alone, it is significant that they can be so successful without advertising. (You wouldn't send a friend to a place you'd been dissatisfied with.) Some of these places have no furnishings at all on their showroom floors; some have quite a lot. Most of their sales are from manufacturers' catalogs. Buying furniture this way will usually enable you to save from 20-40%. You'll pay for freight and delivery one way or another, whether they quote just one price or a breakdown on the costs. Most do not have credit plans other than Mastercharge or VISA.

CONTRACT DESIGN ASSOCIATES, INC.

5525 College Avenue (between Broadway and Bart), Oakland 94618. Phone: 654-2200. Hours: M-F 9am-5am. Purchases: MC, VISA. Parking: Street (watch the meter!).

Contract Design Associates offers personal service and discount pricing on a wide range of home furnishings. There are no showroom displays of furniture, just catalogs from better lines of major furniture and carpet companies. Discounts range from 20-40% depending on the particular source, freight costs, and prices they pay. With no showroom, I'd suggest you shop around a bit to ascertain what styles and brands appeal, then you can browse through their catalogs and make final selections. The staff feels they can provide the best service when working by appointment. That way when you're ready to do business, they'll be free to accommodate you. Deposits of 50% are required on most orders.

CONTRACT DESIGN CENTER

1985 San Ramon Valley Blvd., San Ramon 94583. Phone: 838-1772. Hours: M-F 9am-5pm, Sat 9am-4pm. Purchases: MC, VISA. Parking: Lot.

Southern Alameda County and Contra Costa residents can now buy all their furniture closer to home at discount prices. Except for the prices, service approximates that of other retail stores. Their showroom is notable for the many fine quality furniture groupings in the moderate to higher price ranges. Furniture is discounted 20-30% which *does not* include freight and delivery. Wallpaper from any book is 25% off, wood shutters are 30% off, and upholstery and drapery fabrics are 20% off. Other areas covered are carpeting, vinyl flooring, window coverings, lamps, patio furniture and mattresses. All furnishings in the store are tagged with the retail price and the discount price is provided by the sales personnel. Refer to their catalogs from major, fine furniture companies for additional choices that can be custom ordered. Phone quotes will be given, how nice.

DEOVLET & SONS

1660 Pine Street, San Francisco 94109. Phone: 775-8014. Hours: M 8am-9pm, T-Sat 8am-6pm. Purchases: MC, VISA. Parking: Validated parking, Union 76 Station at Pine and Franklin.

This store has been around for a long time and for good reason. The children of their original customers are returning to get the same good values and prices that their parents received 25 years ago. *Deovlet* has three floors of furniture. They appear to be energy conscious; you have to have someone turn on the lights of the second and third floor if you expect to get a good look at the bed, dining, breakfast and living room furnishings. They have very moderately priced goods in upholstered lines, better quality in case goods for bedroom and dining room and many major lines of appliances. Their carpet selection is somewhat limited but their prices are excellent on what they carry. Don't be shattered by those retail prices, they're just for show. You can count on a 25-30% discount when it comes to writing out the check.

EASTERN FURNITURE CO. OF CALIF. INC.

1231 Constock St., Santa Clara 95050. Phone: 248-3772. Hours: M,T,Th 9:30am-9pm, WF & Sat 9:30am-5:30pm. Purchases: MC, VISA. Parking: Lot.

Upon entering this store which is right off the Central Expressway you'll be greeted by a receptionist. She will provide you with a salesperson who will familiarize you with the showroom. There is a very good selection of quality home furnishings including sofas, chairs, bedroom, formal and informal dining, occasional tables, mattresses, lamps, accessories and even grandfather clocks. All are in the moderate and upper price range. Don't be taken back by the price tags, which may not reflect the bargain price you'd expect, yet you'll pay about 30% less. The styles are traditional, period and contemporary. You can choose from the floor selection or from their complete catalogs. They ask you to be discreet about their prices. It's unfortunate that stores often have their lines jeopardized by the unthinking customer who quotes their prices to other retail stores. Let's not ruin a good thing! To shop here you need a membership card or referral. Check with them to see if your company is on their list, or call to inquire about your shopping privileges.

DON ERMANN ASSOCIATES

1717-17th Street, San Francisco 94103. Phone: 621-7117. Hours: M-Sat 9am-5pm. Purchases: MC, VISA. Parking: Street.

This company has been established for many years, but recently moved closer to the center of the home furnishings industry in the City near Showplace Square. Basically they work like most other outfits that offer quality furnishings at discount prices. They will work closely with you in making selections from their extensive catalog collection of the better furniture manufacturers; also carpets, floor coverings, fabrics and wallpapers. They will take serious customers to the Galleria or Showplace to evaluate potential choices. It's nice to have a chance to sit, touch, and feel the merchandise before ordering. I found their staff to be most accommodating, never pushy, and very knowledgeable. Pricing is straight forward. They subtract 40% from the retail price, then add freight and delivery. Of course, charges for freight and delivery can vary considerably from item to item which also effects the final percentage of discount. Appointments are appreciated but not required. Their store is just off 17th St on Carolina.

FRENCH BROS.

1850 Market St. San Francisco 94102. Phone: 621-6627. Hours: M-F 9:30-6pm, Sat 9:30-4pm. Purchases: Cash or Check. Parking: Street and Lot.

If it weren't for the sign right at the edge of the parking lot you might never find this furniture store. When you reach the door and see the stairs leading to the showroom, you marvel at the success of such an unconventional location. *French Bros* has been in business in San Francisco for 27 years. They are an excellent resource for appliances, and home furnishings. They have recently expanded their carpet selection to cover a price range from $7/yard to $60/yard, installed. In addition to residential jobs, they also specialize in apartment and commercial installations. Their showroom has three vignettes of lovely home furnishings for starters, then you have their catalog resources from fine furniture companies. For those who want to sit and feel, they will take you to two local sofa manufacturers to make selections.

GALLERY WEST

130 De Haro (between Alameda & 15th Sts.) San Francisco 94103. Phone: 861-6812. Hours: T-Sat 9am-5pm. Purchases: MC, VISA, Financing available. Parking: Street.

Gallery West has an absolutely beautiful showroom with many traditional groupings of furniture. Combined with their gracious service and considerable expertise your shopping excursion should result in complete satisfaction. Like others they complement their showroom selection with many catalog resources and samples from leading manufac-

turers of sofas, chairs, bedroom and dining room furnishings, occasional tables, lamps, accessories, draperies, window coverings, carpeting, vinyl and hardwood flooring, appliances and TV's. In short, they provide one-stop shopping. With their recent move next to the Showplace Square area, their serious customers have access to all the wholesale showrooms of the area in making their furniture selections. Their staff of design professionals can provide complete design services at no extra cost when combined with major purchases. Their prices usually reflect a discount of 25-30% off the prices of conventional retail stores, and their appliances are sold for "their" cost, plus 10%. Delivery is extra. *Gallery West* works closely with many employee groups providing cards of introduction. Check with your employee credit union, personnel office or employees club to see if arrangements have been made for your group and, if not, suggest they be made.

HOMEWORKS

522 Center St. (bet. Longs Drugs & Safeway) Moraga, 94556. Phone: 376-7750. Hours: T-Sat 10am-4:30pm. Purchases: MC, VISA. Parking: Street.

This store in Moraga provides convenient shopping for Contra Costa shoppers. The store is small, more like a posh decorator's studio, but the resources for home furnishings are extensive. You can order carpeting, vinyl and hardwood flooring, drapery and upholstery fabrics, shutters, wallpapers, furniture and accessories from their samples and catalogs. Customers are pampered here, with excellent service from their design and sales staff. Savings range from 20-40% off retail prices, depending on the price they can get. Delivery and freight are extra. They request a 50% deposit with the order and the remainder on delivery.

HOUSE OF KARLSON

351 9th St., San Francisco 94103. Phone: 863-3640. Hours: M-Sat 9am-5pm. Purchases: Cash or Check. Parking: Street and validated parking.

The biggest advantage to doing business with *House of Karlson* is their beautifully displayed, well-stocked 30,000 square foot showroom. They show a selection of very fine copies of English and American antiques, many familiar brands of high priced furniture lines (usually displayed in elegant splendor in the posh trade magazines), plus moderately priced lines in teen bedroom sets, game room tables, family room wall units, and other furnishings for every room in the house. If you're really in the dark about what you want, a visit and stroll through their showroom will give you a good overview of the many styles, qualities, and options you have in making your choices. They do a very good job with carpet prices specifically on their special purchases of Class A seconds that they can sell at original wholesale prices. Their discounts range from 25-30% off retail and you save more when you can handle delivery yourself and in many instances do minor assembly.

HOUSE OF VALUES

2565 So. El Camino Real, San Mateo 94403. Phone: 349-3414. Hours: M-Sat 9:30am -5:30pm, Fri eve 7pm-9pm. Purchases: VISA MC. Parking: Street.

It seems like *House of Values* has swallowed up several stores on this block. Just when I think I've seen everything I'm directed out the door and down the street to their next showroom. Many people reported on the outstanding selection and savings offered. I have to agree after shopping their merchandise for comparison. Although they sell no carpeting or draperies, their in-store selection of fine quality dining room furniture is quite extensive. You can save a minimum of 33% (including freight and delivery) and also have immediate delivery on showroom furnishings. They will also custom order furniture from their catalogs or from designer showrooms at Showplace Square if they don't have the pieces you want.

HOUSE OF LOUIE
(See **Appliances**)

LAWRENCE CONTRACT FURNISHERS
(See **Carpets and Floorcoverings**)

MASTER MART

2515 El Camino Real, San Mateo 94403. Phone: 345-5271 or 341-3246. Hours: M-Sat 9am-6pm, evenings by appt. Purchases: VISA, MC. Parking: Street.

Their cost, plus 10% is the inducement for many customers who've done business with this small store. They quote one price which includes all services, freight and delivery. Basically a custom catalog operation, I'd suggest that you shop around first because they have only a few pieces of furniture to show. They also sell appliances and carpets, window blinds, shutters and draperies. With 30 years experience, they can provide intelligent advice based on their in-depth research on important new products. Once you've bought your new furniture, talk to them about buying your old stuff. They own a used furniture store, and may be willing to add your furnishings to their selection.

MILLBRAE FURNITURE COMPANY

1781 El Camino Real, Millbrae 94030. Phone: 761-2444, 344-6782, 589-6455. Hours: T, Th 10am-6pm, W,F, 10am-9pm, Sat 9am-5pm. Purchases: VISA, MC. Parking: Street, City Lot (side of bldg.)

Three floors of furniture, appliances, carpets, draperies, TV's, VCR's and stereo equipment make this a one-stop resource for consumers. In their back room there are cabinets full of manufacturers' catalogues that provide additional resources for their customers. On most items the savings run about 30% off prevailing retail prices; however, appliances are 10% over cost. Like most discounters they rarely advertise but do a steady business based on referrals.

MONROE SCHNEIDER ASSOCIATES
(See **Carpets and Floor Coverings**)

DAVID MORRIS CO.

253 So. Van Ness Ave., San Francisco 94103. Phone: 861-6111. Hours: M-Sat 9am-5:30pm. Purchases: MC, VISA, 30-90 day cash payment plans. Parking: Private Lot.

This is a small company with few furniture pieces on their floor, yet they offer good savings on custom orders from major catalogs and carpet samples. They also sell major brands of appliances including VCR's and stereos. You'll save 30% on almost all purchases including freight and delivery. For those making large purchases, decorator assistance is available. A deposit is requested at the time the order is placed with the balance due on delivery.

NOREIGA FURNITURE

1455 Taraval (at 25th Ave.), San Francisco 94116. Phone: 564-4110. Hours: M,T,W,F 10am-5:30pm, Th 1pm-9pm, Sat 10am-5pm. Purchases: VISA, MC. Parking: Street.

Noriega Furniture is highly appealing for two things in particular: their beautiful showroom and their personable decorator consultants. Their specialty is expensive high-quality furniture; you can order from their manufacturers' catalogs everything you could conceivably need to decorate your home — furniture, carpets, draperies, wallpaper, and beautiful accessories — at savings of at least 20% and as much as 30%. *Noreiga Furniture* stresses quality and in doing so everything is inspected and serviced in their shop prior to delivery into your home. They ask that you stop by the showroom to get an idea of what you want, though their decorators will go to most Bay Area communities with samples. You deposit 25-30% of the total when you order, and pay the rest on delivery (delivery is included in the price). All sales are final — no returns. They can arrange financing for you too.

PIONEER HOME SUPPLY

667 Mission St. (4th floor), San Francisco 94105. Phone: 543-1234, 781-2374. Hours: M-F 9:30am-5:30pm, Occasional Saturdays (call first). Purchases: Cash or Check Only. Parking: Street or Pay Lot.

Real bargain hunters love to compare their "war stories" after shopping at this store: like how long they waited, how the sofas are standing on end (there's not enough room to set them down), how they wrote up their own order, how many times they phoned before getting through — but they're really not complaining. When considering the money they've saved, they're perfectly willing to accept a few trade-offs.

The delightful owners (they're Sam and Lucille to everyone) have been in business for over 30 years on the strength of their reputation and referrals that pass from one satisfied customer to another. They don't advertise, and you'd have to be psychic to discover them on your own. Their only problem is that they have too much business, and not enough help. Therefore, be warned. There's no one to hold your hand while you leaf through catalogs, no design service, it's strictly tell them what you want, and they'll give you a price — a very good one. They operate with the smallest markup around on home furnishings and appliances.

When you buy something off their floor, or from their stock rooms they'll give you "such a deal" just to keep the merchandise moving. Custom orders from catalogs of living, dining, bedroom sets, sofabeds, recliners, patio furnishings, etc. will be about 35-40% off retail. The markups on appliances like TV's, refrigerators, dishwashers, disposals, microwaves, etc. are computed on a "minimal" cost plus basis. Many popular appliance models, TV's, and mattresses are stocked for immediate delivery. Their carpet prices are especially good and in this area they do try to find the time to help you with such an important purchase. A 50% deposit is required with the order and balance on delivery. For bargain parking try the 5th Street & Mission garage.

PLAZA FURNITURE & APPLIANCE CO.

647 El Camino Real, South San Francisco 94080. Phone: 583-7050, 761-0866. Hours: M,T, & Th 10am-6pm, W & F 10am-9pm, Sat 9am-5pm. Purchases: MC, VISA. Parking: Street or Lot.

You know after visiting this store that the entire staff has been in business for a long, long time. Their experience shows as you discuss the merits of one piece of furniture over another, and which is the best value for the money you have to spend. I was particularly impressed with the selection of bedroom furniture for adults and children, although other types of furnishings are also well represented. The selection on display represents many moderate and better manufacturers. On the price comparisons I made, I would estimate you'll save 25% on almost all of your purchases except appliances. Here's what you can buy: sofas, chairs, tables, appliances, TV's, lamps, carpeting, and vacuums. On many furnishings and appliances you get quick delivery if they have your choice on hand in their warehouse nearby. Of course, other selections ordered from their catalogs will take longer.

SAN FRANCISCO GALLERIES

979 Bryant Street (betw. 7th & 8th Sts.), San Francisco 94103. Phone: 864-8787. Hours: M-Sat 9am-5:30pm. Purchases: Cash or Check. Parking: Street and Private Lot.

A small but choice selection of home furnishings fills this showroom with most room groupings reflecting the traditional mode. Chances are you'll end up perusing their catalogs assisted by their staff in making your selection which will ultimately lead to a 30% savings. An exception might be an area like lamps or lighting fixtures, where freight charges are so high compared to other goods, and when a good discount may be only 20% off retail. The staff can assist with interior design services and also provide opportunities to see potential lines under consideration at the nearby Showplace Square design center.

Their catalog resources include moderate to higher priced lines of living, bed, dining room, and occasional furnishings as well as carpeting, draperies and accessories like grandfather clocks. Parking is very limited in this area, a problem I'm always concerned with since meter maids find me whenever I'm six inches or one minute into violation. Yet, given the fact that everyone on the staff is an "old pro", in addition to being very gracious, they're well worth consideration for your next big investment. A 50% deposit is required with your order.

WESTERN CONTRACT FURNISHERS

175 Stockton, San Jose 95126. Phone: (408) 275-9600. Hours: M-F 9am-5:30pm, Sat 10am-5pm. Purchases: MC, VISA. Parking: Private Lot.

☞ **Other Stores:** San Francisco, 861-9600, Carmel Valley, (408) 624-0971, Sacramento (916) 927-2942.

Long time customers will be surprised to note the change in operation at most of the *WCF* stores. No longer will you find a vast selection of furnishings, they've opted to reduce their overhead by reducing the cost of maintaining an extensive showroom inventory. However, their Sacramento and San Jose showrooms still have a fairly good selection of furnishings. One of the "originals" in the furniture discount business, they still offer good discounts, good service, and an extensive selecton of catalog resources. San Francisco clients have ready access to the resources of Showplace Square and *WCF* design services when they are contemplating big purchases.

JOHN R. WIRTH CO.

1049 Terra Bella, Mountain View 94043. Phone: 967-1212, (408) 736-5828. Hours: T-Sat Noon-6pm, Th, Fri 7pm-9pm. Purchases: Cash or Check. Parking: Lot.

For years you needed a referral to gain entrance into *John Wirth's* showroom, now you only need to mention you've read *Bargain Hunting in the Bay Area*, and you understand the ground rules, i.e. payment in full with order, no credit cards or plans, no returns. This is the place for South Bay and Peninsula residents who want to stretch their home-furnishings dollars. Serious buyers will want to check their showroom selection of mid-to-higher priced lines of furniture. The 1st floor showroom is well stocked with living room, dining room, bedroom, patio furniture and accessories. Look for the special reductions on furnishings that have been marked to clear at less than wholesale prices. Upstairs you can spend hours pouring over wallpaper books, fabric swatches for draperies or upholstery, and an almost overwhelming selection of carpet, vinyl and hardwood flooring samples. They can handle any window covering or treatment, including shutters. If there's anything else you want in home furnishings, and it's not in their showroom, you can go to the catalog resource files for additional choices. Their sales staff is experienced and helpful, but not pushy. They'll even provide a cup of coffee while you plot and scheme how to spend your money. The prices on furnishings (including freight and delivery) are discounted from 20% on a small percentage of merchandise to a more likely 35% on the rest. They also pass on extra savings to customers when they participate in manufacturers' authorized sales. You get their discount, plus the manfacturer's discount. They do not give phone quotes. Take note of their atypical hours. Directions: Heading South on 101, take the Stierlin offramp West. Terra Bella is the first street on the left, go 1 1/2 blocks.

Office Furniture

(Also see **Furniture and Accessories — Catalog Discounters**)

ARVEY PAPER CO.
(See **Paper Goods, Stationery**)

BERKELEY OUTLET

800 Heinz Ave., Berkeley 94710. Hours: T-Sat Noon-5:30pm. Purchases: Cash or Check. Parking: Street.

They definitely need a bigger sign on the outside of their building; I drove by three times before locating their doorway. The warehouse is somewhat dark, musty, and piled and jammed with office furnishings that range from old and ugly to nearly new and up-to-date. The furnishings come from major corporations around the Bay Area who relieve themselves of used office furnishings by soliciting bids from businesses like the *Berkeley Outlet*. Because they have minimal overhead, no sales staff (other than the owners), buy in huge lots, and provide no services, prices are very low. Many businesses find their stock particularly valuable because they often have better quality pieces — like heavy duty file cabinets from insurance companies (they take a lot of use). Weekend mechanics scour the warehouse for old bank carts that serve very nicely as tool drawers at half the price of the real thing. Weekends are particularly busy, and if you need help, be prepared to wait. Most of their furnishings are geared for the offices or businesses where the "real work is done", rather than providing front office glamour or image. Deliveries will cost plenty, because frankly, they hate to make them, so if you insist they'll make you pay.

THE DESK DEPOT

310 W. Evelyn, Mountain View 94041. Phone: 969-3100. Hours: M-S 9am-6pm. Purchases: MC, VISA. Parking: Lot.

This place specializes in used office furniture. One day you may find a selection of metal desks (what I call California State modern) that an earthquake couldn't dent, another day, an entirely different selection depending upon their sources. You can also buy chairs, coat trees, tab card files, chalk boards, school desks, wastebaskets, etc. They have some new office furniture at 20-40% off of list prices. If you don't see what you want, leave your name in their "want book", and they'll give you a call when it arrives.

I.O.F. (INSTANT OFFICE FURNITURE)

2744 East 11th St, Oakland 94601. Phone: 532-1525. Hours: M-F 8:30am-4pm. Purchases: Cash or Check. All sales final.

Wear warm clothes when shopping here for office furniture. *I.O.F* is the place to head for if you're in need of a typing chair, file drawers, table, or sturdy desk, etc. A division of Beier Gunderson, this warehouse is where all the rental returns, special buys, trades, and closeouts are banished. Prices range from $19 to $1,000's depending upon the item, age, condition and original cost. Of course, I zeroed in on the $19, virtually indestructible, secretary's chair that was clearly old in age and style, but in nearly mint condition. Large metal, standard, double pedestal desks with file drawers and new formica tops were $49-$79. These would never do in a front office where image is important, but in the den turned office at home, or for the back room of a business, they're perfect.

Pricing is almost always negotiable, especially on the more expensive items. It's perfectly O. K. to make an offer; if it's not ridiculous, you may wind up with a good price. Office furnishings are usually never sold at a list price, rather on a competitive bid basis; therefore, wheelin 'n' dealing is part of the game. Delivery can be arranged at your expense. You'll probably end up dealing with one of their "old pros". They really know the business, the products, and they're willing to share the savvy they've acquired throughout the years. This is truly a warehouse and tricky to locate. From 29th Ave. heading West towards Fwy 17, turn right on East 10th St., right on Lisbon one block directly into the parking lot. From the lot follow the signs to the *I. O. F.* door, if locked, yahoo at the loading dock, so someone will know you're there and the sales staff will magically appear. They are closed at lunch.

RUCKER FULLER SOUTH

601 Brannan St., San Francisco 94107. Phone: 495-6895. Hours: 8am-5pm, Sat 10am-2:30pm. Purchases: MC, VISA. Parking: Lot.

This is the clearance warehouse for **Rucker Fuller**, a firm that deals in many of the best brands of office furniture. Their biggest customers are large companies willing to pay the price for quality and durability. Samples and manufacturers' closeouts are sent to this warehouse from the main store. There's also a large selection of good-quality used furniture received as trade-ins. The savings on the samples and closeouts may range from 40% off retail to below cost. The used furniture is priced according to condition and original price; you can expect to save from 40-60% off the original cost. All the defects or signs of wear are carefully pointed out to you before you buy.

General Merchandise

Catalog Discounters

The catalog showroom has become a fixture among Bay Area retailers. Companies like *Best Products, Consumers Distributing, and Service Merchandise* advertise frequently, have many locations in the area, and consistently offer excellent values to consumers. With this fifth revised edition, it is hardly necessary to list them individually since they are so prominent in our communities. They are certainly an important resource for consumers for all types of merchandise, but particularly in housewares, giftwares, consumer electronics, jewelry, toys and sporting goods. They have almost every area covered except major home furnishings, apparel, and major appliances. They are very competitive with each other but comparative shopping pays off in dollars if you take the time to check out all the catalogs before you buy. All catalog sales operations have the same basic policies: returns are accepted within a certain period of time; there are no lay-a-ways; every article is guaranteed as described in the catalog. Prices quoted in their catalogs are subject to change, but are consistenly stable for the duration of the catalog unless unusual market conditions require a change. Frequently, other retailers will suggest that the merchandise is substandard, or possibly less than first quality. As far as I can determine, this is not the case. It is true that manufacturers will sell products specifically to the catalog showrooms that are *minutely* different from those sold to traditional retailers. The differences may be as insignificant as a different color, decorative design, or absence of some very minor feature. The basic integrity and function of the product is not compromised. But these little changes allow the manufacturer to sell to both retailers — without putting the retailers and catalog showrooms in competition with each other for the identical product — where the catalog showroom would always be able to undersell the traditional store because of their high volume, low overhead type of business. Overall, the catalog showrooms offer good quality merchandise (but not always the most expensive model or higher end merchandise that a manufacturer has to offer); adequate service, but those lines prior to Xmas can get very long; and are fair when dealing with problems and returns.

Discount Stores

(Also see **Part II: Damaged Freight Outlets**)

You don't always have to drive miles out of your way to go bargain hunting. Throughout the Bay Area discount stores like *PayLess, K-Mart, Gemco, Long's Drugs, and Pay & Save* do a respectable job at pricing their merchandise lower than full service retail stores. If you're in the habit of comparison shopping, and you can recognize a genuine sale price, you can do very well just by taking notice of the ads from these discount stores. Then, snap up those loss leaders they use as a lure to get you into the store. If you can resist buying nonsale merchandise at these times, you truly come out ahead. Don't overlook them!

BETTER BUYS

4615 Clayton Rd., Concord 94521. Phone: 671-0827. Hours: M-Sat 10am-6pm, Sun 10am-5pm. Purchases: MC, VISA. Parking: Lot.

☞ **Other Store:** 15 Boyd Rd., Pleasant Hill.

You can really get hooked on this store which acquires merchandise through liquidations, factory overruns, bankruptcies, manufacturers' overstocks, freight salvage and closeouts. While they have a huge selection of merchandise, they may have only one or two of some items in stock. You don't go shopping here with a list; you peruse the selection and buy whatever is available that day at a good price, and then buy as much as you can. They tend to carry most types of merchandise that you find at grocery or drug stores, primary sources of their liquidated stock. They also buy samples from gourmet and gift trade shows. Be sure to get on their mailing list for notice of special shipments. They do very little advertising, and who wants to miss out on these prices that are 30-70% off retail. All sales are final, except food refunds are given with no questions asked.

COST PLUS IMPORTERS

2552 Taylor St., San Francisco 94133. Phone: 673-8400. Hours: Daily 10am-6pm. Purchases: MC, VISA. Parking: Lot.

☞ **Other Stores:** Concord, Fremont, San Mateo, Mountain View, Oakland, San Jose, Daly City, Greenbrae.

Cost Plus is the largest and probably the best-known importer in the Bay Area. Their largest store, near Fisherman's Wharf, has almost become a San Francisco landmark. All that, and it is still probably the best place in the entire Bay Area to save money on all kinds of imported goods! This main store is so large that it is now housed in three adjacent buildings. The main store (the one that started it all) contains a complete dish and glassware department, and sections for clothes, baskets, toys, cookware, and paper goods. Furniture, objects d'art, and a nursery are in the other buildings. Some people have practically furnished their entire home from *Cost Plus*. Young adults in particular find their furnishings very affordable for that first apartment. There are few amenities, but the merchandise is so interesting, the whole environment is so eclectic and stimulating, that if nothing else, a visit to *Cost Plus* is fun anytime for a good browse.

FASHION BRANDS INC.

126 Old County Road, Brisbane Village Shopping Ctr., Brisbane 94005. Phone: 467-5000. Hours: M-F 10am-5:30pm, Sat 10am-4:30pm. Purchases: MC, VISA. Parking: Lot.

This store is like buried treasure because few driving down the Bayshore Fwy. would ever think to detour into Brisbane to unearth the bargains. *Fashion Brands* specializes in buying closeouts and special promotions in the following categories: linens, housewares, clothing, accessories, toys, luggage and many other basics. Primarily first quality namebrand merchandise is discounted 20-60% off regular retail prices. I think this is a particularly good resource for grandmothers and mothers who are buying infant and toddler clothing, and equipment (bottles, diapers, etc.). There are usually many enticing special buys like the ones I spotted during my last visit. J. G. Durand French Crystal (1st quality glasses, goblets, bowls etc.) at 50% off; electric blankets at 40% off; the toy specials are just as impressive: 50% off and more on electronic games and tabletop arcade games. Although the store is not large, every inch is filled with bargains. Garanimals is always discounted 20%, as is BVD underwear. You won't leave empty handed!

LAZZARI FUEL CO., INC.

11 Industrial Way, Brisbane 94005. Phone: 467-2970. Hours: M-F 8am-4:30pm, Sat. during season, call first. Purchases: Cash or Check. Parking: Lot.

Many presitigious restaurants renowned for their grilled or barbecued meats and fish insist that Mesquite is the magic ingredient! Most food experts and gourmets agree. Mesquite charcoal is made from the mesquite tree. It burns longer, hotter, and is a 100% natural product. The absence of chemicals results in a much better flavor. It is carried occasionally in some supermarkets in 10 lb. bags, yet if you want to stock up, you'll want to go where the pros go. *Lazzari* sells and distributes mesquite in several sizes. Their most popular consumer size is the 40 pound bag for $13.95. This is a supply and demand market, so prices do fluctuate. They also sell chips and wood for smoking food, fireplace coal and charcoal for planters. *Lazzari* is near the Cow Palace. Enter off Old Bayshore, one block south of Geneva Ave. Their large warehouse is smack in the middle of the Southern Pacific yards that are full of potholes and difficult to navigate on rainy days.

PIC 'N' SAVE

75 Weller Lane (Between Abel & Main), Milpitas 95035. Phone: (408) 262-9967. Hours: M-Sat 9am-9pm, Sun 10am-7pm. Purchases: Cash or Check. Parking: Lot.

☞ **Other Store:** 521 Redwood St., Vallejo (707) 552-9214.

It's isn't elegant or trendy and it doesn't even do much advertising, but this Southern California based chain with a total of 85 stores in six southwestern states has shown it knows a few things about retailing. Unlike many retailers, who buy merchandise in normal distribution channels and then display it amid glossy promotions and carpeted coziness, *Pic 'n' Save* is strictly bargain basement. It buys carloads full of "close-out" merchandise and sells it at deeply discounted prices (40-70%) from pipe racks and cluttered shelves in austere, warehouse-like stores. Goods include such diverse items as candles, jewelry, linens, toys, books, housewares, giftwares and clothing. This is definitely not for snobs or elitests, unless they're bargain hunters at heart. They have a great selection of Xmas ornaments and goodies every year which is when I make my annual visit. Some of their merchandise will not interest you at all, but when you find your particular "I can't wait to tell everyone" bargain, the whole outing is worthwhile. Once hooked, you'll be a regular customer.

PRICE CLUB

2300 Middlefield Road, Redwood City 94063. Phone: 369-3321. Hours: For wholesale members only — Tues & Thurs 10am-Noon. Group members: M-F Noon-3:30pm, Sat 9:30am-6pm, Sun 11am-5pm. Purchases: Cash or Check Only. Parking: Lot

☞ **Other Stores:** 22300 Hathaway Ave., Hayward. Phone: 783-1745; 6930 65th St., Sacramento.

The arrival of *Price Club* in the Bay Area was applauded by those residents (transplanted from Southern California) who have missed their profitable shopping forays into the huge warehouses of this San Diego based merchandising company. So what is a *Price Club*?

A price club is a wholesale cash and carry membership warehouse selling merchandise and services to business people. In addition, each price club sells to certain credit union members, employee groups and selected other groups at wholesale prices plus 5%. Cash and carry for the business (wholesale member) means that the member picks the merchandise and takes it out through the registers, paying by check or cash only. This provides the following advantages: considerably lower prices; immediate availability of goods; the opportunity to buy in small quantities, because the prices do not vary with the quantity purchased; the opportunity to expand a business by selling new products and services without large inventory investments; and the opportunity to purchase merchandise for personal use at real wholesale prices.

Each wholesale member pays an annual membership fee of $25, which entitles the business to one membership card, which is assigned to an individual. Up to two additional cards can be obtained at an annual fee of $10 each. If within 90 days after joining, the business is not completely satisfied, its membership fees will be refunded. In order to join, the potential member must bring in a copy of the business license or resale permit, or business documents for proof of qualification as a governmental entity. You may shop the same day your application is accepted by the membership department. Bring comb, pictures are taken for the membership card. Wholesale members also have special hours for shopping that are not available for individual members.

Individual members are referred to as group members, and they must show that they are one of the following: a member of a qualifying credit union; a civilian governmental employee, Federal, State, County, or City; an employee of a bank, savings and loan, credit union, scheduled airline, railroad, or telephone/gas & electric company; a member of a qualifying depositor club. Group membership is $15. In order to join, the potential member must bring in proof of membership qualification. The member and spouse are given membership cards on the spot when they come into the *Price Club*.

Finally, if you find you qualify for membership this is what you'll find in their 100,000 sq. ft. warehouse where you can mix with the forklifts and pluck bargains from their pallets: office supplies, tires and automotive supplies, tobacco and candy, janitorial supplies, hardware, health and beauty products, televisions & microwaves, small appliances, consumer & institutional foods, paper products, vending machine products, housewares & gardening supplies, stereo and Hi-Fi, major appliances, calculators, computers, typewriters & watches, photoprocessing, apparel, plants, and lots more.

Since the opening of their first store in Redwood City, their customers' favorite pastime is telling their latest *Price Club* story: like what they bought, how much they spent, how long they waited in line, how crowded it was, etc., etc. People go shopping to make a "haul". It should be noted that while there is a tremendous selection of goods, you can't buy everything on your grocery list or any list, only those foods or products that *Price Club* has been able to buy at a spectacular price so that they can undersell everyone else. Everything is stacked high on industrial shelves, sans any retail amenities, so that you'll be able to buy at prices that Scrooge would have loved. Truly, at times they need traffic cops just to help the crowds navigate down the aisles. Check with your credit union, employer, bank, etc. to see if membership privileges are available to you; if not, send roses to your friends that belong and maybe they'll take you as one of their two allotted guests. Psst! You fill the basket or dolly, they pay for it, and you pay them. This is one company I wish I'd bought stock in before they became so successful.

THE SHARPER IMAGE SALE STORE

406 Jackson Street (Between Sansome and Montgomery), San Francisco 94111. Phone: 391-0563. Catalog Request: 800-344-4444. Hours: M-Sat 10am-6pm. Purchases: MC, VISA, AE. Parking: Pay Lots.

The *Sharper Image* catalog is full of intriguing innovations selected to appeal to the executive. The best of the world's newest products including state of the art electronics, desk and office accessories, apparel, jewelry, furnishings, ranging in price from a modest $10 to thousands depending on the item, are featured in each catalog. Many appear to be designed for the man or woman who already has everything, and some exotic whiz bang gadget is all that's left to surprise them with. This catalog skyrocketed to fame, the owner to fortune, since its inception a few years ago.

The *Sharper Image Sale Store* is stocked with discontinued products, overstocked bargains, demos, and one of a kind wonders. The stock is always changing, but the bargains are consistently reduced 20-50% off original retail. There's always a selection of watches on hand, frequently executive computer products, and the latest exercise gadgets. If your line of work calls for a bullet proof jacket, you might find one here. There were leather jackets, mini sewing machines, futon chairs, fireplace sets, clutch bags, $5 foot massagers, a $2,500 suit of armor and hundreds of other exotic bargains in the store for bargain hunters during one visit. To get a fix on what might be coming into the *Sale Store*, call and request one of their catalogs. There's a ten day return on demos, a 30 day trial on other merchandise. To see the very latest discoveries you might want to mosey over to their large main store at 680 Davis between Broadway and Jackson.

THE WAREHOUSE

15 Dodie Street, San Rafael 94901. Phone: 456-5090. Hours: M-Sat 10am-5:30pm, Sun Noon-4pm. Purchases: MC, VISA. Parking: Lot.

If you're going to be visiting the post office or Marin Surplus in East San Rafael, go just a little bit further and size up the bargains at this small store which specializes in liquidated merchandise, closeouts and overruns. It has the atmosphere of a variety store and with the same types of merchandise, but the prices are much lower. This store falls in the category of "you name it, and we might have it" type. This can include stationery, toys, paper goods, hardware, pet foods, giftwares, and at times, luggage, clothing and even athletic shoes. With markdowns of 40-70% it's worthwhile stopping when you find yourself in this part of town.

THE WHOLE EARTH ACCESS STORE

2990 Seventh St. (corner of Ashby), Berkeley 94710. Phone: 845-3000. Hours: M-Sat 9am-5:30pm, Sun 11am-5pm. Purchases: MC, VISA. Parking: Lot.

☞ **Other Store:** 863 E. Francisco Blvd., San Rafael. Phone: 459-3533.

This is the contemporary version of the general store. Their merchandise will appeal to people who are energy conscious and quality minded. In kitchen equipment, they carry the best brands in food mixers, grain mills, food processors, coffee grinders, espresso makers, electric dough makers, and a complete selection of cookware. These Kitchen Aid, Hamilton Beach, Krups, Foley and other brands are discounted according to the margin they have to work with. Discounts will range from 15-30% on all their merchandise. Their Henckel's cutlery is 25% off and their price on Kitchen Aid mixers was about the lowest around. Power and hand tools, wood burning stoves, tillers, windmills, cameras, binoculars, consumer electronics, video, TV's, computers, plus a large selection of natural fiber clothing geared for casual and outdoor activities fill the store. The Frye boots at 25% discounts are naturally very popular. A comprehensive selection of books relating to the home, energy conservation, food preparation, cultivation and nutrition will provide hours of intriguing browsing. If you're tired of planned obsolescence, you owe it to yourself to check out the carefully selected quality merchandise that I've briefly described.

TWICE AS NICE — A GENERAL STORE

210 San Mateo Rd. (turn right at 1st stop light in town), Half Moon Bay 94019. Phone: 726-6330. Hours: Daily 9am-6pm. Purchases: MC, VISA. Parking: Lot.

☞ **Other Stores:** 1690 Tiburon Blvd., Tiburon. 435-1666; LITTLE PEOPLE — TWICE AS NICE, 180 San Mateo Blvd. (next to Thriftys), Half Moon Bay, 726-6343.

The owner of this unusual store travels the country to find liquidated merchandise, bankruptcies, closeouts, samples, discontinued items, etc. Buying right to help other people get rid of their problems, enables the owner to price almost everything at 50% off original retail. This is like an old fashioned general store with a little bit of everything. Cosmetics, nylons, costume jewelry, toiletries, drug items, tools, housewares, gift items, electronics, jewelry, shoes and apparel are neatly displayed — a remarkable feat considering the ever changing status of the inventory. I wouldn't suggest driving miles out of your way to visit this store, but many consumers are just 15 minutes away *over the hill* and others may pass through Half Moon Bay on the way to the beach, or to try one of their charming restaurants.

Just one block away from their main store is a much smaller *Little People Twice As Nice* devoted to children with a selection of toys and clothing geared for the preschooler. You can take the bite out of birthday parties by picking up several gifts at one time. The clothing and toys are bought in the same way as all their other merchandise, so prices are discounted, many as much as 50%. Some merchandise is just slightly lower than competitors' prices since it was purchased through conventional channels to round out the selection. Marin County residents will want to check out their store in Tiburon where there is a nice selection of fine jewelry.

Liquidators

(Also see **Part II, Damaged Freight Outlets**)

CONSUMERS DISTRIBUTING CLEARANCE CENTER

4950 Almaden Expressway (Betw. Blossom Hill & Branham), San Jose 95123. Phone: (408) 448-0191. Hours: M-F 10am-9pm, Sat 10am-6pm, Sun Noon-5pm. Purchases: MC, VISA. Parking: Lot.

You can't be as big as *Consumers Distributing* and not have some problems. Discontinued, overstocked, slightly damaged and returned items all end up here at their large (20,000 sq. ft.) clearance center. The savings on merchandise just boggle the mind, 20-50% off the catalog discount price! Prices depend on how many pieces they have of a particular item, and how long it stays in the store. You can expect to find anything here that is featured in their catalog except jewelry. The selection changes so frequently and so intriguingly, frequent stops are a must. I peeked in one day when they had just received 300 bread boxes discontinued from their catalog. These were priced at $10 in the *CD* catalog, priced to clear at $6, and will probably end up priced even lower. An $89/67pc. set of china was priced to clear at $31.90 while a child's riding horse was marked down from $22 to $13.00.

MONTGOMERY WARD DISTRIBUTION CENTER

3000 Alvarado St., San Leandro 94577. Phone: 357-7800. Hours: M-F 10am-9pm, Sat 10am-6pm, Sun 11am-5pm. Purchases: Cash, Check, Store Charge. Parking: Lot.

☞ **Other Stores:** Richmond, Oakland.

This huge clearance center is where all catalog returns, discontinued, freight-damaged, and overstocked merchandise is sent. You can find just about anything that might be sold in their catalog from ankle socks to tractors. There are racks and bins of clothing and shoes, furniture, linens, carpets, home improvement items, garden tools and equipment, TV's, appliances, etc. There is a 30-day guarantee on appliances or entertainment items that are labeled "as-is" or freight damaged. There is a delivery charge on this merchandise. Credit terms can also be arranged. Savings at the clearance center range from 10-50%.

Ward's has another store in Richmond at 211 Cutting Blvd., (just furniture and appliances). Their newest clearance center is located at the old *Montgomery Ward Store* at 2825 East 14th St., Oakland. It covers the whole first floor of this huge building and features a larger fashion selection than the San Leandro store.

Giftwares

(Also see **General Merchandise — Catalog Discounters;
Dinnerware and Accessories; Jewelry and Diamonds**)

BLUEGATE CANDLE FACTORY OUTLET
(See **Arts, Crafts, Hobby Supplies**)

BALBOA GIFTS AND GREETINGS, INC.
221 Oak St., Oakland 94607. Phone: 893-1937. Hours:
M-F 9am-5pm. Purchases: Cash or Check. Parking: Street.

Balboa is a catalog company selling greeting cards,
wrappings, novelties, toys, stationery, gifts, and costume
jewelry. Their catalog ads are similar to all those little ads
you see in the back pages of the Sunday newspaper's
magazine section or the ads in back of ladies magazines.
Their gifts and novelties sell for modest prices ranging
from $1 to $5. These are typically ''cutsy,'' many are
perfect for little kids buying for grownups, or many items
are geared as stocking stuffers for children. Their showroom has shelves of catalog items at 1/3 off or past season
merchandise like Easter and Xmas items at even less. The
next time you want to stock up on little gifts or doodads,
you won't spend more than you can afford at *Balboa*.

CHAR CREWS
(See **Dinnerware and Accessories**)

CLASSY GLASS
1310 A-Fulton Ave., Sacramento 05823. Phone: (916)
971-1118. Hours: M-F 10am-5:30pm, Sat 10am-5pm. Purchases: MC, VISA. Parking: Lot.

While this store is far afield for Bay Area shoppers, it's
good news for those in the Sacramento area. Basically,
Classy Glass scours the various wholesale trade shows and
pounces on every opportunity to acquire samples, promotional merchandise and closeouts. They have also developed some very good connections with many well known
manufacturers so that they buy their seconds and discontinued merchandise. All of these 'goodies'' are discounted
10-60% in their store. They stock Arabia dinnerware and
glassware plus sell most of the line for 42% off retail.
Mikasa dinnerware is approximately 15% off; Waterford
crystal is 20% below retail!; Toscany, Colony and J. G.
Durand stemware are sold for discounts which are related
to their own purchase price. You can buy lovely gifts in
brass and copper. The owners will even ship merchandise

if you can tell them exactly what you want. If you plan to visit, *Classy Glass* is in the Northeast section of Sacramento between Arden Way and Hurley Avenue.

COST PLUS IMPORTERS
(See **General Merchandise**)

CRESALIA JEWELERS
(See **Jewelry and Diamonds**)

DANSK DESIGNS
(See **Dinnerware and Accessories**)

THE DISH FACTORY
159 West Napa Street, Sonoma 95476. Phone: (707) 938-1029. Hours: Daily 11am-5pm. Purchases: MC, VISA. Parking: Street.

This ceramic manufacturer's factory store is right in front of the factory where the ceramics are made, kiln dried, painted and shipped. They are best known for their country inspired ducks, geese, and rabbits that are prominent in many stores selling fine giftwares, or European and country antiques. Many of their other items, garlic and butter keepers, collector's plates, tureens, casseroles, trivets, etc. are sold through fancy catalogs as well as retail stores. These are all first quality, ovenproof, microwave and dishwasher safe. Their newest line is bone china dinnerware with a nostalgic Christmas scene. The styles are charming even while being very functional! Prices at the outlet are 40-50% off retail. Prices are very modest ($5. for a trivet) to high priced ($125 for a handpainted large Canadian goose) reflecting the quality and labor involved in this handcrafted line. Directions: On Highway 12, 1/2 block North of the Plaza in Sonoma.

EDAR MANUFACTURING CO.
Hunter's Point Naval Shipyard, Bldg. 351, 4th Fl., San Francisco 94124. Hours: Wed 10am-3pm, Sat 10am-1pm or by appointment. Purchases: Cash or Check. Parking: Lot.

The *Edar* line of cosmetic bags and travel accessories is sold through major department stores, luggage and gift shops and status catalogues. All the bags and accessories, such as tall draw string totes, jewelry rolls and cases, old charm carriers etc. are high fashion quality in sophisticated fabric designs. They not only make wonderful gifts, they're terrific if you do a lot of traveling. Prices are 30-50% off original retail and many items range from $3-$4. Don't let the offbeat location deter you from a visit. From Fwy.'s 101 or 280 take the Army St. exit going East. Turn right at Third and then left at Evans. Follow Evans all the way to the Shipyard main gate. At the gate you must stop and get a pass and directions to *Edar* from the security guard. It's a piece of cake. Really!

FASHION GIFT OUTLET

674 4th St. (at Townsend), San Francisco 94107. Phone: 982-2450. Hours: Th & F Only 10am-5pm. Purchases: Cash or Check. Parking: Very limited street.

This is the outlet for a major San Francisco importer of several lines of giftware. Like all businesses, each year their line is re-evaluated, new lines and directions are chosen, and old lines and trends, samples, and damaged goods are marked for liquidation. That's where savvy shoppers enter the picture. Their outlet, next to their corporate offices, is in a small room with limited hours. Parking around the outlet is very limited, yet they are located right across the street from the Southern Peninsula Terminal. People coming from the peninsula might want to check their salesroom before catching a bus downtown; or anyone downtown, can catch a bus to the S. P. Terminal to shop the outlet.

Since this is a minor part of their business, the importer has not invested a lot of time or money in displaying the merchandise, but rather, giftwares seem to be plopped wherever an empty space is found. Therefore, you have to scrutinize all the nooks and crannies to make sure you don't miss something important in their eclectic selection of merchandise. Prices are reduced 25-50% off retail. Flawed goods are priced very low, more current and popular merchandise may be somewhat higher. At any time you may find giftwares from their porcelain oriental line of bowls, platters, and cups; ceramic picture frames; mugs; miniature boxes; country-motif trays; trivets; charming country designs on kitchen gourmet cookware; wood country primitives; miniature carousel animals; weathervanes; nested oval boxes; and many appealing cartoon inspired mugs, cookie jars, plus the current popular animal motif on a wide range of giftwares. Overall, most of their collection is whimiscal, fun, and sometimes bizarre. The quality is generally very nice.

IMPORTS EUROPA

530 Broadway, Sonoma 95476. Phone: (707) 938-1414. Hours: T-Sat 10am-4pm, Sun Noon-4pm. Purchases: MC, VISA. Parking: Street.

Imports Europa is a wholesale importer of brass and copper. Most of their line is imported from Holland. These are antique reproductions of planters, buckets, pour cans, candle holders, milk cans, scuttles, etc., and mostly handmade. Their low overhead plus their volume buying power helps to keep their prices as low as possible and provides the continuous great quality of fine Dutch workmanship. Fortunately they operate a small retail store selling their slightly damaged, dirty, and discontinued items at reduced prices. First quality merchandise is reduced from 20-25% off retail, while the grubby stuff may be priced at wholesale and occasionally less. They also use the store to test market new imports for their line, letting the customers interest indicate to them the market potential for a given item. In additon to their Dutch imports, they have clocks, candle sticks, brass vases, brass tables from Italy; plus Taiwan brass imports of hooks, kitchen racks, nautical items, weathervanes, candlesticks, hat racks, figurines, and firetools. The store is small, crowded, but has a wonderful selection of all things *brass*. Prices range from a few dollars to quite a lot, depending on the item.

IRISH CRYSTAL CO.

5540-A Springdale Ave. (next to Best Products, in the Stoneridge Shopping area), Pleasanton, 94566. Phone: 463-0240. Hours: Tues-Fri 10am-6pm, Sat 10am-5pm, Sun Noon-5pm. Purchases: VISA, MC. Parking: Lot.

The Irish Crystal Company is a wonderful resource for Bay Area bargain hunters. They sell only quality crystal directly from their factory in Ireland. While Pleasanton is not exactly central to Bay Area consumers, one visit will establish their credentials and future buying can be done conveniently through their catalog with UPS delivery.

The Irish Crystal Company sells Tyrone Crystal gift items and fine crystal stemware that contains well in excess of 30% lead oxide enabling the crystal to merit a full lead "superior" rating by international standards. This very high lead content contributes to the weight and brilliant clarity, and outstanding prismatic qualities of the crystal. Each piece is an individual work of art that is mouth blown, hand cut, and polished twice. (Be sure to take a few minutes to view their charming, short video tape that tells the story of Tyrone Crystal and gives one an appreciation for their traditional fine craftsmanship.)

Now for the best part: prices are about half of what you would expect to pay for crystal of this caliber. They have over 200 pieces on display which are immediately available from open stock. They offer classic Irish patterns which are complementary with Waterford, Galway, Cavan, and many other crystals. Each piece is guaranteed. The collection includes stemware (17 glasses per suite), accessories, bowls, vases, and art pieces. Other services include bridal registry, lay away, and various trophy or award presentation packages geared for companies and organiza-

tions. Their price advantage is due in part to special tax considerations given to the company by the Irish government and the absence of value added tax.

Typically, when you compare the price of Tyrone Crystal to other prestige brands of Irish crystal you'll find comparisons like these: the most standard sized wine glasses are about $25, compared to about $45; decanters are $99, compared to $190; lamps are $299, compared to $865; etc., etc. In my opinion, Tyrone Crystal is every bit as lovely as those *other* famous brands — just half the price. I particularly appreciate the selection of modestly priced gift items like the $12 jigger (a great "little gift"); the Make-Up Bell, perfect for a wedding gift with sizes and prices ranging from $18-$50. This bell is rung when one partner is ready to "make-up" and end any little quarrel that may take place during their marriage. It is expected that each partner will take their turn ringing the bell, and not the same partner every time. Also, they have many lovely vases, jam pots, and cream and sugar sets for less than $50. Finally, every piece is packaged in a classy, heavy, paper foiled tube that makes a lovely gift package without any additional wrap. The *Irish Crystal Company* will surely become a popular gift resource for all of us who need to buy, from time to time, a lovely gift for a special occasion.

JEWELS OF LIGHT — CRYSTAL FACTORY OUTLET

777 Florida (at 20th St.), San Francisco 94110. Phone: 550-1712. Hours: T-Sat 10am-5pm. Purchases: MC, VISA. Parking: Limited Street.

This 2nd floor outlet has a large variety of crystal gift and jewelry products from Europe. Among the most well known items are the Austrian 32% lead crystal figurine collectibles and hanging prisms. You can spot these same dazzling and colorful pieces at many gift shops in the Bay Area. Other Austrian 32% lead crystal products include jewelry, paperweights, mobiles and ornaments. You will also find assorted fine and unusual crystal products from Italy, Germany, Sweden, and France such as hand formed solid spheres (great gifts for stock brokers), traditional etched pendants, perfume bottles, oil lamps, candleholders, boxes, etc. The outlet's selection is a mixture of discontinued, slightly imperfect, and factory surplus items. Prices are wholesale or less. You can buy jewelry that is popular with teens, or exquisite table top accessories for your living room. After you've overdosed on crystal, hop upstairs to the third floor and check out the *Better Dress Outlet* for fine silk dresses.

JUST A SECOND

1276 Oddstad Drive (faces Fwy. 101), Redwood City 94063. Phone 368-2663. Hours: *Take Note* — Tues-Fri 10am-2:30pm. Purchases: VISA, MC. Parking: Lot.

When calling this store they'll say "Just a Second", you'll think you've been put on hold, but that's the name of the store. Peninsula residents have been blessed with a delightful little outlet that features not only the wonderful Grainware line, but also a classy selection of gift show samples and manufacturers closeouts. Their lucite Grainware is sold all over the Bay Area. Because the manufacturer is right next door, you have a chance to buy all the seconds and discontinued merchandise from the factory at 40% off and more. The clam shell serving bowls and individual sized salad shells that are often seen used by fancy restaurents when serving seafood salads and entrees make wonderful bridal and shower gifts. The blems are microscopic! For the fun at heart, their toilet plunger with clear lucite handle is too pretty to believe, and so functional!

The samples and closeouts of soft luggage, top quality gourmet and table top items, utensils, and containers, general housewares, pots and pans (including the status lines), colorful plastics, and other goodies are discounted 30-50% off retail. Their back room is jammed with super bargains, check it out. Even though they may seem off the beaten path, they're really conveniently located and worth a frequent visit to scrutinize the latest arrivals. Directions: From 101 North, take Whipple exit, straight on Veterans Blvd. 5 lights, turn left on Maple, right on Oddstad. From 101 South, Woodside Road Exit, right at Veterans Blvd., right at First St., Hansen to Oddstad, turn left.

LUNDBERG STUDIOS

131 Marine View, Davenport 95017. Phone: (408) 423-2532. Hours: M-Sat 10am-3:30pm. Purchases: MC, VISA. Parking: Street.

Davenport is little more than a wide spot in the road ten miles north of Santa Cruz on Hwy. 1. Jim Lundberg is the recognized leader in Tiffany art glass reproductions. His pieces sell in fine galleries and world renowned stores. At any one time there are usually 150 seconds in the studio which are discounted 50-75%. A Lundberg paper weight retails for about $85, a Tiffany lamp in the thousands! These seconds in lamps, paper weights, vases, crystal and glass perfumes, as well as tiles may have minor flaws, an off color, a pattern that was not pleasing to the artist, minute bubbles, or they may be simply discontinued. In exchange for the low seconds price you may have to forego *Lundberg's* prestigious signature on the piece. If you are a collector of art glass the trip to Davenport is worth your while.

MARJORIE LUMM'S WINEGLASSES
(See **Dinnerware and Accessories**)

MARSHALLS
(See **Apparel-Family**)

MASLACH ART GLASS STUDIO & SECONDS STORE
(See **Dinnerware and Accessories**)

NOUROT GLASS STUDIO
670-A East H Street, Benicia 94510. Phone: (707) 745-1463. Hours: M-F 10am-4pm. Purchases: MC, VISA. Parking: Street.

If you would like to own a museum-quality piece of art glass that is individually crafted in the ancient tradition, be sure to get on the *Nourot* mailing list for their special sales where selection is the best and bargains abound. Approximately three times a year, they have a sale with other Benicia master glass makers of *Yuba Arts*: Zellique, Kathy Erteman, and Smyers Glass. These sales are usually scheduled on the weekend before Mother's Day, 2nd weekend in August, and the 1st weekend in December. Prices at retail are steep, but the quality of their designs is impeccable, and the sale prices that are reduced 50% make them more affordable. Works by the *Nourot Glass Studio* are included in the collection of the Corning Museum of Glass. Pieces from the studio are also shown in museum shops and contemporary art galleries across the country as well as in Europe and the Orient.

POTTERY WORLD
12000 Berryessa Rd., San Jose Flea Market, Space I 26-27, J 13-14. San Jose 95133. Phone: (408) 289-9170. Hours: Sat & Sun 9am-5:30pm. Purchases: MC, VISA. Parking: Lot.

Pottery World has been a fixture at the San Jose Flea Market for years. They also maintain spaces in several Southern California flea markets selling ceramics from 25 companies and their own Los Angeles company. Basically, you'll find whatever is new and popular in consumer trends reflected in their inventory. When the country inspired blue-speckled dishes and ceramics (many with duck designs) were popular, they had them in the thousands at half the prices of other retail outlets. This past spring, large cylinder shaped planters, pots, and vases, in jade, raspberry, black and other trendy colors were widely featured in all the home furnishings ads. *Pottery World* of course had them but at much lower prices. If you're looking at ads right now for ceramic pots, vases, dinnerware, etc., chances are you'll find the same or very similar items at *Pottery World*. Most of their ceramics are first quality, but occasionally they have seconds too. Their low prices are related to their overhead: no advertising, minimal rent expenses, and their own direct factory-to-consumer sales approach.

ROBIN'S NEST SAMPLES 'N' SECONDS

140 East Napa Street, Sonoma 95476. Phone: (707) 996-4169. Hours: M-Sat 10am-5:30pm, Sun 11am-5pm. Purchases: MC, VISA. Parking: Street.

Going to the wine country? Then stop off at this delightful little shop that sells kitchenwares, giftwares, gourmet cooking accessories, small kitchen appliances and kitchen linens for 30-60% off retail. You can save money because these are seconds, closeouts, or discontinued items and samples from gift shows.

ROSE'S BARGAIN EMPORIUM

(See **Apparel-Women's-Neighborhood Stores**)

THE SECOND LOOK

510 Broadway, Seaside 93955. Phone: (408) 899-4442. Hours: M-Sat 11am-5pm, Sun Noon-5pm. Purchases: MC, VISA. Parking: Street.

Don't sulk when your spouse is on the golf course. Instead, hop in the car and make a beeline for the *Couroc* outlet, a quick 15 minute trip to Seaside. This classy line of giftware consisting mainly of bowls and trays is unique for the finished designs that are permanently fused into phenolic resin with heat and thousands of pounds of pressure, then buffed into the unique luster and satin blackness that is distinctive to *Couroc* products. These products are sold in fine gift stores around the country. Tourists can find lovely and functional trays and bowls with designs relating to California, while natives find any and all of their designs appealing. Prices on the seconds and discontinued designs are reduced at least 50% off retail. A real relief when you consider that typically a large tray retails for $50. Shipping boxes are sold at the outlet for the convenience of travelers.

R. STRONG SECONDS STUDIO

1235 4th St. (at Gilman), Berkeley 94710. Phone: 525-3140. Hours: T-Sat 10am-4pm. Purchases: MC, VISA. Parking: Street.

R. Strong is associated with a distinctive line of handblown art glass and sculptured glass. In the seconds studio the vases, goblets, paper weights, and perfume bottles are sold for wholesale. They have slight flaws, may be somewhat irregular in conformation or size or may have been rejected from the regular line for aesthetic reasons. Prices in the outlet range from $15-$150. I was particularly tempted by the large ornamental plates which are not only functional but would be lovely on display. When you go to the studio, ring the bell and wait for a few minutes until someone opens the door.

THREE D BED & BATH

(See — **Linens**)

THRIFTY GOURMET

216 Strawberry Village, Mill Valley 94941. Phone:
388-COOK. Hours: M-Sat 10am-5:30pm, Sun Noon-5pm.
Purchases: MC, VISA. Parking: Lot.

The selection of fine quality gourmet cookware at
Thrifty Gourmet is tops! The prices are "rockbottom"
because the owner has some terrific connections with many
manufacturers and she also buys samples and closeouts
from trade shows. Her store, removed from the main-
stream, is ideal for those manufacturers who need to
dispose "discreetly" of their seconds, samples, closeouts,
and overstocks.

Always prevalent in her selection is a large quantity of
white ceramic platters, casseroles and soup toureens from a
well known manufacturer that is always discounted 50%
whether perfects or seconds. In addition, you'll find copper
cookware kitchen accessories discounted 40%, stainless
steel pots and pans, wine coolers, picnic baskets, gadgets,
coffee mugs, cookie jars, salt and pepper sets, knives,
plastics, linens, glassware and other gems all at 20-70%
off. Villeroy & Bach is one of her biggest sellers, plus
she'll special order anything in their line and pass along a
tidy savings. Obviously, the owner is buying "right" to
pass on such hefty discounts. The *Thrifty Gourmet* is a
wonderful shop for weddings, anniversaries and birthday
gifts. They don't gift wrap or have gift boxes for many
items, a minor detail.

(Also see **Apparel — Family, Women; Luggage; Shoes**)

GRIFFCO HANDBAG CO.

373 4th St. (Mezzanine), Oakland 94607. Phone:
444-3800. Hours: M-F 9am-5pm, Sat 9am-4:30pm. Purchases: MC, VISA. Parking: Side lot.

For casual, genuine soft leather handbags, you'll never
find a bigger selection than right here at the *Griffco
Factory Store*. They manufacture more than 28 styles in a
wide array of colors. This is a mom and pop operation,
and the service couldn't be friendlier. These handbags are
not for elegant dressing, but rather for everyday, day in,
day out use. Factory prices range from $9.50-$30 on the
handbags. The small back packs, men's bags, shaving
bags, are well priced with the soft sided briefcases topping

the price range at $47. Occasionally they pick up merchandise from other lines which they discount 25-35%; these are more expensive refined handbags, wallets and briefcases. To utilize all the scrap leather accumulated in the sewing room downstairs they've filled a showcase with coin purses, wallets, credit card holders and other leather goodies. Another aspect of their business involves ladies and infants sandals made to fit. This outlet is off Broadway in the vicinity of Jack London Square.

JADEL CO., INC.

953 Mission St. San Francisco 94103. Phone: 495-3940. Hours: M-F 10am-6pm, Sat 10am-4pm. Purchases: MC, VISA, AE. Parking: Street, 5th & Mission Garage.

☞ **Other Stores:** McArthur-Broadway Shopping Ctr. & Eastmont Mall, Oakland; 237 Kearny, San Francisco.

I watched this company for a few months, somewhat apprehensive about making a recommendation on discount prices for designer handbags. News reports and features have shown that these well known lines are often sold fraudulently. (I would think that anyone buying a designer bag at 50-80% off retail would know they're buying a fake.) *Jadel* in Oakland and San Francisco sells well known names like Givenchy, Christian Dior, Bally of Switzerland, Pierre Cardin, Valentino and Lanvin at 20% off the retail prices at major stores. After looking at the documentation provided by the owners, I have no doubts these are the genuine products. The quality is evident.

If you're not up to the status stuff at $200 plus on some handbags even at discount, you'll be satisfied with their own line of American made (in New York) handbags that are copies in genuine leather, of popular styles being sold at much higher prices everywhere else. I've paid $20 and $22 for casual bags that were almost identical to bags selling elsewhere at $30-$35. Their most popular styles are the ladies briefcase bags at $49-$69. B. H. Smith Bags are 25% off, and Rolf wallets are 30% off.

Jadel also sells Seiko, Bulova and Longines watches at a 25% discount. Always look for the posted authorized dealer number assigned by Seiko when buying discount or you will not be able to get your watch serviced at U.S. repair centers. If you're knowledgeable about gold jewelry and pricing, you'll want to check their prices which they feel are very good. Finally, they had a small selection of colognes (famous brands) at 25%-30% off. These were a special buy from a liquidation sale.

Jewelry and Diamonds

(Also see **General Merchandise**)

AZEVEDO JEWELERS & GEMOLOGISTS, INC.

210 Post St. (Room 321, 3rd floor), San Francisco 94108. Phone: 781-0063. Hours: T-Sat 10am-5pm. Purchases: MC, VISA. Parking: Pay Lots.

For substantial savings and a beautiful selection of diamonds, colored stones, gold jewelry and watches, this is a place well worth seeking out. *Azevedo Jewelers* has been in the same third floor location for more than 45 years. Their success is owed to low overhead, careful and selective buying, and referrals from satisfied customers. Appraisals are done by graduate gemologists. This is one of six A.G.S. stores in San Francisco.

CRESALIA JEWELERS

278 Post St. (next to Gump's), San Francisco 94108. Phone: 781-7371. Hours: M-F 10am-5:30pm, Sat 10am-5pm. Purchases: AE, MC, VISA. Parking: Union Square Garage.

This store has been located at this address on the second floor since 1912. It is evident that this is a very fine jewelry store when you alight from the elevator and enter the immaculate, luxuriously carpeted showroom full of gleaming displays of silver and showcases of fine jewels. There are no toasters or waffle irons, just the finest in jewelry and watches. You will also find a nice selection of silverware and dinner accessories here. Savings are substantial, with prices below the usual retail at other fine jewelry stores. (Because jewelry pricing is very complicated and varies from firm to firm, no hard-and-fast percentage can be quoted). In addition to sales, *Cresalia* has a complete gemological laboratory, managed by graduate gemologists from the Gemological Institute of America to help you in the choice of any diamond or gem, and to grade and appraise any jewelry you may already have.

LAVIN AND JACOBSON

3343-C (2nd fl.) Vincent Road, Pleasant Hill 94523. Phone: 937-9570. Hours: *By appointment* M-F betw. 8am-6pm. Purchases: Cash or Check. Parking: Back lot.

It's often the case that the best values are found in the most unlikely locations and this jewelry resource is no exception. I took a tour of this jewelry manufacturing facility and was impressed with the exacting craft of the jeweler that involves goldsmiths, diamond setters, gem experts, finishers and jewelry designers. Lavin and Jacobson have been in business for sixteen years manufacturing jewelry in the European tradition. Most of their business is done on a national scale with jewelry stores who utilize their custom fabricating, diamond setting, and repair services. They are essentially wholesalers. However, they are not adverse to dealing directly with the local consumer. They don't claim to sell at wholesale prices to consumers (how refreshing), but they certainly are in a position to offer substantial savings over prices of local retail establishments.

This outfit is not appropriate for Looky Lou's, because while they have a display case with many dazzling rings, most of their available settings are kept in trays or are represented in wax patterns numbering in the hundreds that you can try on. (In fact, surveying all the possibilities is worse than picking out wallpaper.) I would suggest that if you're interested in buying a piece of fine jewelry, that you look around first so that you have a good idea of what you like, and you will also get a feel for pricing. Then when you make an appointment as a serious buyer, you will really be in a position to appreciate their pricing, selection, and the savings. Another time saving idea is to bring in a picture, if they don't have the exact setting they can certainly duplicate the design.

Finally, you can be sure that even though you're getting a good "deal", there is no compromise on quality and craftsmanship. Many volume oriented, discount priced operations sell at what appears to be a good price, yet often the shanks are too thin, and the setting of the stones insecure. For the forgetful, you can get quick service if you've just remembered a birthday, anniversary etc.; however, custom designs usually take 14 days or so. Their

services include repair, remounts, sizing, repronging, reshanking, polishing, etc. If you have unset gems bring them in, otherwise you can make a gem selection that fits your budget from their trays of loose stones which include diamonds, jade, lapis lazuli, pearls and other precious and semi-precious beauties. Their business is not limited to rings; they can also make earrings, necklaces, pendants, bracelets, charms and more.

It is essential to make an appointment. When you arrive at their business, the doors are locked and you'll be admitted after knocking and identifying yourself. That may sound forbidding, yet once inside, you'll be treated in a comfortable, friendly fashion. Naturally, with the kind of inventory they maintain, security precautions are a priority. Directions: From Buskirk (next to Fwy. 680) turn onto Mayhew, left on Vincent.

NIEDERHOLZER JEWELERS

140 Geary St. (4th Floor), San Francisco 94108. Phone: 421-7871. Hours: M-F 9am-5:30pm. Purchases: MC, VISA & TERMS. Parking: Union Square Garage.

For many years this has been a resource where "people who know" go for better quality jewelry at lower prices. The showroom on the 4th floor is just a block off Union Square. There are substantial savings on prestige brand watches, sterling silver flatware, hollow ware, personal gold and silver accessories, jewelry, diamond rings and rings or precious stones. The salespeople are interested in customer satisfaction which means attentive service and fine quality merchandise.

THE SMALL THINGS COMPANY

760 Market Street (Phelan Bldg. Suite 741), San Francisco 94102. Phone: 397-0110. Hours: *By Appointment Only* M-F 10am-4pm, Sat Noon-4pm. Purchases: AE, MC, VISA. Parking: Pay Lots.

The owner of this small company offers very special services and values. Her talent lies in finding maximum value for the best price utilizing connections developed over the years from markets in New York, Europe and the Orient. If you're interested in a special gift, whether it's pearls, lapis, jade, diamonds, precious gem stones, gold or silver, the owner will probably have it in stock, or she'll find it — and usually at a price 30-40% lower than street level, conventional jewelry retailers.

If you need a watch repaired, pearls restrung, jewelry repaired or remodeled, custom design, or appraisals, it can be done. Creating innovative wedding rings is their special pleasure. This business is not confined to the "affluent". You can purchase gift items that start at $15 and end only when your money does. A selection of small items, appropriate as gifts for business associates or members of the wedding are always available. It's really essential to call for an appointment and discuss your jewelry needs so that a selection of merchandise is ready for your perusal.

ZWILLINGER & CO.

760 Market St. (At Grant Ave.), San Francisco 94102. Phone: 392-4086. Hours: T-F 9am-5pm, Sat 9am-3pm. Purchases: MC, VISA. Parking: Downtown garages.

This 60 year old jewelry firm is owned and actively managed by the original family. To find *Zwillingers* first look for the Phelan Building on Market, then make your way up to the 8th floor to Suite 800. You'll feel like you're entering a bank vault as you pass through their security doors. You'll feel more comfortable if you wear your Sunday best while in the presence of such beautiful jewelry.

For those great occasions in life — engagements, anniversaries, and graduation — where the remembrance you desire should be very special, a fine piece of jewelry can be purchased here at considerable savings. Their prices on 14-carat gold jewelry were very impressive as well as their prices for watches and diamond rings. They have extended hours at Christmas.

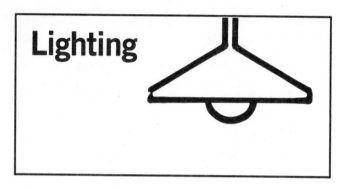

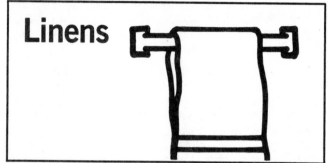

I have to concede defeat in locating a super discount for lighting fixtures. I'm sure that everyone shares my disappointment because even the plainest fixture can cost an arm and a leg. In my research I've found that most retailers offer a 30-40% discount off the manufacturer's list price. Since everyone seems to be doing this, (some will whisper it in your ear as if they're the only ones, others will be much more straightforward), you have to assume that the prevailing retail price for this merchandise is the discount price. Occasionally, you can trim the discount even more by watching ads closely for end of season sales, or special item sales. Those involved with remodeling projects and working with contractors may also swing a better deal. Lighting stores seem to have good sales in January, other sale times vary with the retailer. Pity the poor consumer who is working with a decorator who charges the full manufacturer's list price, that really hurts!

(Also see **Furniture — Catalog Discounters; General Merchandise**)

A-1 LINEN COMPANY

1660 Monterey Hwy., San Jose 95112. Phone: (408) 995-5544. Hours: T-F 9am-5pm, Sat 10am-3pm. Purchases: MC, VISA. Parking: Lot.

The *A-1 Linen Company* that sells commercial and institutional linens also sells namebrand towels, sheets, bath rugs, pillows, comforters and kitchen linens to the public at 30-50% discounts. What is most unusual is that these linens are not old "leftovers", but the same colors and styles that you're seeing currently in better stores. For instance, a very luxurious towel that retails for $23 is sold for $14.50. There are several brands and price ranges, all discounted far more than the "tiny" savings offered on white sale prices by major stores. The irregulars, a smaller part of the selection, are discounted even more. Regular and waterbed sheets are sold. Some patterns have been around for a while, although others are as current as your latest department store ad. The sheets are sold in packaged sets. Both standard and electric blankets are well represented along with newer items in the marketplace like duvet covers, bed bags, and goose down comforters. Everything is beautifully arranged. You can discuss the possibility of special orders and, if they can, they'll try to order for you. Finally, you can always opt for the institutional linens, which are cheaper. For instance a dozen basic white towels like the ones you see in hotels and hospitals sell for approximately $22/dozen.

BED N' BATH

19765 Stevens Creek Blvd., Cupertino 95014. Phone: Pending. Hours: M-F 9:30am-9pm, Sat 9:30am-6pm, Sun Noon-5pm. Purchases: MC, VISA. Parking: Lot.

☞ **Other Store:** Westlake Mall, Daly City. (Fall 1984)

The information on this store was compiled by talking to company executives, and from the recommendations of friends who shop their stores in the Los Angeles area. *Bed N' Bath* originated their successful formula for retailing in the New York area where they solidly established their reputation as a leading off-price retailer of linens for the home. Their first store in the Bay Area should be opening as this book goes into distribution with one following shortly in the Westlake Shopping Center in Daly City.

Their stores are designed to overwhelm the consumer with choices and wonderful prices. Merchandise will be displayed on floor to ceiling high tech shelving in an interior designed to reflect a crisp and clean 1980's ambiance. Manufacturers like Fieldcrest, Wamsutta, Cannon, Springmaid, and Martex are among those represented, with lines from notable designers like Bill Blass, YSL, Marimekko, etc. Prices are discounted 20-40% on current, first quality merchandise every day. On the smattering of seconds or irregulars prices are even lower. Following the trend to fully coordinated bedroom linens, you can start with sheets, add dust ruffles, shams, comforters, drop round cloths, bedspreads and end up with a room that appears to come right off the pages of House Beautiful. The bathroom can be coordinated as well with towels, rugs, shower curtains, etc., plus accessories in the latest trendsetting colors. Their selection of down comforters is geared to accommodate the budgets and levels of quality for just about everyone. Waterbed and flannel sheets, blankets, duvet covers and just about everything found in linen departments is carried in their stores. Their finest line of Dyne goose down comforters from Denmark is expensive even at discount, but would be prohibitive at full retail. Casual kitchen linens get their share of shelf space and hefty discounts. Cash refunds are given if merchandise is returned with a sales receipt within 21 days.

DECORATOR'S BEDSPREAD OUTLET

5757 Pacheco Blvd. (1 mile north of Sun Valley Shopping Ctr.), Pacheco 94553. Phone: 689-3435. Hours: M-Sat 9:30am-5:30pm, Th & F eve till 8:30pm, Sun Noon-5pm. Purchases: MC, VISA. Parking: Lot.

☞ **Other Stores:** 1580 Howe Ave., Sacramento; 15576 Hesperian Blvd., San Lorenzo.

It's so nice to find a store owner who is able and willing to operate a business with a lower overhead, take a smaller markup, and pass on savings to consumers. It helps to have good connections too. The selection of bedspreads, goose down comforters, dacron filled comforters, decorator pillows and dust ruffles has the depth and variety to suit the taste and requirements of just about everyone.

Savings on regular, first quality merchandise (the same merchandise you see in better stores) is approximately 25% below prevailing retail. On custom orders you can save 15%. The best buys are on special purchase items — overcuts, cancellations, or discontinued merchandise from manufacturers — that result in savings of 40-70%. The price range in their selection is very accommodating. There are budget priced goods for lean budgets, and higher prices for fine quality custom-type spreads. The goods are neatly displayed and there are several mock beds, useful for seeing your spread in a home situation. They also have a reasonable trial purchase policy, which allows you to take the merchandise home on approval. Customers who bring in their own measurements will be pleased with the hefty discounts on ready-made and custom-made draperies.

THE HOME SHOP LINEN WAREHOUSE

2313 Stoneridge Mall, Pleasanton 94566. Phone: 484-0670. Hours: M-F 10am-9pm, Sat 10am-6pm, Sun Noon-5pm. Purchases: MC, VISA. Parking: Lot.

The *Home Shop* has several stores in the Los Angeles area all located in shopping malls with bargains in bed, bath and kitchen linens. While they may be the "enemy" to major retailers, they're friends to their customers. Both East Bay stores are beautifully merchandised and a pleasure to shop in. First quality brand name merchandise is always selling as low as the department store White Sale prices, and usually they're marked an additional 10-15% lower. For instance, their Charisma towels regularly $22-$24 are $17.97. This doesn't add up to sensational bargains, yet the selection is on par with better stores that handle quality brands like Fieldcrest, Cannon, Wamsutta, J. P. Stevens and Burlington. There are no tricks to their pricing, just a lower markup. They have a very liberal return, exchange and approval policy. One doesn't expect to find bargains at the Stoneridge or Sun Valley Shopping Centers, but then that was before the *Home Shop* arrived.

HOUSE OF BEDSPREADS

417 Town & Country Village (Stevens Creek Blvd. & Winchester), San Jose 95128. Phone: (408) 244-2148. Hours: M-S 10am-5:30pm, Th till 9pm. Purchases: MC, VISA. Parking: Lot.

☞ **Other Stores:** 320 El Camino Real, Millbrae; 61 Town & Country Village, Palo Alto; 1645 Van Ness, San Francisco; 318 Coddingtown Center, Santa Rosa; Walnut Creek, Hayward, and San Rafael by spring 1984.

With over 2,000 bedspreads and comforters in stock, choosing just one might seem like an overwhelming task. Bring your carpet samples, paint colors, fabric swatches and pillow cushions to make the job of finding the "right" spread a little easier. These spreads are from 11 different companies, plus their own company in Los Angeles. If you can't find something in their vast selection you're really picky. The discounts range from 20-40% below the prices of most department and furniture stores. They've expanded their inventory to include brass beds from J. B. Ross, futons, draperies, plus they're responding to consumer interest in natural fibers with a good selection of cotton, silk and wools. Their goods are first quality.

LINEN DEPOT

300 De Haro St.(at 16th St.), San Francisco 94103. Phone: 861-0786. Hours: M-Sat 10:30am-6pm. Purchases: MC, VISA. Parking: Street.

If you save all those glossy advertising supplements from major stores that relate to their latest home furnishings and linen sales, you'll just love comparing prices on the same merchandise at the *Linen Depot*. They cut the ads and post them around the store so you can see for yourself that their prices are at least 10-20% less than the "big" sale prices in the supplements. I particularly like their inventory that includes many items not often found at discount on a regular basis: bathroom furnishings like hampers, hardware, and wall caddies, in chrome, brass, ceramic, lucite, wicker and a wide selection of soft or padded toilet seats. City apartment dwellers will love the high tech storage and closet accessories. The bed and bath linens are beautifully displayed and reflect the cream of the linen lines. Wrapping up the selection, a complete table top linen department, kitchen linens, and a classy bathroom accessory section including a fragrant abundance of bath soaps. They're located in the Showplace Square area — look for the bright blue building.

LINEN FACTORY OUTLET

2200-C Zanker Rd., San Jose 95131. Phone: (408) 263-8303. Hours: M-F 8am-4pm, Sat 10am-4pm. Purchases: MC, VISA. Parking: Lot.

No, you're not in the wrong neighborhood — not if you're looking for bargains. True, this industrial park is an unlikely area for a factory outlet but this apron and linen outlet is a surprise in many ways. The merchandise is beautifully displayed and neatly organized. New stock flows into the outlet each day as merchandise passes through the manufacturing inspection department. These rejects, overruns, and discontinued pieces may be tablecloths — in all shapes and sizes; placemats — quilted, smooth, tailored or embellished; napkins, runners, napkin rings, table garters — in linen-look, poplins, prints and solids, laces and eyelets. Everything made by this manufacturer is from good quality cotton and polyester blends that wash beautifully and are permanent press. I particularly like their aprons, I've bought several for myself over the years, and many more for gifts. Savings at the outlet range from 40-70% off retail.

LINEN KING

1380 No. Main St., Walnut Creek 94596. Phone: 947-5666. Hours: M-Sat 9:30am-5:30pm, Thurs till 8:30pm, Sun Noon-4pm. Purchases: MC, VISA. Parking: Street.

Yet another entry for the linen consumer. That's *Linen King* in Walnut Creek, a small store with good connections to manufacturers that sell blankets, blanket covers, comforters, bedspreads, dust ruffles, shams, mattress pads, pillows, towels, goose down comforters, bathroom rugs and accessories. Their angle: to sell more expensive merchandise, better quality, more exclusive lines typically carried in our first line stores. So, you'll find soft flannel sheets imported from Belgium, Sybil Shepard dust ruffles, top quality (well filled) goose down comforters, plus 200-220 thread count fine percale bed linens. Being the new kids on the block, they're very accommodating. They'll special order anything you want, if they can get it and pass on a tidy discount in the process. Overall, savings range from 20-60% off current retail. Everything first quality!

LINENS FOR LESS

2650 El Camino Real, Moonlight Shopping Ctr., Santa Clara, 95051. Phone: (408) 249-8636. Hours: M -Sat 10am-7pm. Purchases: MC, VISA. Parking: Lot.

Linens for Less offers consumers discount prices on namebrands like Cannon, Fieldcrest, Wamsutta, Purofied and many others. The selection runs the gamut with bath, kitchen, bed, and table top linens. Discounts range from 30-50% off retail on first quality merchandise, although occasionally there's some seconds. From time to time you'll see good buys on housewares — an indication they got a deal too good to pass up.

LINENS FOR LESS

3191-A Crow Canyon Place, San Ramon 94583. Phone: 820-9302. Hours: M-F 11am-6pm, Sat 10am-5pm. Purchases: MC, VISA. Parking: Lot.

This *Linens For Less* is not associated with the other store with the same name in Sunnyvale. This store is more like an exclusive design studio or boutique that specializes in finer linens for the bedroom, kitchen and formal dining at discount prices. Their aim is to provide a complete package that includes not only the linens for these rooms, but also the wall and window treatments. Their prices on mini-blinds, vertical shades and other window treatments are very good, and wallpapers are carried at modest discounts. Many of their quality lines in bedspeads, comforters, table linens, place mats, blankets, and decorative pillows are not carried by the other off-price linen stores which makes this a nice resource for customers seeking the *designer look*. Overall prices are discounted 20-40% off on linens, up to 50% on window coverings.

LINEN'S UNLIMITED

6632 Dublin Blvd., Dublin 94566. Phone: 833-8222. Hours: M-Sat 9:30-6pm, Sun Noon-5pm. Purchases: MC, VISA. Parking: Lot.

☞ **Other Stores:** Clayton Valley Shopping Ctr., Concord; Oak Park Shopping Ctr., Pleasant Hill; Foothill Plaza, Los Altos; 1299 4th St., San Rafael; 3566 Mt. Diablo Blvd., Lafayette; plus stores opening in Vallejo, Fremont, San Ramon.

Linen's Unlimited has mushroomed from its innocuous beginning in Lafayette, to over nine stores with great savings on factory overruns, closeouts, first quality and select irregulars from major manufacturers. Unlike some of their competitors, they have not gone high class with gorgeous decors, but rather fill their stores with plain tables piled high with goods and cover their walls with shelves 12 ft. high. Their lines are impressive: Wamsutta, Cannon, J. P. Stevens and designer percale sheet sets by Bill Blass, Pierre Cardin, and Calvin Klein (which sold for $23.99 for a "Queen set"). Large bath size "Grand Manner" irregulars were $7.00, while bath sheets rarely sell for more than $9.99. They also carry comforter sets, matching dust ruffles, and pillow shams for the full treatment. Their selection changes all the time: reason for regulars to stop in to see the latest choice merchandise, and some that is merely so-so. They consistently offer savings of 30-70% off the original department store prices, and cover nicely just about every item in bed, bath and kitchen linens.

MARSHALLS
(See **Apparel — Family**)

ROSS DEPARTMENT STORES
(See **Apparel — Family**)

STROUDS LINEN WAREHOUSE
700 El Camino Real, 120 Menlo Station, Menlo Park 94025. Phone: 327-7680. Hours: M-Fri 10am-9pm, Sat 10am-6pm, Sun Noon-5pm. Purchases: VISA, MC. Parking: Lot.

☞ **Other Stores:** Cala Center, 1111 W. El Camino Real, Suite 107, Sunnyvale 94087; 565 Contra Costa Blvd., Pleasant Hill.

Strouds has been a force in the Los Angeles area for years. Their arrival in the Bay Area in 1984 delighted everyone who desires good linen values. *Strouds* is a specialty off-price linen operation that offers a large selection of top quality linen products at the lowest possible prices. This translates into lower-than-white-sale prices every day of the week. Their fine quality brands include Burlington, Cannon, Fieldcrest, Martex, Springmaid, Wamsutta, Dan River, Croscill, Reflections and designer labels like Laura Ashley, Bill Blass, Marimekko and Vera. In short, they have virtually everything for bed (including down comforters), bath, and tabletop. Their selection includes many of the same current colors and styles seen in major department stores that are so hard to find at discount.

Prices are discounted from 10-60% off retail. Typically, a $15.50 towel would be $9.99, a $24 towel would be $15.99, etc. Their stores have high vertical fixtures that create a sense of being surrounded by walls of linens. Everything is immaculately displayed and organized by their attentive sales staff. Their return policies are very liberal. If a customer has a cash or check receipt, they give a cash refund. With credit card purchases, a bank card credit.

THREE D BED & BATH

1637 Hollenbeck Rd. (Loehmann's Plaza) Sunnyvale 94087. Phone: (408) 720-0722. Hours: M-Sat l0am-6pm, Sun Noon-5pm. Th & Fri eve till 9pm. Purchases: MC, VISA. Parking: Lot.

☞ **Other Stores:** 508 Contra Costa Blvd., Pleasant Hill, Phone: 676-8246; Marin Square, San Rafael.

There are 28 stores in the *Three D Bed & Bath* chain in the U.S. The first two opened in the Bay Area in early December extending our linen bargain options. It's almost too much after years of no linen bargains for the Bay Area. What sets *Three D* apart from the other new chains is their housewares and gift departments. The "HOMEWARES" departments carry a large selection of namebrand gourmet and basic dinnerware, cookware, utensils, glassware and endless gift ideas, all at prices considerably below those of department stores. *Three D* has adopted a fashion look in the appearance of their stores that helps customers select merchandise that fits in with their lifestyle and home decor. This sets them apart from the bargain basement/warehouse look favored by some retailers.

Their discounts range from 30-60% off department store prices. Merchandise is first quality from leading manufacturers like Wamsutta, Fieldcrest, Cannon, Martex, Burlington, Marimekko and others. Their selection is up-to-date with the latest fashions and colors. The one hitch is their returns policy. There are no refunds, no MC or VISA

credits issued, only a store credit. That's fair, and the policy is posted prominently, but buy with care!

TOWELS PLUS

3585 Industrial Drive, Santa Rosa 95401. Phone: (707) 525-9800. Hours: M-F 10am-7pm, Sat 10am-6pm, Sun Noon-5pm. Purchases: MC, VISA. Parking: Lot.

Towels Plus started small but they're getting bigger and better year by year. They specialize in bed, bath and kitchen linens, with a few extras to set them apart from their competitors. They offer a decorator service called "Window Shopping" with discount prices offered on mini-blinds, wallpaper, and various types of window coverings. Their section of closeouts, manufacturers' specials, and irregulars is where you'll find the best prices (up to 50% off retail), while the first quality, current merchandise is discounted from 15-25%. *Towels Plus* is located in the *K-Mart* shopping area on the west side of the parking lot.

(Also see **General Merchandise; Sporting Goods**)

AAA LUGGAGE REPAIR DEPOT

585 Howard Street (near 2nd), San Francisco 94105. Phone: 781-5007. Hours: M-F 8am-5pm, Sat 9:15am-12:30pm. Purchases: MC, VISA. Parking: Street or Pay lots.

You'll wonder where you are when you walk in the door because all the luggage, attache cases, trunks, totes, portfolios and wallets are in the back room. *AAA* is the authorized repair station for most national brands of luggage. Their specialty is trunks made from vulcanized fiber over plywood that is very strong and sold at great prices.

AAA is not a retailer, but specializes in airline repairs and replacement. Their back room has therefore become a

clearance center for samples and department store returns, plus some factory special clearances. All deficiencies have been taken care of. Savings range from 20-50% off. You may not be able to buy six matching pieces of luggage from their shelves, but if one or two are your "bag" you should have no trouble. Their attache cases range from the very inexpensive to the deluxe quality, and if special features are required, their shop is equipped to install, or revise, or make from scratch.

FACTORY OUTLET

344 139th Ave., (off Washington Ave.), San Leandro 94578. Phone: 352-1778. Hours: M-F 8am-4pm. Purchases: MC, VISA. Parking: Street.

If you would like some colorful travel accessories like garment bags, suit carriers, duffle style totes, backpacks and sport totes then you should give this outlet a visit. These accessories are made from tough 100% nylon parapack cloth or quilted nylon taffeta. Discounts range from 20-50% on overruns, seconds, and discontinued styles or colors.

GETAWAY LUGGAGE

2046 Fourth Street, San Rafael 94901. Phone: 485-1343. Hours: M-Sat 10am-5:30pm, Sun Noon-5pm. Purchases: MC, VISA. Parking: Private Lot.

If you'd like to bag some bargains for next vacation, do it painlessly by shopping at *Getaway Luggage* in San Rafael. This small store is crammed with soft luggage from the "major" quality line manufacturers. (I promised not to put their names in print.) You can fill your trunk with garment bags, pullmans, carry ons (remember to fit under an airline seat they have to be 21'' X 14'' X 9''), and many sizes of duffel bag. Additionally, they have camera bags, sport totes, golf bags, etc. For executives, leather attaches as well as the latest cordura attaches are priced to appeal. My favorite item?: the classic canvas and wood umbrella for $18.95 instead of $30 that is soooo elegant! If you plan on shaving, ironing, doing laundry, etc. while on your vacation, you'll want to give their travel accessory display shelves close scrutiny. Everything is discounted. The average discount on current line merchandise is at least 20% off retail, with special promotions on selected merchandise providing 40-50% discounts. They will special order merchandise or if they run out of the ''specials'', they will order more and give you the ''special'' price. Plans are being made to stock some fine quality American and European made ladies handbags at 20-35% discounts. *Getaway Luggage* is right next to *Seconds Best Mountaineering*, a great resource for down jackets and down comforters.

HARBAND'S LUGGAGE

517 Mission St., San Francisco 94105. Phone: 986-2751. Hours: M-F 9am-5pm. Purchases: MC, VISA, AE. Parking: Street, Pay lot.

The extensive selection of portfolios and attache cases make this a very good gift shopping resource for the executive man or woman. Fine quality leather is their specialty, although vinyls and hard cases are also available. Lark, Skyway, Ventura, Samsonite, Bayley Bags, Halliburton, and Atlas and Schlesinger business cases are some of their lines but there are many more. The discounts are a modest 20% off manufacturers' list prices but some items are not available anywhere for discount. I was particularly pleased with their selection of better wallets, passport cases and travel accessories. Please note: they're closed on Saturdays.

LUGGAGE CLEARANCE CENTER

828 Mission St. (betw. 4th & 5th Sts.), San Francisco 94103. Phone: 543-3771. Hours: M-F 10am-6pm, Sat 10am-5pm, Sun Noon-5pm. Purchases: MC, VISA. Parking: Lot.

First class as well as economy-minded budget travellers know where to head for a great selection and discount prices. Originally, the *Luggage Clearance Center* started as a clearance vehicle for Burke's and Taylors' luggage stores, now they've become a force to be reckoned with on their own. These luggage pieces are first line merchandise, closeouts, and special purchases from companies like American Tourister, Skyway, Samsonite, Lark, Amelia Earhardt, Airway, Halliburton and others. There are no seconds. Their savings range from 30-65%. The selection is about equally divided between soft and hard luggage, with an accommodating selection of travel accessories, totes, attaches, and wallets. They will make exchanges and even give refunds with a receipt and that's almost unheard of in a clearance center!

LUGGAGE TO GO

75-H Bellam Blvd., Marin Square, San Rafael 94901.
Phone: 459-5167. Hours: M-F 10am-9pm, Sat 10am-6pm,
Sun 11am-5pm. Purchases: MC, VISA. Parking: Lot.

This owner is no novice to luggage retailing. His family
has been in the luggage business for generations, and he
also owns a classy luggage store on No. Beverly Drive in
Beverly Hills. Not wanting to miss the trend to off-
price retailing, he's opened this store to pass on savings of
20-60% to consumers on better lines of luggage (many
current styles and fabrications), plus bonus pricing on
special manufacturers' promotions, purchases made directly
from European factories, plus leftovers from the Beverly
Hills' store. Attaches, soft and hard luggage, travel accessories and almost anything required for packing, carting, or
carrying goodies on a trip are carried. The selection is
particularly choice for those wanting better high-end lines
not often found at discount.

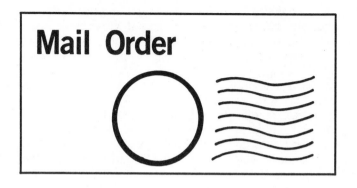

GRAND FINALE

Post Office Box 819027, Farmers Branch, Texas,
75381-9027. Phone Info: (214) 385-2727. Hours: Central
Time M-F 7am-11pm. Purchases: MC, VISA, AE.

Love bargains but never get out to shop? Take heart.
Grand Finale is a separate subsidiary of one of the poshest
catalog houses in the country. Their *Grand Finale* catalog
is full of bargains gleaned from the excess inventory,
closeouts, etc. of other prestigious catalog companies, plus
wonderful items from importers, manufacturers and anywhere else a good buy can be found. The catalog has
"originally" high ticket items, little budget gifts, and
everything in between. You can easily find just the right
gift or treat considering the variety of merchandise offered
in their catalogs. Recent catalogs showed giftwares, practical housewares, fine china and linens, handbags, jewelry,
apparel (silk dresses, raincoats, robes, etc.), desk accessories, executive toys, bed linens, brass beds, small elec-

trics, reproduction antiques, area rugs, closet acccessories, etc., etc. Everything looks deluxe! If you receive many catalogs, you may even guess which company featured these products originally. Savings appear to range from 20-65%. There is a liberal return policy. Just to make sure I ordered a handbag, and returned it without any problems. They'll forward your gifts in a gift box, with golden cord and gift card with your personal message for $1.25 extra. The shipping charges are usually offset by the absence of California sales tax. To get on their mailing list send $2.00 for a year's worth of catalogs (about 10/year) to the address above.

CURRLIN'S MUSIC CENTER

448 So. Winchester Blvd., San Jose 95128. Phone: (408) 241-2051. Hours: M-Th 9:30am-8pm, Fri 9am-6:30pm, Sat 9:30am-5pm. Purchases: MC, VISA. Parking: Lot.

Parents are usually thrilled when their children express interest in learning how to play a band instrument — then they find out how much it costs. If money becomes an obstacle to your budding musician, consider the different options at *Currlin's*. Along with low rate monthly rentals, they have one of the largest stocks of used instruments available for sale (generally 50-60% off of current new prices). For those wishing to buy new instruments, their discounts range from 10-40% off, including hard to find instruments. Another angle is their consignment department. They will sell those old unwanted horns, guitars, or whatever on consignment. They take 20-25% to handle charge card fees, salesman's commission and profit. The folks at this store are very helpful in getting you started within your budget and will even quote prices over the phone.

GUITAR CENTER

1563 Mission St. (corner Van Ness), San Francisco 94102. Phone: 626-7655. Hours: M-F 10am-9pm, Sat 10am-6pm, Sun Noon-6pm. Purchases: MC, VISA. Parking: Street.

☞ **Other Store:** 96 North Second St., San Jose.

At *Guitar Center* their motto is "Don't go on stage without us." From all reports this "the" source for the Rock'N'Roll crowd. With seven stores nationwide they operate on a volume basis which enables them to offer prices to the consumer that the competition just can't beat. Prices are negotiable, so sharpen your horse trading skills. Watch their ads for heavily discounted promotions that are the stuff dreams are made of. For professional quality musical equipment, P.A. equipment, keyboard equipment and accessories, you have a chance to buy maximum value for the money you have to spend whether you're a rank amateur or a big money professional. They will take your old equipment in trade, offer lay-a-ways, haggle, do anything to make that sale.

Paper Goods and Stationery

(Also see **General Merchandise — Discount Stores, Liquidators**)

AMSTERDAM ARTS

(See **Arts, Crafts and Hobby Supplies**)

ARVEY PAPER CO.

2275 Alameda St. (corner of Potrero), San Francisco 94103. Phone: 863-3664. Hours: M-F 8am-5pm, Sat 9am-2pm. Purchases: Cash or Check. Parking: Street and lot.

☞ **Other Stores:** 229 Castro St., Oakland; 1381 No. 10th St., San Jose; 1101 Richards Blvd., Sacramento; 1445 Veterans Blvd., Redwood City.

Arvey caters to small-to-medium businesses, organizations, printers, churches and offices. Your average consumer gets a fair shake too! They offer a unique, selfservice, warehouse store that's got it all: cut-size printing papers of every description, envelopes, announcements, graphic supplies, copy papers and toners, mimeo/duplicating papers and supplies, small printing equipment, janitorial supplies, packaging supplies and on and on. Their office supply section is bigger and better priced than most office supply stores. The stores aren't too fancy, but that keeps their overhead and prices low. They've entered the computer age along with everyone else, with computer papers, printer ribbons, and diskettes at 15-40% off. People come in, wander up and down the aisles to get what they need (and probably a few things they didn't plan on buying), and often wait in line more than a few minutes before checking out. Checkout seems to take forever, as each item is listed, priced and totaled. For most people this documentation is essential for tax purposes, but geez I wish they'd develop a more efficient system!. If you're a big user of stationery supplies, get on their mailing list. I zoom in every few months for super sales on the special items I need.

CASH AND CARRY WARHOUSE
(See **Food**)

PRICE CLUB
(See **General Merchandise — Discounters**)

SUTTER PARTY SALES
6121 San Pablo Ave., Oakland 94611. Phone: 655-5366. Hours: M-F 10am-6pm, Sat 10am-3pm. Purchases: MC, VISA. Parking: Street.

Sutter is a very popular resource for party planners. They have favors, streamers, confetti and all the other props for children's parties, plus the paper plates, napkins, invitations etc. For grown up occasions: weddings, showers, and other social events, the paper goods selection is not only reasonably priced, but the color range in plates, cups, and napkins is delightful to contemplate when developing a theme for an occasion. Long, banquet sized table cloths in colors, prints, both plastic coated and in traditional paper are available. Heavy cut glass plastic serving trays, bowls, and platters are sturdy enough to last through many parties. Doilies, paper place mats, and other paraphernalia for party planners constitute a convenient one stop resource.

Shoes

I have tried to include those shoe stores with the best quality shoes at the lowest prices. Since you will be saving 20-60% off retail prices, you should be prepared to forgo some of the creature comforts of a regular shoe store. Many stores are selfservice, and you have to dig into a pile to find what you want. To try on your discoveries, you may have to perch on a hard wooden bench or even lean against a wall. For the most part, the inventory in these stores consists of factory closeouts, samples, cancellations, seconds, and overruns, resulting in a limited selection of sizes, colors, and styles. Typically, when shopping for shoes think in terms of "hit' or miss"; you may or may not find what you want on your first sortee. It pays to select particular stores that are most likely to have the selection that appeals to you and then shop them frequently.

ATHLETIC SHOE FACTORY STORES
320 Walnut (Peninsula Boardwalk), Redwood City 94063. Phone: 932-9056. Hours: M-F 9:30am-9pm, Sat 10am-6pm, Sun Noon-5pm. Purchases: MC, VISA. Parking: Lot.

☞ **Other Stores:** Alameda, Citrus Heights, Colma, Concord, Campbell, Cupertino, Los Gatos, Merced, Modesto, Mountain View, Napa, Newark, Palo Alto, Petaluma, Oakland, Sacramento, Redwood City, Rancho Cordova, San Jose, San Francisco, San Lorenzo, San Mateo, San Rafael, Santa Cruz, Santa Rosa, Stockton, Sunnyvale, Vallejo, Walnut Creek.

If anyone in your family is engaged in running, tennis, basketball, soccer or racketball, or just prefers the comfort of athletic shoes, they'll find a terrific selection and good prices at this chain of stores. About 90% of the inventory is new, first quality merchandise. These first quality shoes may also be closeouts, discontinued styles or colors from any and all of the big time manufacturers. The rest of the selection is priced ultra low because they are seconds or "blems". If you look carefully you may note a smudge of glue on the canvas or suede, the stitching may be crooked or overstitched for correction, or you may be hard pressed to find the flaw. Anyone following the shoe scene can't help but notice that shoe styles and colors are more abundant and seem to change faster than the car models each year. Of course, this is all contrived to keep the fashion-minded jogger back into the stores to get the "latest". They have a good size range for men, women, and children and everyone in the family can readily help themselves. These stores are geared for selfservice. After you've selected your new shoes, you can check the discounts on active sportswear. Warm-up suits, jogging shorts, shirts and socks and many other accessories all geared to the jock are available. Shoe prices are consistently 15-40% off retail.

BOOT HILL

3191 Crow Canyon Place, San Ramon 94583. Phone: 820-8164. Hours: MT & F 10am-6pm, W & Th 10am-8pm, Sat & Sun 10am-5pm. Purchases: MC, VISA. Parking: Lot.

☞ **Other Stores:** 1375 Blossom Hill Rd., Princeton Plaza, San Jose, (408) 978-9122; coming to Fairfield, Sacramento.

Jeff the owner says: "I've brought boot prices back to reality". With an aggressive pricing policy based on volume sales, a lower markup, and vigorous advertising, Jeff fulfills his promise and offers a solid 20-35% discount on all major brands of western boots. Prices start around $52 and can go well over $500 on the most expensive fine leather, handmade exotically designed boots. Brands like Lucchese, T. O. Stanley, Justin, Zodiac, Dan Post, Tony Lama, Frye, Durango, Wolverine and others are well represented in the 2,500-3,000 pairs of boots on display in sizes 7-15 in mens and 5-10 in womens. Styles run the gamut from very low key to those that would meet the wardrobe requirements of a top country/western recording star.

BROWN BROS. SHOE WAREHOUSE

848 Lincoln Ave. (at 9th St), Alameda 94501. Phone: 865-3700. Hours: M-Sat 9:30am-6pm. Purchases: Cash or Check. Parking: Street.

Brown Bros. has been in business for over 48 years with little fanfare or advertising. Many men have returned here over the years like geese flying south to pick up their shoes for work, leisure or the corporate office life. They don't turn their noses up at the lack of class in decor, because there's class enough in the selection. Their shoes are all first quality, purchased in volume lots or in special make-up orders from manufacturers like Freeman, Walk-Over, Stacy Adams, International, Santa Rosa boots, Sperry Top-Siders, Puma, Chippewa and Brooks. Many are sold under the *Brown Bros.* label. Shoe sizes in boys range from 2 1/2 to 6, with men's sizes in 6-14 to EEE widths. Their athletic shoes by Nike and Converse are sold for solid discount prices. They have some of the lowest prices on Santa Rosa boots that I've been able to find, which is why so many hardworking fellas go miles out of their way to do business with them. You'll always find a good shoe, at a reasonable price, usually 25-40% off retail. Exchanges and refunds allowed.

CLOTHES RACK
(See **Apparel — Women's, Chain Stores**)

CASBAH II

751 Bridgeway, Sausalito. Phone: 332-2018. Hours: M-Sun 10:30am-7pm. Purchases: MC, VISA. Parking: Lot.

The *Casbah I* store in Sausalito is known for fine quality high fashion shoes. To handle the end-of-season, broken size lots, odds'n'ends, they opened *Casbah II* which is a few doors away and upstairs. At *Casbah II* you also find special purchases, manufacturers' overruns, plus all the *Casbah I* rejects. Sizes for women are 5-10. The selection includes casual styles like espadrilles, moccasins, sandals, also casual and dress heels, boots, but no jogging shoes. Some styles are very current and still sold in other styles at high prices while others have passed their season.

CHILDREN'S BOOTERY (JUMPING JACKS FACTORY OUTLET)

2335 Buchanan Road, Antioch 94509. Phone: 754-7774. Hours: M-Sat 10am-5:30pm, Sun Noon-5pm. Purchases: MC, VISA. Parking: Lot.

☞ **Other Stores:** 51 Almaden Plaza, San Jose (408) 265-1931; 20694 Stevens Creek Bl., Cupertino, (408) 255-9012

Jumping Jacks shoes are familiar to most parents who have bought white high tops for their little ones. Prices on these basic styles have certainly gone up since I bought my last pair 14 years ago. At the *Children's Bootery Jumping Jacks Factory Outlet*, all their shoes are discounted at least 30% below retail. These are the first quality overruns. Shoes with yellow tags are discounted 50% and most often

are "blems" with tiny imperfections that do not impair the quality or functional aspects of the shoe. They may also be last season's styles.

In addition to baby and toddler basics, they have a complete selection that encompasses the needs of children from infants through teens. Styles include dress, loafer, patent, athletic, deck, oxfords, saddles, low heeled pumps, sandals, etc. Forget the frustration of shoelaces with one of the many styles that have velcro closing tabs. Sizes range from 0 to ladies size 10, (teen styles) or boys size 7. Basically self service, the fitting needs of children and infants are given careful attention upon request. Little Capezio, owned by Jumping Jacks, is also sold at the same discounts. A liberal return and exchange policy adds up to a perfect children's resource. Note: The Antioch store is right next to the *Carter's Factory Outlet*.

FAMOUS FOOTWEAR

2064 El Camino Real (Mervyn's Plaza), Santa Clara, 95050. Phone: (408) 554-0766. Hours: M-F 10am-9pm, Sat 10am-6pm, Sun Noon-5pm. Purchases: MC VISA. Parking: Lot.

☞ **Other Stores:** Howe & Hurley Way and Lake Crest Shopping Center, Sacramento; Sunrise Hills Center, Citrus Heights; Fremont Hub Shopping Center, Fremont.

Famous Footwear's merchandising concept: good shoes — good prices, leading to one of the best selections of fine quality brand name shoes at the lowest possible prices. Their buying is done in three different ways: in stock shoes, closeouts, and make-ups. In stock shoes are bought directly from the manufacturer. These are basic brand name items like Air Step, Naturalizer, Bass, Candies, etc. They are able to get a complete range of sizes and styles in these shoes, because they are manufactured on a daily basis and are available in stock. Closeouts are styles of shoes that have been discontinued by a company. They also may buy a line of name brand shoes that were to be purchased by another retailer, but were cancelled for some reason. Occasionally a supplier overproduces a particular style resulting in an overstock — these shoes are also considered close-outs. They purchase these at a lower than wholesale price than they would originally have had to pay. This method of buying ensures their customers of substantial savings on namebrand shoes. Make-ups are specifically designed shoes that are patterned after brand name shoes. These shoes can be sold at a lower price because they have them made especially for *Famous Footwear*. Their make-ups are unique to the industry, and have begun to gain a popularity and acceptance of their own.

Each store has approximately 20,000 pairs of shoes in a selection of styles geared to suit the needs of an entire family. Bring in infants, grandparents, boys, girls, teens, men and women, for casual, school, playground, work, backpacking, dress, office, etc. Their size ranges include medium, in greatest selection, but with a respectable offering of wide and narrow shoes. Women's sizes: 4-12, Men's 7-13.

Now for the best news: prices are discounted a minimun of 10% to a maximum of 40% off retail. Prices on their athletic shoes, i.e. Nike, Puma, Converse etc. are close to competitors' prices, yet they claim they will match any price with the exception of seconds or blems. Their strength lies in the selection of what I call "sensible" shoes for women, although they don't ignore the latest trendsetting styles either. Most ladies casual and dress shoes are priced from $20-$40. For the woman who usually buys fine shoes at prices of $100 and up, this may not be the store for you. Their basic market is the woman spending $35-$75 at full retail pricing. Some brand names to whet your appetite: Women's — Naturalizer, Cities, Capezio, Connie, Fan Fair, Air Step, Palizio, LifeStride, Old Maine Trotters, Joyce, Cities, Bass; Men's — Bally, Bostonian, Sperry Topsider, Freeman, Florsheim, French Shriner, Roblee, Dingo, Stacy Adams, Acme, Street Cars, Big Country, etc.; Children's — Jumping Jacks, Robin Hood, Buster Brown, Capezio, Stride-Rite, Crickets, etc. Not too bad!! *Famous Footwear* is geared for selfservice, yet they will give you as much help in terms of fitting and measuring as you need.

KUSHIN'S HAYWARD SALE CENTER

22443 Foothill Blvd., Hayward 94541. Phone: 537-2411. Hours: M-Sat 10am-6pm, Thurs & Fri eve. till 8pm. Purchases: MC, VISA. Parking: Pay Lot.

☞ **Other Store:** 39166 Paseo Padre, Fremont, 793-8079.

Two of *Kushin's* regular shoe stores have been converted into an outlet for all the shoes that didn't sell at their other stores. Moreover, they buy factory samples, cancellations, and special factory make-up orders from namebrand manufacturers that they private label and sell for considerably less than the branded merchandise. Familiar *Kushin's* labels are Red Cross, Joyce, Cobbie, Sabicca, Bear Traps, Famolare, and Freeman plus Hush Puppies for men. Discounts on all these shoes may range from 30-75%

depending on how dated the styles may be or the manner in which they were purchased by the store. There are usually about 5,000 pairs of shoes on racks for convenient selfservice and many more in the back room that can be brought out by the sales personnel.

KUTLER BROS.
(See **Apparel — Men**)

LA GOSHIG
264 Eastmont Mall (Betw. Penney's & Mervyns), Oakland 94605. Phone: 638-2299. Hours: M-F 10am-9pm, Sat 10am-5pm, Sun Noon-5pm. Purchases: MC, VISA. Parking: Lot.

☞ **Other Stores:** 733 Laurel St., San Carlos; McArthur/Broadway Shopping Center, Oakland; Bayfair Mall, San Leandro.

Nickels, 9 West, Life Stride, Caressa, Palizzio, Cities, Nina and other well known brands are sold at discount at all *La Goshig* stores. On current styles the discount is usually 25% off retail, while end-of-season closeouts are more like 40-50% off. Sizes are 5-10. Many styles are the same as those being currently sold at major stores (but the colors may be different) and are appealing for office or dressy occasions. This is basically a selfservice operation which suits me just fine. Don't leave the stores without checking the selection of better leather handbags priced at discount from $18-$60.

L & L OUTLET
(See **Apparel — Active Sportswear**)

MARSHALL'S
(See **Apparel — Family**)

ON A SHOESTRING
75-L Bellam Way, Marin Square, San Rafael 94901. Phone: 454-2552. Hours: M-Sat 10am-6pm, Sun Noon-5pm. Purchases: MC, VISA. Parking: Lot.

☞ **Other Stores:** Crow Canyon Place Shopping Ctr., San Ramon; 1207 Bridgeway, Sausalito.

The motto here is "Nothing but the very best for the best price." By keeping in close touch with Los Angeles jobbers, and buying in-season closeouts and cancellations, the owners are able to offer 10-60% savings on their selection of better brands. You won't find any cheap imitation leathers. Some of the brands you'll consistently spot are Amalfi, BeeneBag, Joan & David, Andrew Geller, Palizzio, Innocence, 9 West and Pappagallo in narrow and medium widths. Their stock changes frequently. You won't always find all the shoes in a complete size or color range. Styles include casual flats, dress heels, canvas fashions and boots.

PATTI QUINN'S
(See **Apparel — Women's, Chain Stores**)

DONNA PILLER'S
12 Clement St., San Francisco 94118. Phone: 752-9106. Hours: M-Sat 11am-6pm. Purchases: AE, MC, VISA. Parking: Street.

This small boutique is associated with *Jerry Piller* in Los Angeles (a favorite with bargain hunters in that area). She has a dedicated following of women who are searching for clothes with high-fashion appeal and clothes noted for fine quality. The *Jerry Piller* family buys sale apparel from the finest boutiques around the country and call themselves a "sale" store, not a discount store. You'll find a lot of designer clothes. Be prepared for a long looksee when checking out their shoe selection upstairs. There are boxes of French and European designer shoes to prowl through. I find going through all those boxes tedious, while others find it exciting. The shoes which range in sizes 4 1/2 to 10 in narrow and medium widths sport some very prestigious labels. Charles Jourdan, Walter Steiger, Alberto Molina, Miguel Hernandez, Bally and others are sold for 25-50% off retail. You won't find many shoes for under $50 even at reduced prices because many of these shoes are priced from $100-$250 at retail. This is just the place for the "shoe freak".

ROSS DEPARTMENT STORES
(See **Apparel — Family**)

SAMPLE SHOE SHOPPE
202 Clement St., San Francisco 94118. Phone: 386-4582. Hours: M-Sat 10:30-6:30pm. Purchases: MC, VISA. Parking: Street.

For good shoe buys this small store offers some real possibilities for those who can stop in now and then. Discounts from 15-50% prevail on ladies shoes in sizes 4-10, with a selection for those who wear sample sizes 6 and 6 1/2. Each shoe is marked with the size range available in that particular style. Men's samples are also available in sizes 8-8 1/2.

THE SANDAL FACTORY
420 Maple St., Redwood City 94063. Phone: 365-4077. Hours: M-F 10am-6pm, Sat 10am-4pm. Purchases: MC, VISA. Parking: Street.

At the *Sandal Factory* all products in their factory store are sold at the current wholesale price plus 10%. This represents about a 40% savings to the customer on their Paw Print (similar to Birkenstock) sandals, men's and women's wallets and many other small leather goods. All of their products are made of leather produced and tanned in the USA. Their comfortable sandals come in women's sizes from 5-10, and men's sizes from 6-12.

SHOE CITY, U.S.A.
1910 El Camino Real, Mountain View 94040. Phone: 969-8393. Hours: M-Sat 9:30am-6pm, T & Th till 9pm. Purchases: MC, VISA. Parking: Lot.

The owner of this shoe store buys cancelled orders and overruns directly from manufacturers as well as from several jobbers. If it weren't for stores like this manufacturers would suffer real losses. You win at the cash register by saving 33-60% off retail prices. The shoes are all first quality, often in current styles, but some are definitely the leftovers from previous seasons. Quality is in the middle range, with lines like Joyce, Nina, Cobbies, Daisy, and Life Stride plus many others. For men, Nunn Bush, Bostonian and Frye Boots are popular brands. Sizes for women range from 4-12, AAA-W; for men, 6-15 A-EEE. This is a selfservice operation; however, the salespeople are helpful without being pushy. It's hard to spend more than $46; you'll probably spend less than that on their shoes that range in price from $20-$60 at retail.

SHOE FAIR
2147 Junipero Serra Blvd., Daly City 94014. Phone: 755-0556. Hours: M-F 9am-9pm, Sat 9am-6pm, Sun 11am-5pm. Purchases: MC, VISA. Parking: Lot.

☞ **Other Stores:** Oakland, Cupertino, Campbell, South San Francisco, Pleasant Hill, San Lorenzo, San Jose, San Mateo.

Shoe Fair, the "House of Famous Brands", is a large complete family shoe store. They have a satisfying selection of sizes in casual, sporty, athletic, and dressy shoes.

Styles in ladies shoes range from very conservative to terribly trendy; brands range from obscure imported labels to well known names like Joyce, 9 West, Sabicca, and on occasion some surprises with status brands like Bruno Magli and Christian Dior. The men's selection is very complete with dress shoes from Nunn Bush, Stacy Adams, Jarman, British Walker etc., casuals from Hush Puppies, Street Cars, Levi's, etc., work books from Gorilla, Wolverine, Santa Rosa, etc., and western boots from Frye, Durango, Dingo and Abelene. Watch their weekly ads featuring special sales and promotions to know when to "buy right."

THE SHOE HOUSE
1299 Washington Ave., San Leandro Plaza, San Leandro 94577. Phone: 352-7800. Hours: M-Sat 10am-6pm, Sun Noon-5pm. Purchases: MC, VISA. Parking: Lot.

Three generations in the same family of women can stop in and each can leave with just what they want: sensible walking shoes for grandma, office/career dress shoes for mom, and the latest trendy teen fashions for daughter. The shoes are moderate lines that at discount prices range from $14.99-$34.99, a savings of 30-60% off retail. The real bargain prices are always on their clearance racks or their red tag specials. With 5,000 pairs of shoes in sizes 4-12, narrow, medium and wide widths, it's easy to find something that suits your budget and your needs.

SHOE MART

1014 W. El Camino Real, Sunnyvale 94087. Phone: (408) 738-9836. Hours: M-F 9am-9pm, Sat & Sun 10am-6pm. Purchases: MC, VISA. Parking: Lot.

☞ **Other Stores:** Millbrae, San Carlos.

A complete shoe store for the entire family, this *Shoe Mart* offers nationally known and advertised brands of shoes for men, women and children. Making large purchases of overstocks allows these stores to sell shoes at considerably lower than retail prices. The styles are fair to great, some up-to-date, some over-the-hill. Outstanding values are standard on work boots for men, sandals for women, and play shoes for children.

SHOE-TOWN

33 Westlake Mall (near Loehmann's) Westlake Shopping Center, Daly City 94015. Phone: 991-9080. Hours: M-F 10am-9pm, Sat 10-6:30, Sun Noon-5pm. Purchases: MC, VISA. Parking: Lot.

☞ **Other Stores:** 5136 Broadway, Rockridge Shopping Ctr., Oakland. 700 El Camino Real, Menlo Station, Menlo Park; 1691 Willow Pass Road, Park and Shop Center, Concord, 680-6249.

The executives at this company suggest that "*Shoe-Town* is to shoes what *Loehmann's* is to women's clothing". They operate nearly 200 stores nationwide consistently offering first quality merchandise at prices substantially below those of department and independent shoe stores. A typical *Shoe-Town* store has thousands of pairs of branded shoes from the world's leading manufacturers. All are first quality and all retain the famous designer labels like Bally, Jacques Cohen, Bandolino, Sasson, Jordache, Life Stride, Red Cross, I. Miller, Evan Picone, Andrew Geller, Nina, Liz Claiborne, Charles Jourdan, Amalfi, etc. Every *Shoe-Town* carries fine handbags, hosiery and related accessories geared to one-stop footwear shopping.

In addition to buying from top manufacturers in the United States, they purchase from Italy, Spain, South America and a number of other countries offering quality product lines. Since they buy in volume, they buy for less, and they pass the savings along to their customers. A typical *Shoe-Town* store carries 20,000 pairs of shoes; an average female *Shoe-Town* shopper, for example, can expect to find from 600-900 pairs of shoes in her size alone, many in the latest designer fashions. New shoes arrive every few days, an inducement for customers to stop in frequently.

Price, of course, is the bottom line. Shoes are discounted from 20-60% depending on what kind of buy *Shoe-Town* makes. There is a mix of current, past season, and overruns, plus closeouts from the finest department and specialty stores. Each shoe has two prices and you can expect to find the smaller discounts on the most current shoes. The selection will include everything from slippers to jogging shoes, with a good selection of boots.

SHOE WORLD

880 El Portal Center, San Pablo 94806. Phone: 236-8121. Hours: M-F 9:30am-9pm, Sat 9:30am-6pm, Sun Noon-5pm. Purchases: MC, VISA. Parking: Lot.

☞ **Other Store:** 6972 Amador Plaza Rd., Dublin. (Children's shoes only).

Excellent values in shoes for the whole family! There are many fine quality name brands available in prices from $14.99-$34, which represents savings from 25-75%. The shoes are purchased from volume lots, short lots, make-up orders, and manufacturer's overstocks — complicated buying techniques resulting in low prices. Hard-to-find sizes are available as well as a complete selection of styles to suit every taste. Some of the ladies shoes are not necessarily the latest style, but if you've a mind of your own and wear what you like regardless of what Madison Avenue dictates, you can really find some fine-quality classic styles. On current styles the discount is 10-20%. Many shoes are sold under their private label but are actually from quality makers such as Red Cross, Air Step and Cobbie. I was especially pleased to find some children's shoes from Jumping Jacks and Capezio that are factory irregulars and first quality at great discounts available here. This is also a clearance center for *Carlin's* quality shoe stores.

SLICK CHICK SHOE AND SHIRT STOP

3160-D Danville Blvd., Alamo 94507. Phone: 838-2658. Hours: M-F 10am-5:30pm, Sat 10am-5pm. Purchases: MC, VISA. Parking: Lot.

☞ **Other Store:** 1012 School St., Moraga.

Although this store sells clothing I am far more intrigued by their shoe selection. Their discount prices are available because they buy from jobbers, closeouts from manufacturers, and they buy some styles at regular wholesale prices and take a smaller markup. Sizes range from 5-10 in narrow and medium widths for women. Prices are reduced up to 50% off retail.

STANDARD SHOE MART

300 El Camino Real, Millbrae 94030. Phone: 697-4014. Hours: M-Sat 9:30am-6pm. Purchases: MC, VISA. Parking: Lot.

Standard Shoe Mart has been in the same location for so long it's easy to take them for granted or to forget they're still there. Yet, their selection is very good for men and women with many namebrand lines sold at 20-50% off. What appeals to many women is that they have a bigger selection in wide widths than most shoe stores. Not only do they have no nonsense basic styles for comfort and days "on your feet," they also have the latest looks in high fashion styles. All shoes are first quality. Their boot selection in dress and casual styles for women and particularly in work boots for men is very good. Naturally, after being in the same building for 20 years, their overhead is minimal, giving them the advantage in establishing prices and markups.

A STEP FORWARD

3281 Lakeshore Ave., Oakland 94610. Phone: 835-4300. Hours: M-W & Sat 10am-5:30pm, Th & F 10am-6:30pm. Purchases: MC, VISA. Parking: Street.

If you covet the fine quailty and lovely styles of Joan and David shoes, you can out-foot your feet here for a pleasing discount. The store serves in part as a clearing-house for end-of-season, overruns, and slow moving merchandise at 15-50% off. In-season shoes are discounted far less than the stuff on the clearance racks, but that's to be expected. For instance: shoes that retail for $70-$125 are sold for $59-$99. The boots at $115-$275 are $79-$225. This line is simply beautiful as the prices indicate. I try to stop by from time to time to keep up with new shipments.

WHOLE EARTH ACCESS STORE
(See **General Merchandise**)

(Also See **General Merchandise — all headings**)

CS ENTERPRISES

350 East San Carlos Ave., San Carlos 94070. Phone: 595-1060. Hours: M-F 8am-4pm, Most Saturdays 10am-2pm. Purchases: Cash or Check. Parking: Lot.

If you have a pilot, motorcycle enthusiast or frequent traveler in your midst, send them down to *CS Enterprises*. For the biker, the Cordura Moto-X pants (sizes 22-42), Enduro Street Jackets (XS-XL) moped saddle bags, tank bags, seat covers, tank covers, soft saddle bags and neck shields at 30-60% off will sure meet their requirements for quality and price. This manufacturer produces a line of travel gear from virtually indestructible Cordura in sport bags for students, skiers and a neat selection of travel luggage and garment bags. Pilots can meet their needs too with chart bags, tool bags, map pockets and log book holders. All of these exotic items are overruns, occasional irregulars, discontinued colors or styles. *CS* is a little hard to find so I suggest calling for directions to get their back alley location.

EURO SPORT

462 Bryant St., San Francisco 94107. Phone: 957-1619. Hours: Sat. & Sun 10am-5pm. Purchases: MC, VISA. Parking: Street, Pay lots.

Skiing enthusiasts will want to watch *Euro Sport's* ads in the *Chronicle*, *Examiner*, and Oakland *Tribune* that announce their sales which occur nearly every weekend between September and December. *Euro Sport* is associated with Swiss Ski Sports and Swiss Ski Chalet, serving as a clearinghouse for all merchandise that is left over from previous seasons, or represents special purchases of closeouts from wellknown manufacturers. Often merchandise from one year to the next doesn't change that much, a new color or a small modification in style replaces the old. Their warehouse on Bryant Street is close to the Bay Bridge with ample parking on weekends. Everything is organized for selfservice but they have enough salespeople to help the novice at selecting skis, poles, bindings, boots, etc. For the beginner, wary of a major investment, their preassembled packages of skiing equipment represent a very good buy. Savings generally range from 20-50% off the original prices. Some of their best values are found on skiwear for men, women, juniors and children. Bib pants, parkas, vests, ski sweaters and windshirts can be pur-

chased, although lines for the dressing rooms may discourage the impatient.

FRY'S WAREHOUSE SPORTS

352 East Grand Ave., South San Francisco 94080. Phone: 583-5034. Hours: M-F 9:30am-6pm, Sat 10am-5pm. Purchases: MC, VISA. Parking: Street.

☞ **Other Store:** 2235 Lawrence Expwy. at Lakehaven, Sunnyvale.

If you play golf or tennis, you'll be interested in the values and selection at *Fry's*. *Fry's* carries better Pro Shop lines of shoes, clothing and equipment, offers discount prices because of the volume purchasing power plus their ability to buy special make-up orders from top manufacturers.

In the clothing categories they carry Izod shirts and jackets, Adidas warmup suits and shoes, Pierre Cardin, Hagger, Lilly Dache and Munsingwear lines. In equipment you can buy all the little accessories plus the basics from brands like Wilson, Lynx, Power Bilt, Dunlop, Spalding, Hogan, Bag Boy, MacGregor, Rossignol, Etonic and Foot-joy. These are not seconds or closeouts. While a discount operation, they do provide free club fitting with their golfswing computer, tennis stringing, and will take telephone orders using a credit card. In fact, I think it's a good idea to call ahead for availability if you're some distance away. Better yet, the next time you have to pick someone up from the San Francisco airport, go early and stop by their store which is just North of the Airport. Check their ads in the sporting sections of the *Chronicle* and *Examiner* if you want to keep on top of their "extra specials".

GUS' DISCOUNT FISHING EQUIPMENT

3710 Balboa St. (bet. 38th & 39th), San Francisco 94121. Phone: 752-6197. Hours: M-Sat 8am-4:30pm. Purchases: MC, VISA. Parking: Street.

If words like crocodile, pencil popper, super duper mean anything to you, read on. While not claiming any expertise or particular familiarity with the requirements of sport fishermen, I can comparison shop prices on these exotic (to me) essentials of the fishing junkie. *Gus' Discount Fishing Equipment* is an experience! First there's Stephanie a young 90 lb. dynamo who manages the store for her father with infectious enthusiasm, unbelievable energy, impressive knowledge of all things fish related. Next, the prices which entice the regulars to stop in almost daily on their way to the water to see what's new.

Serving as a West Coast wholesale distributor for Master, Ryobi, and Olympic, they also have the opportunity to buy factory overruns, salvage losses, and inventory from store liquidations. *Everything* is discounted from 25-60% off original retail. They have equipment for salmon, trout, freshwater, saltwater, and surf fishing. The terminal tackle selection in bins, boxes and counter displays deserves careful scrutiny. All rods and reels are guaranteed except for the rebuilt rods that sell for $1/ft. There's no time or inclination to set up gleaming displays, and the regulars certainly don't care. What keeps them coming are the prices and the element of surprise as each new shipment is unloaded. If you're a novice don't worry. There's plenty of free advice offered by the regulars when Stephanie or her staff are busy. And finally they buy salvage and surplus "stuff" in housewares, Xmas ornaments, baskets etc. and sell it cheap, cheap, cheap.

MOUNTAIN TRAIL FACTORY OUTLET

2353 East 12th St., Oakland 94601. Phone: 532-5220. Hours: M-Sat 10am-6pm, Sun Noon-5pm. Purchases: MC, VISA. Parking: Street, Lot.

Mountain Trail in Oakland is where Twin Peaks sells all their factory surplus, irregulars, discontinued styles and samples. Twin Peaks manufactures sleeping bags for sale under their own label, and also to sell under the private label of many well known retailers of quality outdoor gear. (The names would impress you but I promised not to tell.) They also make parkas, jackets, vests, booties, and serve as a clearance center for another well known maker of tents, poles, stakes, backpacks etc. They have down filled products and offer the latest advances in textile fibers, constructions, and designs that are available in the marketplace.

Prices at the outlet on these clearance categories are usually reduced a minimum of 20% off retail, and more likely 30-50% off. There are in-store, unadvertised, ongoing specials and promotions all the time. Get on the mailing list for occasional "blow out" sales. If prices seem high on some racks, you're probably looking at new, current season merchandise that is not discounted. To round out their inventory, they've brought in many lines of sweat shirts, T-shirts, shorts, camping accessories, etc., all discounted to please and tempt. Sizes for the whole family.

MERCHANDISERS INC.
(See **Apparel — Men**)

THE NORTH FACE FACTORY OUTLET
1238 Fifth St., Berkeley 94710. Phone: 526-3530. Hours:
M-Sat 10am-6pm, Thurs Eve till 8pm, Sun 11am-4pm.
Purchases: MC, VISA. Parking: Street.

☞ **Other Store:** 605 Cambridge, Menlo Park, 327-4865.

All you Sierra Club types and fresh air fans take note:
The North Face manufactures functional outdoor equipment. Their aim is to provide versatile gear for comfortable and efficient wilderness travel in all climates,
conditons, and places.

Their factory outlet stores feature four categories of
bargain merchandise with savings of 20% on all their
seconds. These include clothing (parkas, hoods, vests for
men and women), backpacks, sleeping bags, accessories,
and even tents. They have hiking boots in limited sizes;
these are mostly old styles, and Cross-country skis and
boots are discounted 40% and more. Wool shirts and
sweaters, discontinued men's and women's shorts and
turtlenecks are available in varying supply and are discounted from 20-50%. The selection of bargains depends
on the season with their biggest sales in November and
May. Their seconds are functional and have only cosmetic
flaws such as a run or snag in the fabric, off color or
patch.

R.E.I. CO-OP
1338 San Pablo, Berkeley 94702. Phone: 527-4140. Hours:
MT 10am-6:30pm, WThF 10am-9pm, Sat 9:30am-6pm.
Purchases: MC, VISA. Parking: Lot.

If you're involved in any activity or sport that requires
special equipment or clothing, *R.E.I.* offers their customers
and *Co-op* members good prices and a complete selection.
For $5.00 you can join their *Co-op* which entitles you to a
dividend at the end of the year based on your purchases.
All the people I know in Scouting, backpacking, skiing,
rafting, golfing, tennis, et al., check *R.E.I.* prices first. On
my comparisons with other sports equipment company
catalogs, *R.E.I.* came out with a good value/quality/
price ratio. In all equipment lines they offer several
qualities and price ranges. It's up to you to determine what
your investment should be depending upon your involve-
ment in your sport and the use you hope to get out of your
purchases. Their clothing department is very nice, but
nearly everything is sold at the regular retail price.

SECONDS BEST MOUNTAINEERING
2042 4th St., San Rafael 94901. Phone: 457-5544. Hours:
M-Sat 10am-5:30pm, Sun Noon-5pm. Purchases: MC,
VISA. Parking: Lot.

This store is just crammed with goodies for the moun-
taineer and skier. You can save on name brands like
Snowlion, Class 5, Campy, Wilderness Experience, Kelty,
Jan Sport, Lowe, and Sierra West. Originally, the store
was filled with seconds. No more. Now they have a good
selection of first quality merchandise all discounted
20-45% off retail as a result of their savvy buying of

closeouts, volume purchases and selected seconds. Not only do they get you ready for the heights, they also have an appeal for local residents who just want to buy a good jacket, (down, Goretex, or poly-filled) vest, or shorts for "round the town" needs. The selection is stylish with many fashion jackets in current colors, and and even includes Vuarnet sunglasses at 20% off. They always carry a respectable array of sleeping bags in summer, and down comforters in winter. Their comforters are the best, and they've got all the fill weights and facts to assure you that you're buying a quality product at the best price. All sales are final. Watch for their ads in local newspapers.

SIERRA DESIGNS

2039 4th St., at Addison, Berkeley 94710. Phone: 548-5588. Hours: M-Sat 10am-6pm, Sun Noon-4pm (may vary). Purchases: MC, VISA. Parking: Street.

Sierra Designs makes mistakes too! You can find their seconds in a corner at each of their three Bay Area stores. Everything is reduced 20-40% such as down sleeping bags, jackets, tents, or occasionally, packs and other related backpacking, cross-country skiing and mountaineering equipment. Overstocked or discontinued "Firsts" are marked down 10-15%. Each year, in the spring and fall, *Sierra Designs* has their super sales. If you get on their mailing list you won't miss out. Men's sizes XS-XL, women's 6-14.

SKI CONTROL WAREHOUSE OUTLET

1717 Solano Way #7, Concord 94520. Phone: 680-6531. Hours: M-Sat 11am-6pm, Sun hours Nov & Dec.-call first. Purchases: MC, VISA. Parking: Lot.

At *Ski Control's Warehouse Outlet* in the Solano Business Park the merchandise has been carefully selected to provide all the essentials for the skier at a minimal price. The more sophisticated, expensive equipment and apparel, geared for the advanced skier is not much in evidence, since their primary goal is to outfit families at an affordable price. Beginning and intermediate skiers can buy boots, bindings, skis, and poles, with a one year guarantee, in new or used packages or individually. They'll be assured of receiving appropriate and adequate equipment for their level. The *Ski Control* Size-Ma-Graph assures you that your equipment is suitable for your height and weight.

The discounts of 30-50% off namebrand merchandise are possible because of their buying techniques and their ability to deal directly with manufacturers in obtaining closeouts at below wholesale prices. Special orders on some lines are made with discount prices and a 10 working day delivery time. Some lines: Head, Raffe, Yamaha, Rossignol, Elan and many more. Sizes in clothing accommodate the whole family.

SONOMA OUTFITTERS

1702 Fourth St., Santa Rosa 95404. Phone: (707) 528-1920. Hours: M-F 10am-6pm, Th till 9pm, Sat 10am-5:30pm, Sun Noon-5pm. Purchases: MC, VISA. Parking: Lot.

In the Sonoma county this is where to go to buy backpacking and camping equipment, climbing gear, down jackets and comforters, GoreTex rain gear, down and synthetic sleeping bags, tents (best selection in summer) and odds'n'ends like sunglasses, soft luggage, and footwear. Discounts range from 10-50% off retail. The best prices are on the small selection of seconds, and end-of-season racks. Sizes for men: XS-XXL; women 6-16; and children 4-16. This is a great place for kids' jackets. Directions: Take College Ave. exit off 101, East to 4th St., left on 4th 1/2 mile.

SPORTS AGAIN

816 "B" Street (betw. 2nd & 3rd), San Rafael 94901. Phone: 453-7090. Hours: T-F 10am-6pm, Sat 10am-5pm. Purchases: MC VISA. Parking: Street.

Two very clever ladies have developed a sure winner! A recycled sporting goods store where anyone with quality used equipment can bring in their merchandise and place it on consignment. There're all the basics, i.e. mitts, baseballs, bats, bowling balls, bicycles, camping equipment, hiking gear and boots, soccer shoes, exercise and weight lifting equipment, plus some pretty exotic stuff like fencing equipment and wind surfers. They'll take just about anything that has good resale value, including clothing. This place is wonderful for families who will appreciate the average 50% savings off new retail pricing. Some new merchandise (probably gifts that never got used) are discounted less, about 30%. They will take consignments at any time and will make sure that everyone agrees on a fair and realistic price. You can expect to get 50% of the selling price. Call ahead if you're looking for something special, the selection changes almost daily.

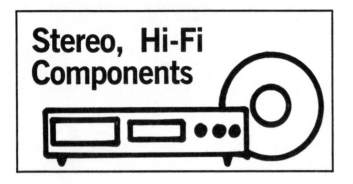

(Also see **General Merchandise — all headings**)

General

HALTEK ELECTRONICS

1062 Linda Vista Ave., Mountain View 94043. Phone: 969-0510. Hours: T-Sat 9am-5:30pm. Purchases: MC, VISA. Parking: Street.

Haltek carries all those esoteric electronic components, i.e. TV tubes, batteries, transistors at 40-50% off. To keep on top of the market involved in ecology and energy saving products, they're selling parts for solar panels, motors for wind power generators, etc.

HOUSE OF LOUIE
(See **Appliances**)

INTERNATIONAL HOUSEHOLD EXPORT
(See **Appliances**)

PACIFIC STEREO

1045 Contra Costa Blvd., Pleasant Hill 94523. Phone: 788-7770. Hours: M-F 9am-9pm, Sat 10am-6pm, Sun Noon-6pm. Purchases: MC, VISA. Parking: Lot.

☞ **Other Stores:** Dublin, Berkeley, Hayward, Larkspur, Mountain View, Sacramento, San Francisco, San Jose, Santa Clara, San Rafael, Colma, Walnut Creek.

Buying a stereo is a complicated purchase for the average consumer. There are so many options, so many systems and configurations, that you can spend a king's ransom if you're inclined to or a few hundred dollars. Purists who are considering spending thousands of dollars to create a system that is state of the art, will want to deal with one of the many fine stereo stores in the Bay Area that specialize in the most exotic and expensive equipment, and they'll pay plenty. For all the rest of us, more modest in our goals, *Pacific Stereo* is probably the best place to go for value. They splash big ads throughout Bay Area newspapers with such frequency that many assume that all their advertising will result in higher prices. Yet, because they are the biggest volume dealer in California, it is possible for them to offer tremendous values on most of their merchandise. You can often wheel and deal and walk out with an entire system at 10% above cost. A lot depends on your assertiveness.

The markup on stereo equipment is about 25-30% above wholesale. There is a higher markup on their own store brands, a smaller markup on some of the finer quality, more expensive lines. The larger markups are on loud speakers, turntables, and accessories. You have the best chance for negotiating a special deal when you're buying a whole system. On their prominently advertised "loss leader" items (that send competitors into a spin) prices are firm. Don't expect to dicker on these low prices. In keeping with their basic philosophy, *Pacific Stereo* has entered the small computer and video markets on a very competitive basis. They offer a good warranty on their stereo equipment and a reliable service department.

QUEMENT

1000 So. Bascom, San Jose 95128. Phone: 998-5900. Hours: M-Sat 9am-6pm. Purchases: MC, VISA. Parking: Free Lot.

Quement is a complete stereo sound center located in a huge warehouse-like building, with 40,000 sq. ft. of electronic parts, components, tubes, accessories, video recorders, projection TV's, antennas, citizens' band, and ham gear. They have most well known brand names, including Dual, Marantz, Sony, Pioneer, Technics, JVC and Panasonic. The prices are very competitive based on their tremendous volume (they even sell to other commercial and industrial outfits in the southern Peninsula area). They also have a complete service department to help you with any problems.

(Also see **General Merchandise**)

THE BEAR FACTORY

725 Bryant St., San Francisco 94107. Phone: 543-6058. Hours: M-T 10am-4pm. Purchases: Cash or Check. Parking: Limited Street.

This well known manufacturer of delightful stuffed animals has their share of seconds, discontinued styles, samples and special promotion merchandise that they are willing to sell at wholesale or less. The shelves which line the small entry area are well stocked with bargains. All their animals are made at their factory with quality materials that wash beautifully. They're best known for their collection of bears, but their other animals such as unicorns, deer, elephants, lions, lambs, etc. are equally appealing and popular. The door to the outlet is always locked and it's necessary to ring and wait a few minutes until an employee can come from the back. Current lines of merchandise can be purchased for a 20% discount.

FURRY FOLK PUPPETS

1219 Park Ave., Emeryville 94608. Phone: 658-7677. Hours: M-F 10am-4pm. Purchases: MC, VISA. Parking: Street.

These very expensive furry puppet animals have become very popular with specialty toy shops because of their unique and appealing life-like appearance. Otters, raccoons, bears, skunks, etc. look like the real animals and are a far cry from the typical puppet. In fact they don't look like puppets at all, but more like stuffed animals. The prices on their selection of seconds with minor flaws are about 50% off retail. They've recently augmented their own classy line with a less expensive line of imported puppets with bears, gorillas, turtles and kangaroos.

GIFTWARES INTERNATIONAL, INC.

1155-A Chess Dr., Suite F & G, (off Foster City Blvd) Foster City 94404. Phone: 341-2884. Hours: M-Sat 9am-5pm. Purchases: Cash or Check. Parking: Lot.

I was very intrigued by the three rooms of giftwares and toys jammed on display shelves all apparently for sale at wholesale prices. I could not begin to calculate the prevailing retail prices on many of their items, so I asked for their wholesale price list. Without hesitation, they provided a copy which enabled me to determine that the showroom prices were the same as those listed on their wholesale lists. So how can they make a profit selling at wholesale prices?

Giftwares Int'l is an importer and distributor of toys and gifts. They sell to stores, wholesale distributors, and catalog companies. The goodies in their offices are broken lots, samples, mis-shipments and returns. So what do they sell? Remote control cars, radio control cars, B/O Toys, Toy China Tea Sets, Toy Pianos, Soft Baby Dolls (12-26in.), dolls, teaching clocks, games with wooden beads, counting frames with wooden beads, do-it-yourself chess, magazine racks, wooden model assembly kits, wooden children's puzzles, wooden skeleton puzzles, children's cloth & vinyl books, musical boxes (West Germany, Japan & Switzerland with Reuge Movement), wooden figurine & porcelain music boxes, musical porcelain dolls, porcelain dolls, clowns, chess games and others. Prices range from $1 to $200 (imported music boxes). You won't always find everything on their wholesale price list available for sale, and you may find samples they've received but decided not to import. Their toys don't look like Fisher Price or Mattel lines, you'll have to check them out yourself to see if they meet your requirements for quality and play value. If you collect dolls or music boxes I'm sure you'll want to plan a visit.

TOYS "R" US

1082 Blossom Hill Road, San Jose 95123. Phone: (408) 266-2600. Hours: M-F 10am-9pm, Sat & Sun 10am-7pm. Purchases: MC, VISA. Parking: Free Lot.

☞ **Other Stores:** Daly City, Hayward, Newark, Pleasant Hill, Redwood City, Salinas, Santa Rosa, Citrus Heights, Sunnyvale.

Just for the record, I do think that *Toys "R" Us* is about the "best" all around resource for toys and children's gifts when you're considering price and selection. Their prices have stood up well in my comparison shopping. Only *Best Products* gives them serious competition in prices, but *Best* has a limited toy selection. For a big operation, I have been impressed with the no hassle, no fuss, exchange and refund policy, when you meet them half way with sales receipts as requested.

PRICE CLUB
(See **General Merchandise — Discount Stores**)

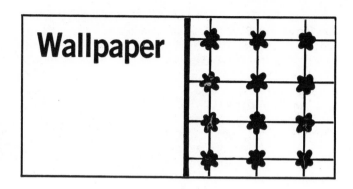

(Also see **Furniture — Catalog Discounters**)

ANN'S FABRIQUE
(See **Fabrics**)

LAWRENCE CONTRACT FURNISHERS
(See **Carpets**)

THE PAPER TREE
12175 Alcosta Blvd., San Ramon 94583. Phone: 828-4696. Hours: M-Sat 10am-5pm. Purchases: MC, VISA. Parking: Lot.

The owner of this wallpaper store handpicks discontinued wallpapers from the distribution warehouses of major wallpaper companies in the Bay Area. This choice selection is sold for $3-$7/single roll. Savings on the discontinued rolls may be 50-75% off retail. All the patterns are displayed on rods that allow you to unroll the pattern and get a good look and overall impression of how each pattern will appear in a large area. For the cautious, you can take rolls home on approval before purchasing. Once you've made up your mind, be sure to estimate correctly, because if you run short, you may not be able to obtain additonal paper. Most discontinued patterns are in vinyl, vinyl coated, foils or vertical string (similar to grasscloth). Discounts on patterns chosen from current wallpaper books range from a minimal 10% off up to 30% during a manufacturer's sale. Martin Senour paints (the best) are always discounted $1-$3/unit and frequently placed on limited specials.

WALLCOVERING & FABRIC FACTORY OUTLET

2660 Harrison St. (near 23rd), San Francisco 94110. Phone: 285-0870. Hours: M-F 10am-6pm, Sat 9am-5pm. Purchases: No cash, Only checks, MC, VISA. Parking: Street.

At this outlet, located on the premises of San Francisco's only manufacturer of quality designer wallcoverings, you will find seconds, overruns, mill ends, and discontinued patterns. They offer wallpaper which normally retails at $18.95 to $60/roll at prices ranging from $1.95-$10.95/roll. They allow you to borrow samples for evaluation. Many of their remnant rolls are sold for small change and are great for gift wrapping. They can help you determine just how much you need for your job, but bring in complete room measurements along with measurements for large doors and windows that will figure in your computations. Designer fabrics, many of which match wallpaper, are priced at $1.95-$9.95/yard. Many fabrics are bought for the outlet from Eastern mills and the values are just mind boggling. For best results, come with an open mind and be prepared to be versatile. If you can start your decorating project with the wallpaper selection *first*, it's a cinch to coordinate the other elements. Note: they do not take cash!

Part Two

Sometimes Tearfully Abandoned, Almost All Previously Owned, Some New, Perhaps Damaged, But All in All, Useful and Useable Merchandise

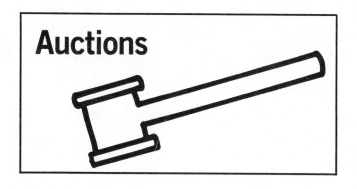

Auctions

Art and nostalgia combined have made the auction big business in California. Sometimes the bargains are fantastic, sometimes they're not.

Auctions must be announced in advance, and this is generally done in the Sunday edition of the metropolitan newspapers, under "Auctions." Most of the art and real estate auction firms have descriptive brochures of items to be sold, and offer previews prior to the sale.

Bidding at almost all auctions proceeds according to the mood and pocketbook of the crowd. Size up your competition: customs, police, and railroad auctions attract average citizens, while art and antique auctions appeal to the moneyed collectors.

Many auction houses require a buyer's registration prior to the sale; others have a loose "walk in and bid" arrangement. Purchases are usually by cash, or by certified or cashier's check.

There are many different types of auctions listed on the next few pages. Take your choice and have fun.

Art and Furniture

Follow the classified ads of the following auction houses for antiques, furnishings, estate sales and art objects. There are many good auctions in the Bay Area, but I have found the following to have auctions more frequently with a selection of merchandise appealing to "consumers"

BAYSHORE AUCTION GALLERY
305 Main, Redwood City 94063. Phone: 364-8888. Hours: Tuesday evenings at 7pm. Antiques, household, collectibles, etc.

BUTTERFIELD'S
1244 Sutter St. (fine arts galleries) or 660 3rd St. (appraisal departments and Butterfield 660 galleries), San Francisco 94107. Phone: 673-1362. Hours: Once a month at each location. Mailing list. Typically handles finer antiques, art objects, oriental rugs, jewelry, etc.

CONCORD AUCTION STUDIO

2350 Willow Pass Rd., Concord 94520. Phone: 689-4884. Auctions monthly usually on Tuesday evenings, previews on Monday's between Noon and 6pm.

HARVEY CLAR'S ESTATE AUCTION GALLERY

4364 Piedmont Ave., Oakland 94611. Phone: 428-0100. Hours: Preview Sat & Sun Noon-5pm, Auctions every 3 weeks M,T,W evenings at 7:30pm (subject to change). Mailing list by request. Purchases: MC, VISA. Parking: Private Lot.

☞ **Other Store:** Redwood City: 2317 Broadway. Phone: 365-8122.

MC COY AUCTION CO., INC.

37400 Cedar Blvd., Newark 94560. Phone: 793-9511. Hours: Every Tuesday 7pm for American and European antiques only (subject to change). Purchases: MC, VISA.

TAIT AUCTION STUDIO INC.

1209 Howard Ave., Burlingame 94010. Phone: 342-8352. Hours: Auctions once a month announced in local papers. Specializing in antiques, fine furnishings, silver and jewelry.

VALLEY AUCTION

3440 Stanley Blvd., Pleasanton 94566. Phone: 846-4860. Hours: Retail store and for auction preview of pre-owned furniture, antiques, appliances, general merchandise, etc., M-Sat 9am-6pm, Sun Noon-5pm. Auctions: Wednesday.

POLICE

Local police departments hold auction sales to dispose of goods which were confiscated in police cases but not reclaimed by their original owners. The range of merchandise is limited only by the ingenuity of the burglar. Bicycles are the hot items at these sales, followed by radios, tape decks, TV's, small appliances, cameras, tools, and furniture. Sometimes there is no prior inspection of merchandise, so bid with care. It's all sold "as-is", strictly cash-and-carry. Bidding depends on the mood and pocketbook of the crowd, and since buyers are usually average citizens, bargain buying prevails. Auction dates must be publicized in local newspapers. Call your local department to find out when the next auction will be, mark it on your calendar. The sales usually begin about 9am and last until mid-afternoon.

San Francisco is the only police department that holds frequent auctions. Starting at 9am they are held at the Hall of Justice, 850 Bryant St., (basement), San Francisco. For dates and information call 553-0123.

U. S. GOVERNMENT

U. S. BUREAU OF CUSTOMS

630 Sansome St., Room 400, San Francisco 94114. Phone Info: 556-7954. Purchases: Cash only. Parking: Street.

Several auctions are held each year by the *U. S. Department of Customs* to dispose of the thousands of items confiscated by San Francisco customs agents for various violations of the Tariff Act of 1930. Many unique articles from all over the world take this route to the auction block. Items up for auction are liquor (which goes for about the same as regular retail, because bidding starts at the amount of federal tax on each item), clothing, cutlery, cameras, watches, lamps, pottery, gift items, jewelry, radios, tools, and some furniture. While some of the auction prices here are close to retail, many sell for 50% or less. Watch Bay Area newspapers for auction dates.

U. S. POSTAL SERVICE AUCTIONS

228 Harrison St., San Francisco 94105. Phone Info: 550-0100. Hours: 3-4 times a year. Purchases: Cash. Parking: Street or Pay lots.

If you love to gamble and you can't make it to Vegas or Tahoe, try the *Postal Service Auctions*. You'll end up with auction fever, once hooked, you'll return year after year, even though you're bound at times to end up with ridiculous buys that defy rational explanation. Part of the attraction of the auctions is the joy of discovery. The Postal Service can't guarantee that what they sell will work or can be fixed. Their policy is "buyer beware". The Postal Service probably has one of the largest stocks of merchandise because it collects so much dead mail. This happens when addresses are indecipherable and there's no return address; goods are damaged and a claim has been paid; or nobody claims them. In 1983 the contents of almost 823,000 dead parcels went up for bid from major metropolitan facilities, netting more than $1.4 million. You might find a box of bibles, boxes of dentures, exhaust pipes, tractor tires, but more likely and appealing, clothing, books, and housewares. Both single items and lots are sold. The dead letter center sends bulletins to all post offices designating times of auctions. It's best to call, though, and have your name put on the mailing list.

OAKLAND MUSEUM WHITE ELEPHANT SALE

Oakland (address to be announced). Phone: 893-4257.
Hours: To be announced. Purchases: Cash or Check.

This sale, conducted by the Oakland Museum Women's
Board, is one of the most successful fund-raising efforts in
the Bay Area each year. In 1984 the sale earned more than
$413,000! It is usually held in a different Oakland location
each March.

Every possible type of merchandise is available for sale,
including large quantities of new, first-quality goods
donated by local merchants. Clothing is popular and
accounts for a substantial portion of the sale; it is always
arranged neatly in department-store style on racks according to size and quality. There is an elegant designer
section, a better-dress section, a nice selection of furs —
and budget dresses as low as $1. There are linens, toys,
housewares, books, records, appliances, and great buys in
furniture. Donations are solicited from August each year in
preparation for the next sale, and they provide an itemized
statement for Uncle Sam. The sale is announced in newspapers and on radio and television.

Flea Markets

Attending flea markets has become a national weekend pastime. On any leisurely Saturday or Sunday, many families leave their all-too-peaceful homes to enjoy the harried, tumultuous bargaining and selling at a nearby swap meet or flea market. Absolutely everything imaginable is for sale, from post World War II surplus wheelbarrows to eggs, bakery goods, and produce so cheap it makes you wonder why everyone doesn't shop here instead of their local supermarket. Most flea markets require a hopeful seller to pay a fee to set up a booth. Sometimes prospective customers are also charged a token amount to park or to enter. The booths are arranged sometimes haphazardly, in a large fenced-in field or yard. Cheerful chaos is the order of the day. Items for sale are those the sellers have carried from their homes (like a portable garage sale) or have acquired through liquidating stores; some items are from closeouts or from auctions or surplus

goods. Some people sell things at flea markets as a regular business, spending the days between weekends collecting stuff for the next sale. Prices are often a problem though, for many sellers are amateurs in the retailing business — sometimes they price too high, sometimes too low. Get into the swing of things — if you see something you want, make an offer (remembering that the seller is as anxious to sell as you are to buy). Haggling is a part and parcel of the flea market way of life.

It may take all day just to navigate through the crowds and see everything. Most clothing must be purchased without trying on, since few vendors have dressing rooms (a few with campers as their base of operations have them inside their vans). Most merchandise is sold "as-is", and it's strictly "buyer beware." Most of the small appliance and home entertainment booths give written guarantees and will make exchanges on defective merchandise if the proper receipt is presented. Most vendors operate on a cash-only basis; only a few accept credit cards.

Listed here are some of the better-known markets in the area; these are held regularly throughout the year. Other markets occur on some other basis — maybe monthly or annually. These smaller fairs can be fantastic sources of bargains by virtue of the fact they are not as well traveled as the others. Check your local paper for notices of these events. The most popular flea markets in the Bay Area are hands down — Marin City, San Jose and Alameda.

ALAMEDA PENNY MARKET

Island Auto Movie, 791 Thau Way (3 blocks south of the Alameda Tube), Alameda 94501. Phone: 522-7206. Hours: Sat, Sun 7am-4pm. Purchases: Cash Only. Parking: Free. Admission: 40 cents/person.

The Penny Market at the Island Auto Movie Drive-in Theatre is a bargain hunter's paradise. Spaces are rented by the day, weekend, or month to anyone wishing to sell merchandise. Many vendors make a handsome living selling namebrand, first quality stereo equipment, tapes, clothing, etc., in this low-overhead type of operation. Clothing, household goods, toys, and furniture (you name it) are available new and used.

BERKELEY FLEA MARKET

Ashby Bart Station Parking Lot (Hwy. 24 & Berkeley exit), Berkeley. Phone: 653-4170 Hours: Sat & Sun 8am-6pm. Admission: Free. Parking: Free.

CASTRO VALLEY FLEA MARKET

20820 Oak St. (at Castro Valley Blvd.), Castro Valley 94546. Phone: 582-0396. Hours: Sat, Sun 6am-6pm. Purchases: Cash only. Parking: Free. Admission: Free.

DALY CITY FLEA MARKET

Geneva Drive In, 607 Carter, Daly City. Phone: 543-3886. Hours: Sat & Sun 7am-5pm. Parking: Free. Admission: Free.

DE ANZA COLLEGE FLEA MARKET

21250 Stevens Creek Blvd., Cupertino 95014. Phone: (408) 996-4946. Hours: 1st Saturday of every month. Purchases: Cash. Admission: Free. Flea market is located in parking lot B & C on campus.

THE LOST FLEA MARKET

1940 Monterey Road., San Jose 95113. Phone: (408) 293-2323. Hours: W-F 10am-5pm, Sat 7am-5pm, Sun 10am-5:30pm. Purchases: MC, VISA. Parking: Free. Admission: Free.

Directly across from the G. E. plant and Stauffer Chemical, the *Lost Flea Market* has between 40-45 individual dealers in their own shops. They deal in antiques, collectibles, records, reproductions, new and used building materials, brass, art deco and miscellaneous items. Items range from inexpensive to moderate. The flea market is built in the style of an old western town with dust and all!

MARIN CITY FLEA MARKET

Location: Donahue and Drake (just off Hwy. 101, Marin City Exit) Marin City. Phone: 332-1441. Hours: Sat & Sun 5am-5pm. Purchases: Cash or Check. Parking: Pay lots. Admission: Free.

Very popular with Marin residents because of the many regular vendors selling prints, posters, T-shirts, and sundry items.

MIDGLEY'S COUNTRY FLEA MARKET

2200 Gravenstein Highway South (off Hwy. 101, left to Sebastopol 5 miles), Sebastopol 95472. Phone: (707) 823-7239. Hours: Sat & Sun 6:30am-7pm. Purchases: Cash Only. Parking: Free.

NAPA-VALLEJO FLEA MARKET AND AUCTION

303 Kelly Road (Just off Hwy. 29, between Napa and Vallejo) Napa. Phone: (707) 643-3977 or 226-8862. Hours: Sun 7am-4:30pm. Parking: 50 cents. Admission: Free.

OAKLAND FLEA MARKET

5401 Coliseum Way, Coliseum Drive In, Oakland. Phone: 543-3886. Hours: Sat & Sun 7am-4pm. Parking: Lot. Admission: Free.

SAN JOSE FLEA MARKET

12000 Berryessa Rd., San Jose 95133. Phone: (408) 289-1550. Hours: Sat, Sun 7:30am-sundown. Purchases: Cash Only. Parking: Pay lot. Admission: Free.

This is one of the biggest flea markets in the Bay Area. The crowds approach *Disneyland* proportions, the vendors and sellers offer a smattering of everything from clothes to furniture. Plants, pottery, toys, flowers, T-shirts and children's apparel are very popular with consumers. *San Jose* has the largest number of regular tenants operating on a year to year basis.

SOLANO DRIVE IN FLEA MARKET

Solano Way & Hwy 4, Concord 94521. Phone: 543-3886. Hours: Sat 7am-4pm. Admission: Free. Parking: Free.

buying this way, when you pay $40 for a dress that probably cost $200 new. You'll find some very sophisticated clothes with designer labels like Givenchy, Oscar de la Renta, Nipon and others, as well as labels from finer department and specialty stores. A really good shop will have merchandise that looks fresh and current unless they're specializing in vintage clothing. It is impossible to list all the many better resale shops which abound in the Bay Area. Your best resource is the yellow pages of the phone book. Check listings under "Clothing: Used."

Here's your chance to have finer clothes at prices you can afford. A resale shop is the "top drawer" of the used clothing business. Usually their prices are higher than thrift shops. The affluent (who often do wear their clothes only a few times and then recycle them) use these shops as a moneymaking outlet for disposing of their apparel. Most of the resale shops operate on a consignment basis. It works this way: the potential seller brings in any items she wants to dispose of, and the store agrees to try to sell the items for her for a certain percentage of the price. Other stores agree on the price the item will go for (the amount depending on item's condition and age), and this is split fifty-fifty with the shop owner. Other shops buy outright. On this kind of a deal, everyone makes some money: the socialite makes a profit, the store owner makes a profit, and you the customer make good buys on clothing you couldn't otherwise afford. You will be saving 50-70%

Salvage — Damaged Freight Outlets

PAUL'S DEPARTMENT STORES

1122 Howard, San Francisco 94103. Phone: 861-1122. Hours: M-F 8am-4:30pm, Sat 8am-1pm. Purchases: Cash Only. Parking: Limited Street.

The insurance writeoffs, liquidations and salvage merchandise are virtually dumped, jammed and crammed into the nooks and crannies of all of *Paul's* stores. It's practically an indoor flea market with all the unpredictability you might expect in a selection acquired in this manner. Sometimes you groan as soon as you walk in the door (things look so tired), other times you're gleeful over nylons, leather jackets, housewares, pajamas or whatever that is of surprisingly good quality and wonderfully priced. This is only for the most serious bargain hunters, dilettantes need not bother.

SELECT SALVAGE

1796 Willow Pass Road, Concord 94520. Phone: 687-0480. Hours: W-Sat 10am-5pm. Purchases: MC, VISA. Parking: Lot.

Shopping at this place is like going to a surprise party. Not even the salespeople know from one week to the next what's going to be in their inventory. This store is a clearinghouse for *Pacific Intermountain Express Trucking*. Every Tuesday a *P.I.E.* truck arrives with merchandise that has been refused by *P.I.E.'s* customers. The merchandise may be slightly damaged, or part of a shipment that was damaged. Most of the items seem to be in perfect condition. The firm is able to recoup some of its losses by selling the merchandise here for prices low enough to insure quick sales to savvy customers. You should note that the store is always open Wednesday through Saturday. Come Wednesday if you want first crack at the selection and don't mind elbow-to-elbow shoppers. You won't always find furniture or appliances, but you can expect to find just about everything else. I loved their sign over a popular poster: "This is somewhere in the store, probably in the last place you'll look."

WORLDWIDE SALVAGE INC.

3906 Adeline, Emeryville 94608. Phone: 653-1902. Hours: M-Sat 9am-4:30pm. Purchases: MC, VISA. Parking: Street.

Regulars of the old M. Jessup Co. in Emeryville will know just where to go to find *Worldwide Salvage Co.* They'll feel right at home too. Like Jessup, the owners are buying liquidated stock, salvage merchandise, and gift show samples. Prices are reduced from 30-70% off retail. The choicest merchandise comes from the gift shows and includes Toscany crystal, Italian tea carts, Oriental vases, silk flowers, craftwares and brass from India, pottery, clayware, Marsh ceramics, etc. Unfortunately, samples come in one-of-a-kind quantities, and the best pieces don't last long. The sundries, household goods, foods, stationery and clothing selections are haphazard at best. Some things look very "tired", but they're priced right! Stores like this are always an expedition into the unknown. You don't know whether you'll end up disappointed or delighted. They are located just where Berkeley, Emeryville, and Oakland come together at the corner of San Pablo and Adeline at 39th St.

AAA EQUIPMENT

745 50th Ave., Oakland 94610. Phone: 261-2443. Hours: M-F 8am-4:30pm, Sat 8am-Noon. Purchases: MC, VISA. Parking: Street.

A sign "Something for everyone" would seem appropriate on the outside of this business, located on three acres near the Nimitz Freeway in Oakland. A sign in the office appropriately boasts "We Talk Hardhat Here." It behooves you to avoid shopping on rainy days, since most of the merchandise is displayed outdoors. You can buy everything here from small hand tools (new and used) to huge pieces of construction equipment. Contractors, firms, and handymen come to *AAA* to avail themselves of the tremendous selection of government surplus and bankrupt stock. Savings of 50% are not unusual on used machinery like air compressors, generators, portable power plants, roller conveyors, and stainless steel items.

This is the place to shop for concrete trucks, crawler

tractors, yard cranes, or fork lifts. The yard man will direct you through the maze of equipment to your special need and will gladly test the equipment for you. Anyone contemplating a purchase is free to bring in outside experts to appraise and evaluate the equipment. All equipment and machinery is in working order when sold. Although no guarantees are given, *AAA* tries to stand behind its merchandise.

BONANZA SURPLUS DISTRIBUTORS

3617 E. 14th St., Oakland 94601. Phone: 534-3030. Hours: M-Sat 8:30am-5:30pm. Purchases: MC, VISA. Parking: Street

This is a gadgeteer's paradise. A friend tells me he comes here when he can't find what he's looking for anywhere else. There are tons of tools, hardware, bolts, tape, cable, chain, compressors, motors, wheels, plumbing supplies, and on and on. You'll probably have to ask for assistance to locate your particular item amid the organized chaos that prevails. I did notice that all nails, screws, and bolts were neatly arranged in boxes according to size, and I was told that a reorganization is under way to label all those cluttered aisles.

All new electrical motors are given a 90-day guarantee; used motors carry a 30-day guarantee and are tested for you in the store. Prices are lower than those of your neighborhood hardware store, since most merchandise comes from government or industrial surplus or from stores going out of business. Special shipments are advertised in the sports section of the Oakland *Tribune* every Friday.

J & H OUTLET

476 Industrial Way, San Carlos 94070. Phone: 591-7113. Hours: M-F 10am-6pm, Sat 10am-3pm. Purchases: Cash, Check. Parking: Street.

J & H Outlet is tailor-made for all you tinkerers with components and audio equipment. It consists of a cavernous room filled with practically everything you could possibly need at low prices. There are literally millions of surplus items — thousands of components, lots of wires, all kinds of parts, and very good buys on copper and brass remnants for jewelrymakers and sculptors. The owner is helpful and nice, plus the staff is willing to help you find what you need or get it for you if they possibly can.

Thrift Shops

have everything priced clearly and arranged neatly for your perusal. We suggest checking out your smaller thrift shop from time to time, too; smaller stores are often less picked over than the larger ones. I've not listed three good old standbys — *Goodwill Industries, Salvation Army, and St. Vincent de Paul Society*. All offer great bargains and there are many located throughout the Bay Area. Check the white pages of your phone book.

Moving, remodeling, marriage, divorce, and death all contribute to the unearthing of items no longer needed but too good to throw away. At least half of the "too good to throw away" items end up being donated to charitable organizations which redistribute them through thrift shops. The donations come from many sources; sometimes a will leaves an entire estate to an organization, or a large corporation redoing its offices will simply hand its old stuff to a thrift shop for a tax deduction rather than incur the headache and expense of moving. Of course, there are also those who are simply cleaning out their attic, closet, or basement, and call their favorite thrift shop to remove the discards. Whatever the reason, many valuable antiques and collectibles with obscure histories often end up here; for the "pro" bargain hunter thrift shops are a must. Most larger thrift stores operate on a similar basis, with the same store policies on exchanges, returns, etc. Most of them

Wrecking and Salvage Yards

If you're leery of putting new wood on top of old, or more likely, if you're just too broke to meet the prices at your local building supply store to redo, make new, and repair your abode, then try scouting the local salvage and wrecking yards. First, wear old clothes and sturdy shoes and take all the pertinent measurements for your project before you head out the door. Occasionally (though not as prevalent in earlier years), you can find newel posts, footed bathtubs, wooden columns and other charming architectural items from Victorian homes. Windows are available in many yards in curved, straight, leaded, stained, or beveled glass. You can take nothing for granted in terms of selection because it depends largely upon what projects they've demolished recently, or what "buys" they've made. What is fairly consistent is the selection of basic building materials like used plywood, paneling, lumber, doors, used windows (ordinary types), used bricks, plumbing fixtures, etc. These supplies are just waiting to be recycled and represent great dollar savings for a thrifty remodeling job or even new construction. Think of saving 50-70% off new prices and the extra time in scouting the yards will not be such a chore. The following list includes yards and companies that produce results for the do-it-yourselfer.

ALLEN ABDO SALVAGE CO.

718 Douglas, Oakland 94603. Phone: 569-2070. Purchases: Cash Only. Parking: Street.

Specializing in large timber, doors, some plumbing and windows.

BERKELEY ARCHITECTURAL SALVAGE

2750 Adeline, Berkeley 94703. Phone: 849-2025. Hours: Sat 10am-5:30pm. Purchases: Cash or Check. Parking: Street.

Decorative parts of old buildings, including moldings, doors, plumbing and lighting fixtures.

CALDWELL BUILDING WRECKERS

195 Bayshore Blvd., San Francisco 94124. Phone: 285-9192. Hours: M-F 9am-5pm, Sat 9am-4:30pm. Purchases: Cash or Check. Parking: Street.

Lumber, wood, bricks, doors, windows and bath fixtures.

CHAS S. CAMPANELLA WRECKING

5401 San Leandro Blvd., Oakland 94601. Phone: 536-7002. Hours: M-F 8am-4:45pm, Sat 10am-4pm. Purchases: MC, VISA. Parking: Street.

Lumber, plywood, doors, windows, plumbing, lighting fixtures, and bricks.

CLEVELAND WRECKING CO.

Cargo Way at 3rd St., San Francisco 94124. Phone: 824-1804. Hours: M-F 9am-4pm, Sat 8am-Noon. Purchases: MC, VISA. Parking: Street.

New and used building materials. Lumber, doors, windows, plumbing fixtures, marble, steel, and brick. Huge yard!

ENVIRONMENTAL RESTORATION AND DESIGN

2140 San Pablo, Berkeley 94702. Phone: 648-3967. Hours: M-Sat 9am-5pm, Sun Noon-5pm. Purchases: Cash Only.

Bathroom accessories and bathroom sinks. Not exactly cheap.

OAKLAND BUILDING MATERIALS

1224 22nd Avenue, Oakland 94606. Phone: 532-7116. Purchases: Check or Cash. Parking: Street.

Very good on roofing materials, plus windows, plumbing and doors.

OMEGA SALVAGE

2407 San Pablo, Berkeley 94702. Phone: 843-7368. Hours: M-Sat 9am-5pm. Parking: Street. Purchases: Cash or Check.

Lumber, windows, doors, plumbing, lighting, bricks, and bathtubs.

SAV-A-BUCK

1940 Monterey Rd., San Jose 95112. Phone: (408) 293-0147. Hours: M-Sat 9am-4pm. Purchases: Cash or Check. Parking: Lot.

New and used building materials.

WHOLE EARTH RECYCLING

1325 6th Street, Berkeley, 94710. Phone: 526-7080. Hours: M-Sun 9:30am-5pm. Purchases: Cash or Check. Parking: Street.

Lumber, windows, doors, plumbing, kitchen and bathroom fixtures, cabinets, electrical fixtures and piping.

Part Three

Related Services, New Trends And Information, Late Additions, Updates and Index

Shopping Bus Tours

Many don't think twice about buzzing into the City for a day of shopping. Others are simply terrified at the thought of parking, one-way streets, city driving, and locating obscure back streets in areas far removed from the familiar Union Square area. There is an easy way out — a shopping bus tour. During the last few years, several companies have developed successful tour programs geared specifically for bargain hunters. Most tours are arranged on a group basis. A tour tailored specifically to the interests of your church, club, civic organization, or employee group can be easily arranged. Individuals can often sign up on a space available basis when there are cancellations on group tours, while a few companies set aside special days expressly for individuals wishing to take a tour.

Popular tours for employee groups are arranged with an emphasis on career apparel and accessories suitable for the sophisticated office environment, others are mother and daughter, junior and teen fashions, updated, trendy or conservative apparel, some include stops for men's clothing, jewelry, household linens, giftwares, the Flower Market, plus general tours with a smattering of everything. Typically 6-10 businesses or outlets are visited. Some tours offer opportunities to visit businesses not typically doing a retail business with the general public, while the majority are accessible at any time to bargain hunters using *Bargain Hunting in the Bay Area* as a guide.

Prices range from $15-$25 and vary according to the distance from the City, the food service offered, and the special arrangements involved in setting up the tour for the particular interests of a group. Lunch is usually not included, unless requested, and then at extra cost. Most tours will provide recommendations for quick service restaurants in the area visited during the lunch period, others suggest bringing a bag lunch to avoid any hassle. Most companies serve a morning and afternoon snack with beverage. Door to door service to each outlet or business is important for most consumers. Wardrobe counseling, seminars, make-up and color analysis services are combined with the tour program by a few of the companies.

Times and dates vary with each company but usually start early in the morning and end late in the afternoon. Although all offer Saturday tours, weekdays are usually scheduled for the convenience of the group, or according to the access available to particular outlets.

I highly recommend starting your bargain hunting forays with a bus trip — especially if you're new to the area, or live a distance away. You're bound to have a marvelous time, especially when you're with your friends. However, intense shopping like this is not for the disabled or the faint of heart. It's both exhilerating and exhausting! Call the companies located in your area, and out of your area (since many have established tour programs originating from several communities in Northern California). They can give you more specifics about their programs, and you can determine which company will suit the needs of your group.

ALLADIN TRAVEL

818 K Street Mall, Sacramento 95814. Phone: (916) 925-0633. Days: By arrangement. Type: Group Only.

ANN'S BUS TOURS

6155 Franciscan Way, San Jose 95120. Phone: (408) 268-7734. Days: Most Saturdays, weekdays by arrangement. Type: Group and individual. Serves many YWCA, church and civic groups in South Bay area. Self guided and escorted tours.

THE BARGAIN BUS

445 Lesser St., Oakland 94601. Phone: 533-0874. Days: Saturdays, weekdays by arrangement. Type: Group or individual. Departure points from Walnut Creek, Oakland, San Jose, Palo Alto, San Mateo. Other shopping tours to Carmel and the wine country.

FASHION OUTLET EXPRESS (DIVISION OF ACTION TOURS)

1275 Teresita Drive, San Jose 95129. Phone: (408) 446-0642. Days: By arrangement. Type: Group. Fashion consulting and specific fashion interest tours arranged.

FIRST FASHION EXPRESS

11 Juana Ct., Walnut Creek Ca. 94596. Phone: 943-1226. Days: Saturdays, weekdays by arrangement. Type: Group. Particular emphasis on custom designed tours for each group. Make-up and color analysis can be arranged. A popular tour caters to the needs of career woman interested in finer fashions and accessories. Tours depart from many points in the greater Bay Area.

PIPER TOURS

4040 Crandall Dr., Sacramento 95825. Phone: (916) 488-2159. Days: Tues-Sat. Type: Group and individual. Special fund raising tours. Departure points from Sacramento, Yolo, San Joaquin, and Butte Counties.

PROFESSIONAL TRAVEL SERVICE

2371 El Camino Avenue, Sacramento 95821. Phone: (916) 482-4744. Days: Saturday. Type: Groups — teachers, lodge, mother-daughter, etc.

SHOPPER STOPPER

P. O. Box 535, Sebastopol 95472. Phone: (707) 829-1597. Days: Wednesday & Saturday. Type: Group or Individual. Popular tours originating from Santa Rosa, with pickups in Sonoma, Marin County and San Francisco. Conducted by tour guides with door to door service. Special interest tours arranged.

SPECIAL SERVICES TRAVEL CENTER

Building 2, Wing #1, Naval Air Station, Alameda 94501. Phone: 869-3716. Days: Wednesdays. Type: Group tours limited to military families and Dept. of Defense civilian employees.

WAYWARD HO! CUSTOM TOURS

P. O. Box 26331, Sacramento 95826. Phone: (916) 363-9743. Days: Saturdays. Type: Shopping stops included on tours which may encompass nature, arts, culture, or interesting off-beat places.

Off-Price/Outlet Shopping Malls

Off-price retailers represent an industry in high gear. Not only are more manufacturers developing their own outlet stores around the country, but major *Fortune 500* companies, are entering the arena to capture a portion of the off-price profits. Perhaps the most exciting development is the Off-Price/Outlet Shopping Center. Their success on the East Coast and in the Mid West is prompting local developers to get on the band wagon. We may never develop a center or area on the scale of Reading, Pennsylvania — the Outlet Disneyland — with over 700 outlet stores. (Three million visitors a year come in cars and busloads to sample the bargains and the exciting milieu created by so many outlets and so much merchandise in one place.) Yet, if all goes according to the plans of several local developers, we will soon see the first truly Off-Price/Outlet Malls in the Bay Area.

So what is *Off-Price*? Existing on the fringes of retailing for many years, off-price stores did not really catch on in a big way until a few years ago. The impetus was two-pronged. Consumers were wearied by inflation, and at the same time, they were developing a taste for nationally recognized brands and designer-name merchandise. To most, these goods symbolize higher quality, not to mention status. Off-price stores fit into a gray area between discounters and full-service or carriage trade stores that sell goods at a full markup. Discount stores pay wholesale prices to suppliers but cut costs on their overhead so they can sell below retail. Off-price stores, on the other hand, often buy below wholesale. They load up on manufacturers' overruns and end-of-season goods, and often get special deals for buying in large quantities. They buy current season merchandise off-price (at inside prices) mainly by foregoing the many perks required by traditional store buyers like advertising, markdown, and warehouse allowances. They may often buy on the spot for cash. Unlike discounters, most off-price buyers concentrate on designer labels or well known brands that have proven consumer appeal. An off-price store with shrewd buyers may sometimes sell a product for less than the same item is selling in the manufacturer's own store. Some off-price stores will sell apparel with the labels out because the manufacturer required that action; other off-price stores may simply use that as a marketing ploy. Some off-price stores aren't eager to clarify confusion about whether or not they're true outlet stores.

Outlet Stores are owned and operated by the manufacturer. Factory stores have existed for decades. But they have typically been at the factory site, as an outlet for seconds and surpluses and as a favor to employees and local residents. Now they often sell first-quality, current-season merchandise and are locating more and more in outlet and off-price shopping centers. Sometimes they're producing their own goods just for their own stores. Examples of outlet stores in this book: *The Outlet Store*, *Vogue Alley*, *Carter's Factory Outlet*, and *Dansk Designs*.

The local developers who are aggressively planning Outlet Malls have many obstacles to overcome. Not only do they have to navigate the tedious route through local planning offices, permits, etc., they also have to persuade Eastern companies to test new markets, which for the most part are far removed from their head offices and proven areas of development. Another problem: the cost of California real estate and development, typically much higher than Eastern costs. However, the Bay Area is appealing because there are no off-price malls.

New Off-price/Outlet centers will have a combination of outlet stores, off-price stores, and highly promotional stores. If the pattern established in other areas of the country holds true, tenant mixes will be composed of approximately 70% apparel, with other categories in shoes, housewares/giftwares, linens, luggage, books, records, food, and just about anything else.

The following developers have projects in the planning stages with completion dates scheduled as early as Spring 1985.

GREAT WESTERN OUTLET MALL

This company, *The Great Western Outlet Company* has sites selected in San Jose, at the intersection of Capitol Expressway and Pearl Ave.; San Francisco, at Second St. and Townsend; the Peninsula, and Santa Rosa.

San Jose mall will be enclosed with 200,000 sq. ft. A spring 1985 opening is scheduled. Other sites will open at later dates.

SANTA ROSA OUTLET MALL

This mall will have over 200,000 sq. ft. of off-price merchandising according to its developer, Codding Evans of Santa Rosa. The site is located on Highway 12, 1 1/2 miles West of U.S. 101. An opening is scheduled for late 1984.

Alphabetical Index

Geographical Index

Subject Index

Late Additions

BREUNERS CLEARANCE CENTER

4946 Almaden Expressway (between Branham and Blossom Hill), San Jose 95118. Phone: (408) 265-9700. Hours: M-F 10am-9pm, Sat & Sun 10am-6pm. Purchases: MC, Visa, Brueners Charge. Parking: Lot.

Unlike the *Brueners Rents Clearance Centers* listed on page 121, their new 20,000 sq. ft. store in San Jose is stocked with the "big stuff", i. e. mattresses, living, dining, bedroom furnishings, plus a huge array of carpet remnants. This clearance center is fed with inventory from all Breuners Northern California and San Joaquin Valley stores. When merchandise arrives it is automatically marked down 30% off original retail, and then is marked down an additional 10% each month it remains on the floor. The quality ranges from Baker, Henredon, Heritage, (the very best) to Bassett, a popular modestly priced line. The merchandise arriving here is sometimes damaged, occasionally customer returns, but usually just discontinued lines or sample pieces. If you're decorating on a budget, you'll want to monitor the weekly new arrivals. Delivery is extra and all sales are final.

P. S. PLUS SIZES

285 Lake Merced, Westlake Plaza Shopping Center, Daly City 94015. Phone: Pending. Hours: Tentatively set for M-F 10am-9pm, Sat 10am-6pm, Sun Noon-5pm. Purchases: Cash or Check. MC, VISA, pending. Parking: Lot.

P. S. Plus Sizes is scheduled to arrive in the Bay Area by October, 1984. Considering their reputation established in Southern California and on the East Coast, they will be heartily welcomed by all large sized ladies. A division of Catherine Stout (a well known retail Eastern chain), their off/price stores will offer sportswear, coordinates, dresses, lingerie, bathing suits, coats, outerware, active and leisure fashions. The size range is 16 1/2 to 32 1/2, or 18-52. The clothing represents great on-the-spot buys, some merchandise from their Catherine Stout retail stores, and is generally considered very current. Brands carried include many well known lines in the moderate to better price ranges plus several status designer brands. Discounts range from 20-50% off retail. Private dressings rooms and a reasonable return policy will surely please all their new customers.

OAKLAND'S OFF/PRICE PLANS

The *Great Western Outlet Company (see page 216)* is putting together an impressive list of tenants for their newest project, an off/price and promotional center that will be located in the former site of the Liberty House Department store at 1501 Broadway in Oakland. This conversion will certainly be welcome by all Oakland shoppers who have seen more stores close than open, and would love to have a close and convenient area for their bargain hunting forays. Completion of this center is scheduled for early 1985.

Corrections to This Printing

Page 36: **Fritzi Factory Outlet** is most recently located at 218 Fremont Street in San Francisco.

Page 40: **Olga Fashion Fabrics & Other Things** has moved to 798-78 Blossom Hill Rd., Los Gatos 95030. Phone: (408) 356-9047.

Page 46: **Vogue Alley** has new stores at the Oaks Shopping Center in Cupertino, and at 373 Geary Street in San Francisco.

∗ Recent Store Openings ∗ Latest Outlet Discoveries ∗ Lower Discount Previews ∗ Special Closeouts ∗ Seasonal Sales ∗ Manufacturer Clearances ∗

The budget conscious shopper needs to be up to date on this information. Help yourself meet your budget by subscribing to Sally Socolich's Bargain Hunter's Hotline.

10 bargain-packed issues for $15.00 or $1.50/issue.

Name _____

Address _____

City _____ State _____ Zip _____

Phone_____

Mail this coupon and your check to Bargain Hunter's Hotline, Box 144, Moraga, CA 94556.